You
Can't
Get
There
From
Here

You
Can't
Get
There
From
Here

A YEAR ON THE FRINGES
OF A SHRINKING WORLD

GAYLE FORMAN

RODALE

© 2005 by Gayle Forman

Illustrations © 2005 by Diane Rios

Rodale books may be purchased for business or promotional use or for special sales. For information, please write to: Special Markets Department, Rodale, Inc., 733 Third Avenue, New York, NY 10017

Printed in the United States of America

Rodale Inc. makes every effort to use acid-free ∞, recycled paper ☺.

Book design by Christopher Rhoads

Library of Congress Cataloging-in-Publication Data

Forman, Gayle.
    You can't get there from here : a year on the fringes of a shrinking world / Gayle Forman.
        p.   cm.
    ISBN-13 978–1–59486–037–9 hardcover
    ISBN-10 1–59486–037–8 hardcover
    ISBN-13 978–1–59486–551–0 paperback
    ISBN-10 1–59486–551–5 paperback
    1. Forman, Gayle—Travel.   2. Voyages around the world.   I. Title.
G440.F73F73   2005
910.4'1—dc22   2004027373

Distributed to the trade by Holtzbrinck Publishers

2 4 6 8 10 9 7 5 3 1 hardcover
2 4 6 8 10 9 7 5 3 1 paperback

For R.D.T.J.
Excelsior

The world is too dangerous for anything but truth
and too small for anything but love.

—WILLIAM SLOAN COFFIN

She goes no more to the places she used to be.
She goes to fly now into life's mystery.

—JONATHAN RICHMAN

Contents

Contents

You
Can't
Get
There
From
Here

Invitation to a
Shrinking World

Twelve weeks before my husband, Nick, and I were due to leave for our long-planned, round-the-world adventure, hijackers sent a trio of airplanes careening into the World Trade Center and the Pentagon, and might have smashed a fourth plane into the Capitol were it not for a handful of brave passengers. As we all know, three thousand people were killed that day. This *is* a travel book, by the way, and a funny one at that, so I don't mean to bum anyone out with this defining moment of darkness, except that it illustrates a point that I didn't fully comprehend myself until I got a gig acting in a Bollywood movie several months later: The world is shrinking.

You only need step out into it to see the signs of this condensing, this converging. The obvious examples are the familiar ones: the McDonald's at the base of Rome's Spanish Steps; the Starbucks in downtown Doha, Qatar; the malls of Bangkok, indistinguishable from their counterparts in Los Angeles. These, along with the oft-decried economic acronym forces—NAFTA, WTO, IMF, ASEAN, etc.—are globalization's harbingers. And, depending on your worldview, they either herald the dawn of a beautiful age of international cooperation or foretell some grim world populated by prepubescent sweatshop workers and a monoculture of Gap-wearing, latte-drinking droids.

Whatever. That globalization is about stuff, product; it's economic, defined solely in terms of dollars and yen and euros. It misses the bigger and far more interesting picture. Globalization is really about people, about what happens when your culture shows up in my living room or when my way of life is tossed into your lap. It's about the marriages—some arranged, some chosen, some forced—that result when everything gets mixed up. And this is no early twenty-first-century phenomenon. Globalization is a messy, incremental, and evolutionary process, going as far back as—who knows?—Neolithic times, when rival tribes ceased fighting and started trading. Globalization is Genghis Khan consolidating Asia, from the coast of China to the skirts of Europe, and introducing a postal system to keep the empire connected. It is Arab traders sailing the oceans, ferrying not only silk and saffron to new markets, but also mathematics and, later, Islam. It is Christian missionaries descending upon South Pacific nations, delivering the Gospel of Christ and Victorian fashions to naked natives. It is Ghanaian slaves making their middle-passage to a life of bondage. It is Central European Jews emigrating en masse from the Old World to the New World. It's the Somali restaurant in downtown Minneapolis. Globalization is what happens when the melting pot explodes.

What makes the world's shrinkage so significant now is that travel, trade, and technology have sped up the process exponentially and, in doing so, altered all the rules. Thirty years ago, it was of little consequence to a Manhattan banker that some guys in a cave in Afghanistan hated everything he and his country stood for. Now, it matters; it matters a lot.

In January of 2002, my husband and I boarded a plane for our trip anyway. First stop: the South Pacific island nation of Tonga. Then onward to the disparate corners of the planet. The terrorist attacks gave us pause, made us reconsider our trip, and ultimately reminded us why we should go: To forget the humanity in others is to risk forgetting your own. Besides, whatever fear we may have nursed soon subsided; the world is so much scarier on a TV screen than it is in a spice bazaar or a tropical jungle. Once I got my toes wet, I started noticing the commonalities as much as the differences. Those freaky Kazak kids who were so obsessed with Tolkien that they spent weekends in the mountains acting out Middle-Earth fantasy games were really just trying to get in touch with their European heritage. I understood that. And the Tongan transvestites were not the beauty-contest-obsessed flits they appeared to be, but a group of men looking for love. I understood that, too.

It's no accident that my global education came not from economists, politicians, or professional opinion makers but from Tolkienists and transvestites. You see, I am a member of the tribe of the odd. Have been since, as a little girl, I came to realize that I was not like an Amy or a Jenny. I was a Weird Girl. As such, I spent a lot of time by myself, daydreaming, bug-hunting, thrift-shopping for Snoopy skirts, dyeing my hair unnatural colors, and doing interpretive dances to the Velvet Underground at my elementary school's talent shows. All of this might make me cool by today's standards, but in 1980s suburban Los Angeles, it was social suicide. Naturally, I became the picked-on person, which was just as well because the alternative was to be a picker-onner and I didn't have the stomach for that.

Mine is not a novel story. The teen-alienation motif has been well-covered in the John Hughes oeuvre. And my tale had a happy enough ending. I was miserable, but eventually the world broadened out enough for me to realize that legions of other outsiders existed. And then I started finding them: the actors, the painters, the punkers, the computer geeks, the black kid at my mostly white school, the queer boys, the antisocial girls who didn't shave their armpits. I understood early on that these people were my tribe and that somehow I would always find them.

They would find me, too. The first time I went abroad was to be an exchange student in England where, by chance, I ended up studying not in a typical parochial school but in an experimental academy without classes and classrooms. My teachers were socialists, and Chumbawamba played at school events. If you weren't a hippie, a punk, a vegetarian, or a sworn enemy of capitalism, *you* were the misfit at this school. A year later, high school diploma in hand, I traveled through Europe. In Florence, I missed the Duomo because I'd taken up with a troupe of street performers. In Paris, it was a clique of gay Moroccan florists who adopted me. In Copenhagen, I got friendly with a klatch of drag queens. This was how it always went, and how it continues to go. When I became a journalist I wasn't drawn to stories about politicians or business leaders or movie moguls. It was the child soldiers, the tree-hugging ecoterrorists, the food cultists who captured my attention. And when it came time to fall in love, I found Nick, a shy punk-rock librarian, who wasn't too cool to sing goofy songs to our cats and who seemed to love me not in spite of my weirdness but because of it.

When Nick began agitating to take a trip around the world for a year, I decided to use the occasion to put my weirdness to the test. This time I would venture to the fringe of the fringes, to seek out the guerilla Chinese linguists and the lost tribe of African Jews. I planned to experience these exotic countries through the eyes of those on the margins. I wanted to see if our otherness would bind us, if our understanding of one another's differences would bridge the cultural chasms that separated us.

But a funny thing happened on the way to the fringe. I started to notice that my freaky friends were in flux. The tentacles of globalization, whether they be in the guise of international DNA tests or the music of Vanilla Ice, were changing everything, and not only for the people in the mainstream but for those on the edges, too. Globalization is remaking India's film industry—and in doing so, creating a new class of starlets. It is remaking Amsterdam's sex trade—and putting more than a few hookers out of work. It is remaking Cambodian society—leaving a generation of street children in a strange limbo.

It is challenging identities, creating new art forms, igniting new obsessions, and uniting long-lost families.

Creation, destruction, reinvention. Things are getting very interesting.

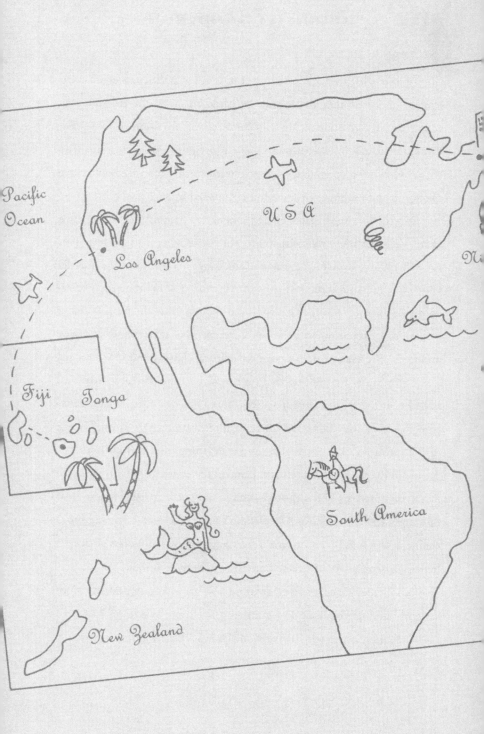

U.S. to Tonga—

January–February

It took eight hours for the homesickness to kick in. Nick and I had left Los Angeles at 6:30 P.M. on January 31st , a gaggle of West Coast relatives waving us off, and arrived in Fiji at 2 A.M. on February 2nd to an empty airport. We'd flown right over February 1st, passing the international dateline. Though we would recoup that day, hour by hour, on our yearlong westward journey, I never got over the sense of feeling cheated.

After landing in Fiji, we collected our bags—two-wheeled behemoths that we christened the Beast and the Beastette—and wandered through the moldering terminal, settling down in a deserted, fluorescent-lit restaurant to await our connecting flight to Tonga. As morning dawned, the café began filling up with throngs of Australians heading home from their beach vacations. The sight of all these happy people with fresh suntans and blond ponytails who had gone away for a week or two made me realize, suddenly and not all that pleasantly, what Nick and I were about to do. This was no holiday. We were going away for a year. Away from family. Away from friends. Away from home. Behind us was stability and normalcy; ahead of us a nebulous twelve months of getting lost, sick, ripped off, lonely, and angry. In that airport restaurant, a little neon sign began flashing in my head. It read: WHAT THE HELL HAVE YOU DONE?

Everyone assumed the trip had been my idea. After all, I'd been a world traveler since my parents dragged me abroad when I was seven. I'd done the whole backpacking thing in my teens and twenties. I even took three years off before college to travel and live in Amsterdam. Now, at thirty-one, as a freelance journalist I globe-trot to report stories from all over the world. Nick, on the other hand, hadn't left the United States until he was twenty-eight, eight years ago. His forays into the world since then had always been crammed into the two-week vacation allotments that corporate America deems sufficient. As he figured it, the choice was to keep seeing the world ten days at a time, or to take the plunge. He started talking about traveling for three months, then six, and finally began lobbying for a year away. He would just quit his job or take a leave of absence. As a research librarian at a television network, he could always pick up where he had left off.

I had my doubts about the trip. My travel bug had been itched plenty. My roller-coaster career was on an upswing, and I feared this hiatus would interrupt that trajectory. Besides, I didn't really want to drop out of my life. I happened to like it as it was. And Nick and I are so different. I am an ambitious, at times career-obsessed social butterfly with a huge extended family and a large crowd of friends. Nick is a quiet, nonobsessive bookworm who has a handful of friends and whose family consists of his mother, grandmother, and uncle. Our yin-yanginess had worked well

*enough for ten years—Nick being my steadying anchor; I, his kick
in the pants—but how might this balance skew when it was just
the two of us?*

*The more I pondered a yearlong trip away, the more the idea
struck me not as glamorous or fun but as exhausting and scary—
and in the end, that was the deciding factor. If the prospect of
travel elicits fear, it's a sure sign that the time has come to shake
loose the dust and ditch the routine. Plus, it was something that
Nick really wanted. I agreed to go, but with ground rules. Rule
one: No running about from A to B to C to D; we would plant
ourselves in one place for weeks, maybe months, at a time. My favorite part of traveling is that moment of alchemy when the man
at the tea shop remembers your name and you are suddenly transformed from tourist to temporary citizen. Rule two: No clinginess.
At home we spend a lot of time apart, hanging out together a few
nights each week and every Sunday. A year's worth of Sundays
could muck up our well-tested formula. So, I'd write and report,
he'd do whatever he wanted to do, and we'd come together when
we came together. Rule three: Start out easy, at the beach.*

*Hence Tonga. It was tropical, English-speaking, and home to
the* fakaleiti, *a strange third gender of half-men, half-women, with
whom I was itching to hang out.*

*At 10 A.M. our flight to Tonga was finally called. It was just
an hour's jaunt eastward, a zigzag back in the direction from
which we had just come. I clutched Nick's hand during takeoff
and looked out the window. From the sky, the sun glittered*

against the Pacific and tinged the waters around the hundreds of flat, sandy atolls with more blues than any crayon box I'd ever seen. I relaxed a little. It looked like paradise. Soon enough, we were coming in over Tongatapu—the largest of Tonga's 171 islands—flying atop groves of wind-stooped palm trees, jagged cliffs, and an angry, foamy sea crashing against the sharp coral reefs. All of a sudden it didn't look like paradise; it looked foreboding. The pit in my stomach lurched. The neon sign in my head blared. The plane jerked onto the runway. We had arrived.

Sex, Love, and Bouillabaisse

Generally speaking, flying coconuts don't portend successful dinner parties. The morning of the *fakaleiti* soiree, as I was setting off to the market, I was intercepted by Heleti. He was the caretaker of the Backpacker's Place, the guesthouse where Nick and I were staying, and our resident weather adviser. "Going to be a cyclone today. Big wind, big wind," he proclaimed. "I called my relatives in Ha'apai and they tell me the waves are very, very big, and the coconuts are flying."

There was no way to prove Heleti right or wrong. I'd been in Tonga for a few weeks already and had found it impossible to get anything resembling an accurate weather forecast. In the country's capital of Nuku'alofa there is no daily newspaper or morning news program with hourly weather updates. There *is* an English-language TV channel, but it broadcasts imported American televangelism all day, so forecasts tend toward the hellfire and brimstone. Perhaps I could've gotten onto one of Nuku'alofa's three public, modem-equipped computers at the bungalow that housed the post office and logged on to the country's single server and even managed to connect to CNN.com/weather or weather.com. Even if I had, the online forecast would have borne little relation to the actual conditions outside. According to the larger world, Tonga is always mideighties and partly cloudy, even when the rain is hammering the palm trees and the waves are pushing twenty feet. Tonga tags itself as "The Land Where Time Begins," being the first nation falling fully west of the international dateline. A more appropriate moniker would be "The Land That Time Forgot." I had imagined Tonga to be like Fiji or Tahiti, but though it was within two thousand miles of each of those places, it was on an entirely different map—or rather, it was off the map.

Of course, there are certain bonuses to visiting a country so remote that most people believe it to be in West Africa (that would be Togo). Oftentimes it is only within the vacuum of isolation that the gloriously odd and unique can evolve. Think of the Galapagos Islands and its finches, or Madagascar and its lemurs. In Tonga, isolation has helped to protect and maintain its population of fakaleiti—men who at an early age shuck off the macho Tongan ideal of manhood and try on something a bit frillier.

I'd heard about these fakaleiti from a friend who'd taught in Tonga in the early nineties. The fakaleiti were not simply gay boys or transvestites in the Western sense, my friend explained to me; they were a third gender who had plotted their own ground on the sexual spectrum.

I was immediately transfixed by the idea that sexuality was something we might concoct however we saw fit. For years I'd vowed to come to Tonga. This trip had provided the perfect excuse.

I spotted my first fakaleiti the day after we arrived. It was a Sunday, and Sundays in Tonga are meant for one thing: church, followed by a picnic. All businesses are closed, so the only thing for a heathen tourist to do is to grab a water taxi to one of the tiny pink-sanded offshore islands near Tongatapu, where a number of private hotels and restaurants have somehow managed to be exempted from the Sunday strictures. Nick and I were happy enough to spend a day lazing on nearby Pangaimotu, swimming in the clear waters, snorkeling around a sunken ship, and holding hands as we waded through the island's mangrove swamps. We pretty much had the place to ourselves until about two o'clock, when boatloads of Tongans began arriving. Some were still dressed in their church finery, but they soon stripped down to bathing suits and began tossing back Ikale beers (the private islands are also, apparently, piety-free zones).

It took me a while to realize that the two striking bikini-clad women with hair kinking down their backs were actually fakaleiti—or *leiti*, as they're called for short. Sleek as mermaids, they stood waist-deep in the turquoise water, glasses of wine in hand, surrounded by husky Tongan lads who were both flirting and horseplaying with them, treating them as though they were chicks *and* dudes. It was then that the complexity of the fakaleiti began to dawn on me. What did it mean to be neither male nor female—or to be both? And what did it mean to be a third sex in a place like Tonga? After all, this was a country so Christian that its constitution bans businesses from opening on the Sabbath and demands the arrest of any man who walks the streets shirt-less. But a silk dress and heels are perfectly permissible?

I had questions about the fakaleiti. Lots of questions. I had to find Joey, who, through "her" membership in Tonga's elite noble class and her connections to Tonga's royal family, was the most influential fakaleiti in town. She ran some sort of civic group, the Tongan Leitis' Association, and owned the aptly named Joey's Unisex Salon, which is where I went to find her.

Leaving Nick at the Backpacker's Place, I hopped on my rented bi-cycle and cruised through Nuku'alofa's downtown, a metropolis of a dozen or so dusty streets, and onto Vuna Road, past the palm-lined seafront where, out in the distance, I could see Pangaimotu. I turned right at the expat hangout of choice, the Billfish Bar, cutting through the suburbs full of wood houses, each with a pig or two rooting in the yard. (Tongans keep pigs like Americans keep dogs, except they eat them.) The salon was in the Kinikinilau Shopping Center, a Third World take on a 1974 American strip mall: a dusty, pothole-pocked parking lot ringed by a grocery store, a buy-in-bulk, a tailor, a pizza place, a financial services office, and the salon. The only thing missing was a donut shop.

The Kinikinilau turned out to be something of a fakaleiti club-house. On my first visit I counted seven of them sitting out front, eating popsicles, fanning themselves with outdated fashion magazines, and chatting in Tongan. I went inside the salon and one of the leiti followed me in. She had frizzy hair and acne and was wearing tracksuit pants, a T-shirt, Adidas flip-flops, and a snarl.

"Hello," I said.

"Yesss," she hissed.

"I'm looking for Joey," I said.

"No," she said.

"No?"

"Not here."

"Do you know when she'll be back?"

"Don't know."

I wasn't quite clear whether Frizzy's attitude was a result of language issues or the universal language of bitchiness. English is widely spoken in Tonga, but many Tongans openly dislike Westerners. When Nick and I had taken an exploratory bike ride around the island a few days earlier, every other person we'd passed had yelled "*P'alangi!*"—a derogatory term meaning "white person." A few kids had even thrown rocks.

I spent the next two days hiding out on Pangaimotu with Nick. I wanted to go back to the salon, but I had to work up my nerve. When I finally did, an overnight storm had left the air heavy and the island half-flooded. The Kinikinilau parking lot was knee-deep in brown water, so I parked my bike on the side of the road and waded to the front door. Frizzy was inside, along with another fakaleiti with floppy hair and a gold tooth that glinted when she smiled.

"Hi. I'm looking for Joey. Is she back yet?" I asked.

"Joey's in Feeeejeee," said Gold Tooth. "On business."

"Do you know when she'll be back?"

"Two, three days. Not sure."

"Is that Joey?" I asked, pointing to the poster-sized glamour shot of a heavily made-up brunette that hung over one of the mirrors across from an illustration of Jesus, light bursting forth from his chest.

Gold Tooth nodded. "Yesss, that's our Joey."

Two days later, I was back again. This time a crew of a half-dozen leiti was gathered in the entrance to the tailor shop, where a leiti with a blonde buzz cut and a flowery skirt was in the middle of telling a joke. The salon appeared to be empty. I cased the crowd from a safe distance while I devised a new plan, brilliant in its simplicity. I strode into the salon as though I had a standing appointment. Frizzy again followed me, just as I thought she would. I explained to her in slow English that I wanted to get my hair dyed. "This isn't my real color, you know?" I pointed to my fresh roots. Frizzy surveyed me from my hair to my feet and then curtly informed me that the salon didn't do redheads.

That night, I dragged Nick to a nightclub. It was an act of mercy on his part; he's not the party-people type, but he must have been feeling sorry for me and my failure to connect with the leiti. The Blue Pacific was a sprawling place, a few miles out of town on the shores of the island's large inland freshwater lagoon. This was *the* place to see and be seen Tongan style, and as our taxi pulled into the circular driveway, the meat market was well under way. The men, bulky as refrigerators in their shimmering button-down shirts, eyed the ladies. The ladies, spiffed up in low-cut dresses, their dark hair flowing, eyed the fakaleiti. The fakaleiti, decked out in microminis, sarongs, headdresses, and incongruously blond hair falls, eyed one another. Nick and I paid our cover fee—seven *pa'anga* for him, or about three and a half bucks; half that for me—and we walked past the beefy bouncers, across the humid dance floor, and onto the back patio, parking ourselves at a table within eavesdropping distance of a large group of gossiping leiti.

"Go talk to them," Nick said.

"I can't. I'm shy."

"You're never shy," he said.

But I was. As much as the fakaleiti intrigued me, they also intimidated me. Perhaps this insecurity was some kind of junior high reflux that a gang of giggling girls can elicit in me, or perhaps it was more a matter of my lingering homesickness. Or maybe it was Tonga. Nick and I had thought that starting the trip here would be a way to baby-step our way into the weirdness, and instead we'd jumped into the deep end with our clothes on. Tonga felt vaguely familiar, which made its essential unknowability all the more disconcerting. Quite a few Tongans I had met treated me with cool disdain or even outright aggression, an anti-Westernism I might have expected—but actually would not experience—in places like Cambodia or Tanzania. In those countries there was ample reason to hate Westerners: war, colonization, silly tourists with cornrowed hair. But Tonga had none of that. It is the only South

Pacific nation never to have been colonized, and is one of the few Polynesian islands that is rarely visited by tourists. It is off the radar—and as discombobulating as any rural African village I'd ever visited.

So Nick and I sat at the table in silence as the fakaleiti clucked and flirted. We were only halfway through our first beer when a bouncer came by and ejected us from our seats. I started to protest, but he put his paw on my shoulder and said, "Show starting." And then, just as the sky opened up and released a late-night tropical cloudburst, the Blue Pacific Fakaleiti Beauty Contest began.

There were six contestants, each of whom took two turns parading down the rain-slicked cement runway. The first competition was formal wear of the Las Vegas variety: One leiti wore a red floor-length gown, the spangles reflecting the fairy lights that festooned the stage; another, Gold Tooth from the salon, went the Sally Bowles route in a severe black bob, short black skirt, and fishnet stockings; while a third seemed to have found her skirted leotard at the U.S. figure skating team's castoff sale. The second set of ensembles was sportswear: hip-huggers and bikini tops, flowery halters and matching billowy pants, peach flight-attendant suits. Some leiti wore heels. Those who didn't tippy-toed in make-believe ones. They changed clothes behind the stage, adding a friend's necklace or plucking a hibiscus from the bush and twisting it into their wet hair. The rain pounded down throughout the twenty-minute show, but the leiti strutted their stuff on the catwalk in practiced supermodel saunters as though they were high and dry in the Fashion Week tents. The crowd, sheltered from the deluge underneath the covered patio, catcalled and cheered with gusto, the fakaleiti making the most ruckus of all, except for one older leiti wearing a coppery sarong and matching turban, who had pulled her chair onto the sand. She sat there alone, quietly watching the show and getting drenched.

Naturally, as soon as the contest was over, the rain let up. I inched toward the contestants, now clustered around the bar. Frizzy was there, too; I was nearly at her side when the emcee returned to the stage to announce the winners. Lasa, aka Gold Tooth, took first place, and a fakaleiti named Viva came in second. When Viva's name was announced, Frizzy speed-skipped toward the stage, waving her hands in the air and screaming, "Veeeevah, Veeeevah." Then Frizzy came bounding back to the bar, looked straight at me, and said: "Oh, hi. You look so pretty," and planted a kiss on my cheek and a rum and Coke in my hand, as though I were her oldest and bestest friend.

Frizzy's actual name turned out to be Rosie, and her English, aided substantially by a half-dozen cocktails, turned out to be quite good. She pulled me over to a table where Susi, the soaking wet senior diva, had been joined by several others. Rosie had transformed herself from the androgynous and semisurly creature at the salon into a beaming femme fatale in a leopard-print dress, her acne artfully hidden by makeup and her décolletage glittering with sparkle dust. I told her she looked great. She tittered and hugged me. She smelled like jasmine. "Oh, thank you. You are so beautiful."

"I saw you in the beauty salon and I wanted to talk to you," I said. "But you didn't seem to want to talk."

"I'm very shy. Except when I'm drunk, and I'm too much drunk now," she said and then erupted into the crescendo of giggles that would punctuate pretty much everything she said that night.

I asked Rosie if she'd ever competed in one of the beauty contests. She spent the next ten minutes detailing her pageant résumé, counting on her fingers, mixing up the dates. "Oh, I'm too drunk to remember. Come to the salon next week and I'll show you my pictures."

Viva, a tall, lanky young leiti with a bobbed haircut and a mole atop her lip, came over looking crestfallen, her second-place winnings of two hundred *pa'anga* in hand.

"You were so good tonight," I said to her. "Rosie told me it was your first contest. And you won!"

"I had a feeling tonight would be the night," Viva said. But there was no joy in this statement, for Viva had been gunning for top girl, not understudy, and not second place to Lasa. "I hoped it would be the night," Viva repeated wistfully. She then pulled out a compact and started touching up her makeup with her fingers. On closer inspection I saw that there was no mirror or compact. Viva was simply miming her beauty routine before an imaginary looking glass in the palm of her hand.

"Are you married?" Rosie asked me.

I nodded.

"Where is your man?"

I'd asked Nick to steer clear for a while, worried his presence would intimidate the girls. This was stupid of me. If the fakaleiti appreciate female attention, they absolutely swoon over the male variety, particularly from an exotic foreigner. Nick was chatting with an expat we'd met, and when he was done I called him over. "Ladies," I said, "this is my husband, Nick." The girls were all over him, lining up cold beers for him to drink.

"You are very lucky. He is very handsome," Rosie said. "Isn't he handsome?" she asked Susi, who had been quietly observing.

"Very handsome, dahling," Susi said.

Nick just sat there smiling. It occurred to me that perhaps your typical straight guy might not be quite so comfy learning about boob prosthesis while several drag queens draped themselves over him, but unflappable, open-minded Nick, who had played punk shows wearing a dress back in the day, clearly wasn't having any issues. He was quietly observing as he always does, soaking in the moment. Just then I wanted to bury my face in his neck. That, however, would have to wait until later.

"She is forty-eight, can you believe it?" Rosie interrupted, pointing to Susi. Susi had creaseless caramel skin—pampered with rain baths and applications of ptui nut that Tongan women chew up and then rub on themselves for moisturizer—and two enthusiastically penciled arches where her eyebrows had once been.

"Yes, I am forty-eight. I am the oldest one," Susi said, before plunking all two hundred pounds of herself on my lap.

A few minutes later the emcee returned to the stage and Susi squealed, "Oohh, it's the floor show." As soon as the Tongan women shimmied onto the stage in tight bodices and long skirts to dance the *lakalaka*, Susi ran to the front of the stage, gyrating and shaking her chest. When the Tongan men began banging their chests as part of the war dance, Susi rolled on the sand in front of the stage, a la Madonna circa "Like a Virgin." Such antics kept up throughout the Hawaiian *hula*, the Tahitian *otea*, and the Samoan *tavallunga*, and escalated further when a pair of fire-eating brothers appeared for the finale, causing Susi to shriek: "The brothers, they are so handsome!" Susi yanked me out of my chair and toward the stage. The boys were indeed adorable, but they were also throwing flaming sticks around, so I hung back while Susi stormed the stage.

The night continued in a friendly state of bacchanal. Rosie piled on the kisses and compliments, invited me to dinner, and inexplicably kept trying to shove a ten-*pa'anga* note into my hand, insisting I'd need it for food later. Viva begged me to stop by the bakery where she worked and promised to make me a cake. Susi invited me round to the fakaleiti netball games. Every invitation was also extended to Nick, who nodded vaguely with a tipsy grin on his face. I arranged to meet Rosie and Lasa at the salon on Monday, and then, at 4 A.M., my feet bitten raw by the sand flies, my teeth hurting from the sugary drinks, and my body adorned with Rosie's sparkles, I bade the fakaleiti farewell.

Back at the guesthouse, things were also starting to get interesting. A strange group of tourists was converging there. We had Dev, a traveling salesman and single father from New Zealand and his dashingly handsome preteen son, George. Next was Ivan, a sixty-eight-year-old Czech émigré and German national yachter, who'd spent the last decade sailing the South Pacific and had just married Mele, a dewy, shy Tongan girl who was all of twenty-two. Rounding out the group were Astrid and Martin, a pair of German doctors and psychoanalysts who had ditched their degrees, houses, and VW Golfs to go tramping around the world indefinitely. They'd been in Tonga for more than a year.

The Backpacker's Place was the cheapest guesthouse in town, although calling it a guesthouse was a bit optimistic. It was a dump: a mobile home trailer where we slept, a loftlike barnhouse that was too mosquito-infested to enter, and a clapboard house with a kitchen. The cozy kitchen was the saving grace, especially after we all started making communal meals. Astrid created lasagnas with whatever she found at the markets. I roasted chicken and tossed together papaya and avocado salads with fruit picked from the garden. Nick did spaghetti. And Dev prepared tongue-searing curries. Ivan and Mele had no cash for groceries and didn't know how to cook, but they were persuaded to join in. We spent hours each day around that table, preparing the meal, eating the meal, talking about the meal, and then talking about everything else. After a week or so the guesthouse felt less like a hotel and more like a home, and this hodgepodge of travelers began to become a temporary family. As with all families, we had our dramas.

Dev was reeling from a double desertion. First his wife had ditched him, leaving him to raise three kids on his own, and now one of his daughters had run away to America. This had convinced him to pull George out of school and move to Fiji where Dev had family, but first he had business to conduct in Tonga. Dev was a raging alcoholic but a disciplined one. Cocktail hour never began before 7 P.M.

Soon enough, Ivan was joining Dev's extended tippling to drown out problems of his own. Ivan and Mele were stuck in Tonga while they attempted to get Mele a visa to New Zealand, so they could sell Ivan's yacht and return to Germany. But the larger issue was that Ivan and his new bride had not consummated their relationship. "Mele is too young, like a flower," he'd announced one morning at breakfast in front of Mele. For her part, Mele had taken to spending her days with twelve-year-old George. The two of them raced around town on bicycles, swam at the wharf, had water fights, and exhibited all the symptoms of puppy love.

"George has a very unhealthy attachment to Mele, like she is a mother," Ivan told Astrid one morning, clearly hoping for a bit of professional help. "He needs help with the psychological," he said, tapping his head.

"Oh, I don't think so," Astrid said. "They're just close in age."

Ivan puffed on his cigarette and frowned.

Meanwhile, as Ivan battled the consulate to get his young wife a visa, the marital bed remained cold. It was a soap opera to be sure, but it was comforting to be engrossed in someone else's problems. The days at the guesthouse began to take on an easy rhythm, the fakaleiti were warming up, and I began to think I might survive this year after all.

On Monday when I turned up for my lunchtime date at the salon, I found Rosie, Lasa, a peroxide seamstress called Princess Mara, a boyish leiti named Baby, a woman named Fina, and Fina's mentally retarded sister, whom everyone called the Halfwit, at an office next door. They were clustered in front of a fan, watching a tape of the 2001 Miss Universe contest. I arrived in time for the interview portion, when the finalists answer those trite questions about their hopes for the world—you know, helping children, promoting world peace, serving Jesus, and the like. Assuming that some claws-out commentary would be appropriate, I began peppering the proceedings with snarky remarks. The leiti politely ignored me at first and became visibly annoyed with me soon after. It dawned on me that this contest was not an exercise in irony; the leiti took Miss Universe very seriously.

After Miss Puerto Rico took the crown, Rosie, Lasa, and I returned to the salon, where I became even more confused. We sat down on the bench in the lavender anteroom and I started quizzing them. I was curious to know about their families, about how they'd become fakaleiti, and about the origin of the fakaleiti. For while there is no in-depth historical record on the leiti—not even from the various Europeans who visited Tonga over the last four hundred years and wrote prodigiously dull accounts of their experiences—anthropologists say that the practice has been going on for generations. One explanation is that when families lacked enough girl children, they simply raised their youngest son female, out of a practical household need. Such fakaleiti dressed like women but were oriented sexually like straight men. Many of them went on to marry women.

Rosie, who was nineteen, and Lasa, who was twenty-one, were not of that tradition. As they told me, no one had forced either of them into a dress. And both of them liked boys. When I asked about the origin of their fakaleitiness, they recited pat and near-identical stories, about growing up knowing that they were different, wearing women's clothing at home from a very early age, and doing so in public during their late teens. This evolution sounded just like the transformation my gay friends back in the States had undergone: an early sense of being a world apart, an affinity for dolls (the gay boys) or lacrosse (the dykey girls) that developed into an attraction to same-sex partners. I told Rosie and Lasa as much.

They were horrified, and more than a little offended. They were not like my friends at all, they emphatically told me, because *they were not gay*. The thought of two "straight"—i.e., neither one adopting a feminine style—men going at it was revolting to them, as was the notion of a girl-on-girl coupling (there's no female equivalent to fakaleiti). They attempted to explain this to me by laying out the rules of sexual propriety in Tonga, which in their minds were universal. Men were supposed to have sex with either women or fakaleiti. Anything else was an abomination.

"Are the men you sleep with gay?" I asked.

"Oh, no, we only sleep with straight men," Lasa answered.

"But how can they be straight if they're having sex with you?"

"They're not having sex with another man; they're having sex with a fakaleiti."

"So does that make you gay?"

"No," Lasa insisted.

"So you're not gay, then?"

"No, no we are not gay; we are poofters," Rosie said wearily, as if this kernel would clarify things.

"Right," Lasa added. "We are just born this way."

"I get that part. But gay people are just born that way, too. If you're not gay, what are you? Are you transsexual? Transgendered? How do you classify yourselves?"

"We are not any of those," Lasa said, slowly, as if trying to explain some basic concept to a thick child. "We are just fakaleiti."

"I got it. I see," I said.

I didn't get it at all.

And it only got weirder. Fina introduced me to Eva, an old-school fakaleiti of Susi's generation. Diabetes and obesity had left Eva housebound, and now she lived with Fina and Susi, where she spent her days watching repeats of *The Little Mermaid* on TV. The first time I stopped by to visit at the square, modest, two-room house, I found Eva reclining on a plaid couch. She talked me into buying her cigarettes, and when I returned, she lifted up her blouse. "All the fakaleiti are jealous of me because I have tits," she said, smiling and showing me her man-breasts. "All the fakaleiti say I look the most like a real woman." Eva did look like a woman—like a trailer park hausfrau in a muumuu, but a natural lady nonetheless.

As long as I kept Eva in cigarettes she would entertain me with a stream of salacious tales about her wild days when she and Susi would seduce and then rob visiting sailors. Unlike many of the other fakaleiti, who were shy and proper when sober, Eva left nothing out—the blow jobs in the cemetery, the arrests for indecency—so I assumed that anything was fair game. One afternoon I asked Eva if she'd ever had sex with another leiti. "Oh, that's sick," she said, putting her hand in front of her face.

Had she ever had sex with a woman? Eva answered by telling me a meandering story about a woman who'd stolen away the guy Eva had been secretly sleeping with, then left him and tried to seduce Eva. "She came over and she was drunk. She wanted me to suck her tits," Eva told me, the look on her face so disgusted that you'd have thought the woman had asked Eva to eat her eyeballs.

"I take it that you're not into women," I said.

"Women belong with men."

Such statements both amused and perplexed me, mostly because even though I'd heard that as a third gender, fakaleiti were neither men nor women, neither gay nor straight, on some level I just couldn't comprehend that. I assumed that cross-dressing was the way Tongan boys expressed the gay gene. Over the next month, I tried to figure it out. I went with Rosie, Lasa, Susi, and Baby to their bars. I primped at their houses before club nights. I visited them up at work and called them at home. I gate-crashed their meetings. I went to a fancy royal gala dinner catered by the Tongan Leitis' Association and even talked Nick into going (much to the girls' delight).

In some ways, the fakaleiti were traditional good girls, buying into the local sexual and gender mores: Men should work and lift heavy things; women should clean house and raise babies. Fakaleiti should do it all. "My family likes me because I do the washing *and* the hoeing," Rosie told me. Moreover, the leiti were just as zealously Christian as everyone else in Tonga, dragging their hungover selves to church every Sunday, taping pictures of the Last Supper over their beds—alongside cutouts of Kylie Minogue. In other ways, however, the fakaleiti, especially the younger set, really did seem just gay: the women's clothes, the sashaying, the lispy falsettos, and the fact that they fucked men. This made their raging homophobia all the more bizarre.

To mix it up further, the fakaleiti possessed such distinctly male and female traits, often on display at the same time. Nowhere was this more apparent than on the netball court, where every Tuesday and Thursday, several leiti would gather for a round-robin tournament. One afternoon, I got Nick to come with me.

Whereas I had been whiling away my days cooking, eating, or fakaleiti-chasing, Nick had actually been exploring Tonga. He saw all the things the *Lonely Planet* guidebook recommended: the underwater caves, the blowholes, the coral beaches. (I missed these, of course. I'm the kind of tourist who visits Paris and skips the Louvre.) He also had hooked up with some local Peace Corps workers with whom he took semiweekly kava ceremonies (kava being a mildly narcotic root that's extremely popular among the South Pacific islanders). Nick wasn't as fascinated with the leiti as I was, and he quickly grew tired of their tittering, but he was intrigued by the netball games. We took our bikes to the rundown courts between our guesthouse and downtown. There, about forty leiti were gathered, decked out in a range of costumes from gypsy fortune-teller outfits to Adidas tracksuits. At four o'clock the whistle blew and the leiti began a fiercely competitive three-hour session of gender-bending ball. They would prance around the court, shouting "Dahling, over here!" when they were open for a pass and do that hand-flappy thing girls do when they run. But when the play got going, the going got rough. Makeup ran with sweat, talons were torn off, torsos bruised with body blows. It was every bit as punishing as the men's rugby being played on the adjacent field.

Nick was mesmerized by the spectacle. "Wow," he said. "They really are both male and female."

I'm glad Nick got the essence of the fakaleiti, because I still didn't. Perhaps all had been clear a few generations ago, when fakaleiti were defined and judged by Tongan standards alone, without the global imports of Christianity and gay rights to muddy the water. But today fakaleiti stand at a crossroads between the Bible and Stonewall, between an ancient identity and a modern one with forces from all sides pulling at them.

The old forces are, of course, tradition and religion. Tonga may never have been colonized by Europeans, but missionaries went to town on the place—so successfully that today, 99 percent of Tonga's population is Christian. The missionaries went about discouraging traditional practices such as nudity, polygamy, and cannibalism. The fakaleiti they left alone.

These days, however, an American-style religious fundamentalism is creeping into Tonga. Mormons and evangelical missionaries are replacing the Catholics and the Methodists, and the new kids in town do not approve of the fakaleiti brand of gender reinvention. Similarly, Tongan television now broadcasts fundamentalist programs like Pat Robertson's *700 Club*—a show obsessed with sinner homosexuals—for hours every day. This constant harping has no doubt made ordinary Tongans aware of what *gay* means and, lo and behold, that they have been unknowingly fraternizing with queers all these years. The leiti, who are just as traditional and religious as everyone else, are loath to be lumped into the maligned "queer" category.

But at the same time, in the last fifteen years the isolation that had kept the rest of the world out of Tonga—missionaries notwithstanding— has slowly been eroding. Globalization is arriving in Tonga, bringing with it, among other things, a new class of sexuality. *Gay* has many couriers. Today, as many Tongans live out of the country (mostly in the United States and New Zealand) as in it. Some of these expats are homosexual, and when they return to the islands they bring their sexuality with them. By the same token, more Tongans, including fakaleiti, are traveling overseas and encountering the West's sexuality buffet—not just men and women and fakaleiti, but men and women, dykes and fags, bis and swingers, transvestites and transsexuals. Given such choice, some fakaleiti opt to take on a more gay persona and then bring that persona back home. The media also do their share to confound the leiti identity. Tonga may be off the radar, but popular culture is a tenacious weed. Elton John, George Michael, RuPaul, and Madonna, among others, have all made inroads here. And then there is Joey.

I finally caught up with the jet-setting Joey at Nuku'alofa's Catholic church, where she directs the choir. Nick and I went one Sunday, taking seats in the cool, cavernous wood chapel, surrounded by ladies fluttering their palm-frond fans. The mass, in Tongan, was a bit on the dull side, but Joey livened things up with her gospel solos—Aretha-esque renditions of "Amazing Grace" and "I'll Fly Away." Afterward, I introduced myself. She was late to catch the boat to Pangaimotu, but we made an appointment for the following week.

We met at Friends, Nuku'alofa's trendy eatery. "You see, I was very blessed," Joey told me in a husky voice that was authentic and a clipped British accent that was not. "I grew up with the Tongan royal family, and I had a family that understood me. But I see that the respect I enjoy, the others do not," she said. Part of that privilege was luck of the genes. Joey's family, being nobility, had money and land. Joey owned a salon, had interests in several local businesses, and traveled all over the world for beauty trade shows. Such glamour contrasted with the lives of most leiti, who tended to have low-paying, "women's" jobs as tailors or bakers or hairdressers and were among the lowest on Tonga's socioeconomic tree.

Determined to use her status for good, in 1991 Joey founded the Tongan Leitis' Association. "Everything in Tonga is *faka* this, *faka* that [the ubiquitous *faka* prefix means "like a"], and you know what that sounds like to international people," Joey told me with a conspiratorial laugh. "We just call ourselves 'leiti.'" It was the first of Joey's many moves linking her organization to the West. The stated reason for the Leitis' Association was to battle AIDS, though HIV rates have remained very low in Tonga.

As the nascent group evolved, Joey modeled it on gay rights organizations she'd seen in full swing in Australia, New Zealand, and the United States. And when it came time to raise funds, Joey decided that a fakaleiti beauty contest would do the trick. Beauty contests were already a staple in Tonga's straight world—the yearly Miss Heilala competition is a big event—but Joey's take on the pageant, the Miss Galaxy contest, was full of over-the-top kitschiness and overt displays of sexuality. In other words, it was a drag show. Miss Galaxy is now a three-day affair that outsells the Heilala contest. Even the royal family attends. It is the pinnacle event for fakaleiti, a time when they are not only visible to all of Tonga but embraced. The popularity of the contests had also spawned a cottage industry for beauty contests. I'd thought I'd been lucky to catch the Blue Pacific competition my first week on the island, but it turns out that you can't throw a tube of lipstick without it hitting some kind of pageant or modeling show.

The only problem with this new gay identity is that the fakaleiti don't want it. Fakaleiti didn't set out to be this way; they claim they don't want to be this way, and to some degree they are still very confused as to what "this way" means. After all, until recently there was no concept of *gay* in Tonga. There's not even a word to describe homosexuality in the Tongan language. Moreover, fakaleiti are savvy enough to recognize that if homophobia is institutionalized into religion, the way it is in the West, and if fakaleiti are considered queer, the way they would be in the West, they may be in trouble. "People treat us like dogs," Lasa lamented over and over again, "because they think we are gay."

I understood her worries, but I wondered if there wasn't something to be gained by tapping into a global gay-rights movement. There is strength in numbers. There is power in pride. By throwing in their lot with the rest of the queers, maybe the leiti might someday realize more rights, or at least that most important one—the right to fall in love.

Love, at least sexual love, is off limits to most fakaleiti. It's all part of this Madonna/whore bind in which the leiti find themselves. "Sluts and Superwomen" is how anthropologist Niko Besnier describes it: Fakaleiti are valued in society because they make great housekeepers and are thought to be smarter, wiser, and craftier than real women. They are the resident vixens, known for a certain in-your-face sexuality, and "straight" guys hit on—and sleep with—fakaleiti all the time. But such exploits are always furtive and temporary. It is both socially and legally unacceptable for fakaleiti to carry on long-term sexual relationships with men. The penalty for sodomy is jail.

I don't completely understand why a culture would at first embrace a third sex and then neuter it. Perhaps historically the fakaleiti, like eunuchs, had never been sexual. Or maybe once upon a time the leiti really were hetero. Or perhaps in pre-Christian days no one cared if males cavorted with other males. But now they do. Almost none of the leiti I met was in, or had been in, a long-term relationship. Instead, they hung out with one another, sublimated their need for affection by participating in beauty contests, and slept around with straight guys in one-night stands. Some of the leiti took money for sex. All of this has made them targets of discrimination, sexual harassment, abuse, and rape.

The one fakaleiti I met who was exempted from this sexual purgatory was Joey. She *was* blessed, and not just because of her wealth or connections to the royal family, but because those things afforded her one very important entitlement: Joey could have a boyfriend.

One night after a few drinks at the Billfish Bar, the talk predictably turned to love. "How did you marry Nick?" Viva asked.

I met Nick in Eugene, Oregon, at college. He played in a popular band about town, and I'd known him from shows and through friends. He was one of those adorable, blue-haired, shy, seemingly asexual punk boys, the kind I'd recently sworn off of as relationship poison. So I nursed my crush on him. But instead of pursuing any kind of romance, I just became his friend, and he and I took to advising each other on our other respective dalliances. This went on for about a year, but shortly before I was due to leave Eugene to go traveling for six months (I couldn't make it through four years of college without at least one trimester of escape), things started to change. Nick was in another band, and he'd asked me to do a number with them. At band practice we started flirting. Then we started spending all this time together, and then finally, on the night before the show, we found ourselves at my tiny studio apartment, baking chocolate chip cookies and talking. And talking some more. We moved from the floor to the edge of the bed. Finally I figured that if I didn't do something, we might stay on the edge of that bed forever, so at 2 A.M. I got up, took off Nick's shoes, and clicked off the light. "Do you want me to stay?" Nick asked. "If you want to," I replied. He did. From there, the progression was easy. After a year, we moved in together, and after six years we realized we had become each other's family, and so we decided to go traditional and get married, though we tempered the tradition part by having a raucous punk-rock Jewish wedding, with Nick's tattooed ex-girlfriend serving as the best man.

When I finished telling the story, I asked the girls if they'd ever been in love. They looked at each other. Rosie said she had, maybe, once. For a month or so.

"Do you want to fall in love?"

Rosie laughed. "No, maybe later."

"It leads to heartbreak," Lasa piped in.

"If it is someone I really trust, I could fall in love with him," Rosie ventured.

"Yes, someone who understands me," Lasa said and looked away.

"You're so lucky to be married," Rosie said.

Then Viva asked, "Do they have people like us in America?" This was a common question, and I answered it broadly, putting fakaleiti under the queer umbrella.

"They do, lots of them."

"Do you know people like us in America?"

I told her that my best friend is gay and that another friend is trans-sexual.

"The people like us there, do they get married?" Viva asked.

"Don't be stupid," Lasa snapped.

Viva looked wounded. I explained to her that, in fact, there was a battle raging on just that question, and in some places, like New York City, gay men and lesbians could live together openly, even adopt or have children. A transgendered man could have sex-reassignment surgery, reapply for a birth certificate as a female, and then get legally married to a man. That was an impossibly long road for someone like Viva to even contemplate traveling, but she seemed excited by the prospect nonetheless. She leaned over and in a quiet voice said: "I just want to fall in love."

That night when I came back from the bar, Ivan and Dev were sitting at the table. Dev was singing his lonely man blues, recounting how his wife, who was Tongan, had left him, and how difficult life had been since. Ivan was reminiscing about meeting Mele at a restaurant on the island of Vava'u and falling for her with all the bumbling shyness of the twenty-five-year-old who should've been courting her.

"I was very confused. I did not know what to say," Ivan said.

"Why not?" asked Dev.

"I was scared, you know. I just wanted love," he said.

I glanced at Dev, drowning his loneliness, and then at Ivan, a love-struck sixty-eight-year-old. I thought of Viva earlier that night, the look in her eyes. *Love.* It is the universal common denominator. I had an idea. The world was already shrinking; universes were already colliding. It was time to merge my two strange little Tongan worlds.

My invitation to a dinner party caused quite the splash among the leiti, especially because it was exclusive.

"Who else is coming?" Susi wanted to know.

"You, Rosie, Lasa, Fina, Viva, Baby," I said. "Plus the people I live with. And Nick."

"Don't tell too many fakaleiti about it," Susi said in an exaggerated whisper that anyone could hear. "Otherwise, *everyone* will come."

On the morning of the party, the killer storm was brewing. After hearing Heleti's dire predictions, I went into the kitchen to make some coffee and consider my options. I could reschedule. Problem was, I'd already postponed the party on account of rain the night before. The kitchen table could comfortably seat six, handle ten in a squeeze. With fourteen coming we'd need to use the patio table, and that would hardly work when it was raining. But I'd sworn not to cancel again, which is why even though today the weather was far worse, the dinner party would have to go on.

Most of the stores in town were closing early because of the storm, so I had to devise a menu with what I already had and what I could find. I'd bought a dozen lobsters a few days before. They were in the freezer and would constitute the centerpiece of the meal. Beyond that, the pickings were slim: tomatoes, frozen tuna, pasta, whatever fruit I could get from our trees. The final menu was to be a rather sad bouillabaisse, served over spaghetti, along with a vegetable casserole, salad, garlic bread, and, for dessert, a banana-papaya crumble. It wasn't my most stylish meal, but whatever it lacked in panache would, I hoped, be compensated for by the cases of beer chilling in the fridge.

It had been raining intermittently since the previous morning, heavily at times. Sometime around four that afternoon the rain began coming down in windows of wet. By 5:30 the sky was too dark to see anything, but the sounds were ominous: branches snapping, glass breaking, and the occasional *crack* of some flying projectile crashing into some stationary object. Heleti was right—the coconuts were flying. The streets, however, were quiet; even the barking, bullying neighborhood dogs had shut up. No one was going anywhere tonight, including, I figured, my guests.

But at 7:30, as Dev and Ivan settled into their gin routine, and Mele and George sat down for a game of cards, Martin called to me: "Someone is looking for you."

Rosie and Viva were in the barnhouse, their meticulous primping showered right off. I crossed the lawn, shin-deep in water and sludge, to fetch them. By the time we got into the kitchen we were all drenched.

"Rosie, Viva, this is Dev, Ivan, George, Mele. You know Nick," at which they both smiled and fluttered mascara-dripping eyelashes, "and here are Astrid and Martin."

Viva blushed. Rosie tittered. She had gone corporate chic in a gray pantsuit. Viva had opted for East Village sexy in low-rider jeans and a shirt that tied up the side. George kept stealing glances at the two, utterly confused, while Astrid and Martin smiled and looked at the floor, upon which Rosie and Viva were leaving puddles of water. Finally, Dev broke the silence.

"You are a hairdresser, I hear," Dev said to Rosie. "I need a haircut." And then, from where I will never know, he produced a pair of professional haircutting sheers. "Will you please cut my hair?"

"Dev, they are guests tonight," I said. "They didn't come to work."

"But I need my hair cut. I will pay her."

"Dev, why don't you just go to the salon? It's a party tonight."

He ignored me. "I can wash it first if that helps," he said, wielding the scissors at Rosie.

"Let's just have a drink," I said.

I handed Rosie and Viva a beer. Viva started small talk with Ivan about New Zealand, while Dev zeroed in on Rosie. "You should open a salon in Fiji. That's where I'm going to live. I'm from Fiji. I'm Indian, and have been living in Auckland, but soon I'm moving back to Fiji with George here. It's a better life, you know." He stopped, took a pull of gin, and continued. "You could make lots of money there. I could set you up in a salon. Make much more money than working in Tonga. I could get you your papers. You could hire a staff. Give haircuts and other things. I have a friend in Fiji. We might start looking for a place."

I looked at Dev. Was he hitting on Rosie? Was he serious? Was Rosie interested? I couldn't tell. I glanced at Nick to see what he thought of Dev's behavior. He gave nothing away. Rosie was sitting with her head half cocked, a small grin on her lips, as though she received such offers every night.

At eight o'clock, Lasa arrived. Viva snorted.

"What's wrong?" I asked.

"I didn't know *Lasa* was coming," she said.

"Of course Lasa would be coming. What's the matter?"

"She's jealous of me because of the beauty contest."

Viva shot Lasa a dirty look. Lasa ignored her and sat down on the floor. Ivan looked confused, staring at Viva and then at Mele, who was ignoring him. Dev continued his pitch. Ten awkward minutes later, Fina arrived with Susi and Baby and a bottle of rum. I was relieved—Susi would have everyone talking in minutes.

Except that Susi, belle of the ball, flamboyant lover of the spotlight, had gone mute on me. She pulled a chair into a corner and proceeded to hold her hands upside down in front of her face, looking like a demented geisha. She wouldn't even return my hello. I offered her a beer. She waved it off with a flick of the hand.

"You're not drinking?"

"It's Lent."

"It was Lent last week, too."

She put her hands back in front of her face but beckoned me forth with a finger. "I can't drink," she hissed. "There are elders here." Except for Ivan, no one in the room was older than Susi. I took the beer for myself.

By 8:30 all fourteen of us were jammed into the kitchen; there wasn't enough bench space for everyone, so Nick, Mele, and George joined Lasa on the floor, while Astrid and I stood against the counter. I tried my best to get people mingling. Dinner parties often start with an awkward period before the alcohol kicks in and the connections form. Back home I had a knack for pulling together disparate people: librarians, punk rockers, fashionistas, academics. It always gelled eventually. In fact, I'd always believed the more diverse the crowd, the more fun the party. But this dinner, prompted by an impulse to spread the love, looked like it was about to be hijacked by discord. Dev kept rambling on about his salon, while Astrid clung to the counter and Ivan stared glumly at his wife, who was flirting, as usual, with George, who was still sneaking looks at Lasa.

"Is anyone hungry?" I asked.

"Oh, no," Rosie said. I looked around the room and the leiti all shook their heads.

"You're not hungry. . . . But I cooked lobster. . . . Um, Nick, can you come here a second?"

"Yes, Miss Gayle."

"What am I going to do?" I whispered. "No one will eat."

He shrugged. Dinner parties were not his specialty. Instead he put his hand on the back of my neck, a kind of Vulcan hold that tranquilizes me. "I don't know. Just keep calm, feed them, and send them home," he said.

"You're right. This sucks. I want this night over," at which point Astrid leaned in and whispered, "It's rude in Tonga to say you're hungry. Just serve dinner and they'll eat."

As Astrid, Nick, and I began dishing out fourteen portions of dinner, there was a flash of lightning, a crack of thunder, and the lights went out.

"Does anyone have a torch?" Martin asked.

Apparently not.

"OK then. Matches?" Several matchboxes were proffered. Martin took one and set off in search of candles, while Nick took another box and stood over Astrid and me, lighting matches for us to work by. Illuminated by the weak light of a ten-second flame, Astrid and I hurriedly dished up servings of spaghetti and bouillabaisse with all the grace of school lunch ladies. Martin returned with the candles, which we lit and distributed around the room.

The wind was blowing, flashing bits of moonlight glanced through the kitchen window, the candles were flickering, and somehow the stew had come out divine. Everyone started to eat. In the semidarkness I could feel a change in the air. There was an exhale, a relief of warm food against discomfort. The murmurs of conversation started; quiet at first, a bit of soft laughter. Then George turned to Lasa and asked the question that had clearly been weighing on him.

"Are you, I mean, do I call you 'he' or 'she'?" he stammered.

Lasa laughed. "We're both," she said.

And with that, the dinner party began.

Nobody had been hungry, yet the ten-quart pot of bouillabaisse, four packages of pasta, three loaves of garlic bread, and a vegetable casserole were all razed. The beer was history. Dev offered his stash. Fina pulled out her bottle of rum, now only three-quarters full, as Susi had been secretly slugging from it during dinner. The lights were still off but the rain had stopped. We moved into the barnhouse, lighting candles and mosquito coils. Nick and Martin hooked up a Walkman to some decrepit speakers and started blasting Fatboy Slim. Everyone danced or played cards or gossiped. Only Ivan stayed out of the action as he watched Mele and grew glummer and drunker. The candles melted all the way down and we lit new ones. The booze was disappearing. Rosie passed that magical alcoholic threshold into sentimentality and started to cry. "I will miss you when you leave, Gayle," she said. "I don't want you to go. You are my friend." Then she paused to think. "But I will leave Tonga, too. I will go to Fiji to open a salon. It will be hard to leave my family, but I will go. I will make a lot of money."

I was on my way out to search for the rest of my guests, who had repaired back to the kitchen, when Lasa leapt out of the darkness and grabbed me. "I have to talk to you," she stage whispered. "It's important, but it's, it's embarrassing."

"What is it?"

She took a deep breath, clutched my arm. "Miss Galaxy. I'm going to be in the Miss Galaxy contest," she said with a small smile. Yes, I said. I'd heard Joey's Salon had just picked Lasa as its contestant. That was great news, especially considering that Joey's contestants almost always won. Lasa looked at me, straight in the eyes, as if trying to telepathically impart something of vast importance.

"When you get back to New York, will you send me an evening gown? And pumps. It's so hard to get shoes my size here."

After disappointing Lasa with the news that I wouldn't be returning to New York until well after Miss Galaxy, I followed Mele to the kitchen. The power had returned. Dev was sitting at the table with a local cabdriver I called Big Pussy because of his resemblance to the *Sopranos* character. Ivan was sobbing something in German, while Astrid tried to comfort him and Viva looked on concerned. Pussy helped himself to the gin. Mele's eyes were dancing.

"What is happening?" she asked in English.

Ivan started sputtering in German.

"Ivan doesn't think you care for him at all," Astrid told Mele. "He wants to know if you love him."

"He said that? He said that?" asked Mele, excitedly.

"The Tongan women," Big Pussy said. "They are difficult."

"Love is complicated," added Dev.

Ivan went on. He loved Mele. Was it a mistake? Did she want to come with him to Germany? Why would she not touch him? Was he a despicable old man to her? Would it ever get better? He wanted to be like a father to her in a way, to teach her things, to show her a better life. He knew he didn't have so many years left, but he thought that his last decade could be a happy one. He would leave Mele better than he found her and she could get married again, have children.

Mele looked overwhelmed. "Did he say that? Did he say he loved me?" she repeated, to which Ivan started bawling all over again. He spat something in German toward Pussy and Dev. Astrid translated.

"He says, 'You laugh at me; you laugh at me because I am a man and I cry over women.'"

Pussy, whose face was usually set into a smirk, enhancing his Sopranoesque qualities, turned serious. So did Dev. "In Tonga, the men cry," Pussy said. "We cry about women. Even when we laugh, we cry."

Ivan looked up, the tears wet in his eyes. He surveyed the room: me, Astrid, Pussy, Dev, Mele, Viva, her eyes glistening.

"We cry," Viva reassured him. "We cry over love."

The party started to splinter. Fina and Susi went home, toting a bag of leftovers for Eva and the Halfwit. Pussy, seemingly moved by the talk of love, offered free lifts to Rosie, Lasa, and Viva. Rosie wasn't ready to leave. Lasa took the ride, but Viva opted to call her own cab rather than ride with Lasa. Astrid and I started to clear up the mess in the kitchen. George went to sleep around 2 A.M. Dev rejoined Nick, Martin, and Rosie in the barnhouse, while Martin played ambient German trance dance music. Ivan and Mele could be seen embracing under the eaves.

By three o'clock, when the rain started up again, everyone else had gone to bed, which is what I wanted to do, but Rosie would not leave. In the barnhouse she was prattling on. Dev was half-dozing, half Rosie-staring in a chair.

"You look tired," Rosie finally told me. "You sleep. I want to talk to Dev here about the beauty salon." I started to object, to try to clue Rosie in, to protect her from her naïveté, but then I looked at her and then at him and saw just who was naïve.

"Oh, well, I'll just clean up some more."

"You do that, Gayle," Rosie said.

I brought an armful of empty bottles and lipstick-stained teacups to the kitchen and washed and dried a batch before going back outside. I crept to the front steps of the barnhouse, ostensibly to grab more cups. Dev was laid out on the couch, Rosie sitting next to him smiling. I scurried back to our room to tell Nick of the liaison.

"Maybe she'll go to Fiji and they'll live happily ever after," I said.

"Stranger things have happened," Nick offered, grabbing my hand. "Come to bed."

I crawled next to him, and we lay there listening to the crickets. After ten minutes we heard the low rumble of talking, then Dev going into his bedroom, rustling around for something, then the door slamming, more talking and a cab pulling up and then driving away. The dinner party was over.

In the morning, the rain stopped—an intermission before the next two major storms hit. When the skies finally cleared, I stopped by the salon to say farewell. I saw Dev's name scrawled in the scheduling book. I don't think he kept the appointment. Within a week of the party, Mele's visa was approved and she and Ivan immediately decamped for Auckland. Dev and George left for Fiji soon after, Dev's hair looking as shaggy as before.

Tonga to China—February

In the pre-trip planning phase, people often asked Nick and me if we were going to Australia and New Zealand. Nope, we told them, too First World. But then it turned out that our flight from Tonga to Hong Kong would take us via Auckland, and an eleven-hour layover turned into a two-week camper van tour across the North Island. It was very pretty but kind of lonely. New Zealand's total population is, oh, four million people (forty million sheep, though) spread out across 103,000 square miles. New York City has eight million people crammed into 321 square miles. We didn't meet very many humans on our Kiwi tour, and the two of us, stuck in such close quarters, started bickering over everything from who drove too fast to where to park the van for the night.

Hong Kong was another incidental stop. With its population of 6.8 million shoved into 423 square miles, Hong Kong should not have been a lonely place, and yet we spent ten days cheek-by-jowl amid a bustling multiculti melee of Chinese, Indians, Filipinos, Africans, and Europeans of every stripe and spoke not a word to anyone, save for our hotel's owner, Charlie Chan, and a team of teenage girls conducting passenger surveys at the ferry terminal. Never had I traveled anywhere and failed to meet at least one local friend.

"Aren't you lonely? Don't you need other people around?" I asked Nick.

"No," he said. "I have you."

I began to fear for what mainland China—and the rest of the trip—would be like.

About ten minutes after boarding the train for the twenty-four-hour trip north to Beijing, I relaxed. If Hong Kong had been all business, the vibe in the train felt familial. Our fellow passengers, many already changed into pajamas and slippers, were gathered in the carriage's narrow hallways unpacking their tin lunch boxes. Kids raced up and down the aisle, ducking around the young woman attendant who was filling up our thermoses with hot water. No one spoke to us; instead they smiled and raised their teacups.

Nick and I made our way to our four-berth compartment and met our cabin mates: an old man with yellowing teeth and a gray pointy beard, and a teen girl, presumably his granddaughter, chattering into a cell phone. Grandpa beamed at us and boomed what sounded like "Air gwow tow" over and over. He smiled and nodded. We smiled and nodded. After repeating himself about ten times, he pulled out a flask, poured a few shots, handed them over, and said again, "Air gwow tow."

"Oh," I said to Nick. "It must mean 'Cheers.'"

Actually, it meant ehr guo tou, the ubiquitous and potent Beijing rice whiskey. It went down like gasoline, but it did make communication easier. We drank a few shots and Grandpa and his granddaughter began teaching us how to count in Mandarin. Our accents must have echoed down the halls, because we were soon joined by Matt, the other American in our carriage. An expat who lived in Beijing and Hong Kong, Matt was fluent in Mandarin, and through him Grandpa started talking to us about all he'd lived through: wartime occupation, liberation, civil war, communist revolutions, cultural revolutions, leaps forward, leaps back. Things were OK now, he said, though the Communist Party still stoked nationalism as a way to hide larger problems, like corruption, economic injustice, and human rights. But at least they were rid of the tyrants for a while. Tyrants always come in three, you know, Grandpa told us, and China's tyrannical triad of Mao Zedong, Chiang Kai-shek, and Deng Xiaoping was history, although Jiang Zemin hadn't been handling the Falun Gong situation so well. As he translated, Matt started looking uncomfortable. Chinese people don't criticize the government, out loud, to strangers, he told us. They certainly don't sympathize with the Falun Gong. It's not safe.

So I changed the subject. I asked Grandpa why the people in Hong Kong had been so chilly.

"Oh, Hong Kong, the people are Cantonese. They don't like strangers. Not friendly people." He took another slug of ehr guo tou and smiled. "But you are in Beijing soon. And in Beijing, everything is different."

Chinglish Lessons

I know lots of swearwords: bastard, beetch, sheet, bloody... " Doctor Bi proclaimed as we rode the escalators down through the mammoth Wangfujing Bookstore in central Beijing. He was speaking in a staccato voice that penetrated the noisy din of the place, and I expected our fellow shoppers to be appropriately horrified. Naturally, they stared at us; a barking Chinese man trailing two bewildered Westerners is still something to look at, but they seemed unperturbed by Bi's barrage of profanity. In most of the world—English-speaking and otherwise—a thunderous and public utterance of such words has the power to quiet a room. But in the political and cultural capital of the most populous country in the world, ignorance was bliss. Wangfujing's shoppers did not understand Doctor Bi at all.

Not that I did either. Nick and I had met Doctor Bi a few hours earlier. It was our third day in Beijing and we were shopping for that ultimate Beijing accessory, a bicycle. Two-wheeling through the Chinese capital is one of those tourist must-dos, like a Venice canal cruise or a

San Francisco trolley ride, but it is also a practical necessity in the sprawling city, which encompasses an area larger than Connecticut.

There are taxis, but Beijing traffic is a constant snarl and even when it's moving, well, there are the taxi drivers. It's not just that they don't understand English—only the most boorish traveler expects locals to speak his native language—they don't speak Chinglish or Mandranglish either. Chinglish is the mangled English Chinese speakers attempt; Mandranglish, the completely useless Mandarin that comes clunking out of foreigners' mouths. Whenever I asked drivers to take me to some famous landmark such as Tiananmen Square or the Sanlitun Bar Street, I got the kind of baffled-bordering-on-offended stare that rich people give to panhandlers. There are buses, of course, more than seven hundred lines, but they are not for the benighted. Bus stops, bus maps, bus schedules, and bus destinations are in Chinese characters, instead of Pinyin, the transliteration of Mandarin words into Roman script. I needed a bicycle not only to navigate traffic, but also to navigate a city that is as illiterate in English as I am in Mandarin.

So this was why on a drizzly early spring morning Nick and I stood near Tiananmen Square, map in hand, trying to make our way to a nearby *hutong*, an ancient warren of narrow alleys and brick houses, where we were told there were a number of used-bike sellers. As usual, we were lost, but in Beijing, particularly near the Tiananmen Square/Mao Mausoleum area, it rarely took more than a few minutes before some eager student bounded up, offering to escort us to a bank, a good restaurant, or a shop selling Chairman Mao tie clips. They wanted little in return—a quick lesson in verb tenses, help in choosing an English name, or a chance to show off their knowledge of U.S. state capitals.

Doctor Bi was no ordinary practicer. A trim thirty-something man in a black leather blazer, he strode up to us with such purpose that I suspected he was a cop, especially when he immediately began interrogating us.

"What is it with this lazy English? I don't understand!" he demanded.

Nick and I stared. Doctor Bi went on.

"Lazy English. People say 'Scuse me' when they want say 'Excuse me.' Or say 'Cause' not 'Because.' The lazy English," he said, his tone implying that this phenomenon was as universally recognizable as Britney Spears.

"I think that's just slang," I told him. "You know how people shorten words in conversation. You must do that in Mandarin, too."

The answer didn't seem to register. Bi spent the next few minutes expressing his perplexity with the American penchant for taking good words and amputating them. For him, this was not a matter of mere personal confusion, it was of grave importance. Doctor Bi claimed to be a pediatric surgeon at Beijing Children's Hospital. He'd apparently cut one too many cancers out of one too many kids because now he was on a crusade to cure the disease. But whereas his colleagues were looking at the link between, say, genetics or environmental toxins and malignancies, Doctor Bi was hoping to achieve his medical miracle by way of lazy English.

"I want to conquer the cancer," he told me. "I think the way to conquer the cancer is doctors to work together, but in China we no have understanding of the efficiencies of English language."

After the lazy-English spiel, Doctor Bi abruptly changed gears. "You know your president, Bush?"—pronounced with a long *o*, like "Boooosh"—he asked. "Your president is George Bush now, but it was President George Bush before, too?"

"The first President Bush was the father, now it's the son," I said.

"Yes, I know the father and son. But how you tell them apart? When you talk about George Bush, how you know which Bush?"

"Lots of ways," I said. "The older Bush is called George H. W. Bush, for George Herbert Walker Bush. His son is just George W. Bush: George Walker Bush. Everyone knows that 'President Bush' means the current president. If we want to refer to his father, we can say 'former President Bush.' Or we can call the older one 'Bush elder.'"

"But why you don't call him George Bush the First and George Bush the Second?"

"I don't know," I said. "Sometimes families will do that. Parents will give a son the father's name. So you'll have John Hancock the First. Or John Hancock the Second."

"The family calls old one John First and young one John Second?" Bi asked.

"Not exactly."

Here, Nick jumped in. "It's like with the Kennedys," he offered.

"We had the president John F. Kennedy, and his son was John F. Kennedy Jr."

"But how you tell George Bush from George Bush?"

In time I would learn that the best way to deal with Doctor Bi was to keep things simple, that offering examples only added hours to the explanation. But Nick and I were still naïve and earnest and too eager to help.

"Sometimes," Nick piped in, "we will call the former president Forty-one and the new one Forty-three because George H. W. Bush is the forty-first president and Dubya's the forty-third. Clinton was Forty-two for eight years."

"Bush is the forty-third? I thought second?"

"Second president?"

"No, the Second. The son is the Second."

I didn't quite know where to go with that one.

"What do *you* call the Bush?" he asked.

"Just the president," I said. "Or President Bush."

"Not 'George?'"

"No," I said. "Not 'George.'"

"Why not 'George'?"

"Because he's the president. It's too informal."

"You wouldn't call President Jiang 'Zemin,'" Nick added.

"Besides," I said, "that would be even more confusing. Then we couldn't tell George W. Bush apart from George H. W. Bush."

"Or from George P. Bush," added Nick.

"There is son of George Bush?" Doctor Bi asked.

"No, no. That's his nephew."

" 'The Little Brown Baby,' as his grandfather called him," Nick quipped.

"But the other George is not the son of the president Bush?"

"No," I said. "He's the nephew. President Bush doesn't have any sons. Just two daughters."

"Are they Juniors?"

I was about to explain that normally one didn't do the Junior thing for girls, and that Jenna and Barbara were named after their maternal and paternal grandmothers, but unpeeling the layers of the political name game, with all its Firsts and Seconds and endless retreads, wasn't leading to any great breakthroughs on Bi's part. After forty-five minutes on the street corner, Nick and I were no closer to getting bikes and Bi no closer to understanding lazy English or the intricacies of naming trends particular to the political elite. And now it had started to really rain. I pointed this out in hopes of initiating our escape.

"Where you go now?"

"We were going to get a bike," I said. "But it's too late. We need to find an Internet café."

"Oh, I show you. You come with me."

We followed Doctor Bi back down Dongchang'an Avenue to the edge of Wangfujing, a consumerist paradise, unimaginable in China even ten years ago. The crowded pink-bricked pedestrian street was packed with multistory department stores, trinket shops, and restaurants, including a Starbucks, a KFC, a Popeye's Chicken, and two McDonald's. It was prime stomping ground for Chinese tourists as well as a romantic dating spot, judging from the number of couples making out there each evening. Bi led us through the throng of tourists, merchants, and ever-present Public Security Bureau officers to a tall concrete building between the Bank of China and the southern McDonald's. We went up to the sixth floor of the Wangfujing Bookstore, where next to the musical instruments (it was a bookstore and then some) sat a bank of eighty new computers. All DSL for the equivalent of a buck an hour. God bless capitalism.

I bade Bi farewell. After six weeks on the road, e-mail time had become sacred. Although Tonga had been stuck in the cyber Stone Age, New Zealand and Hong Kong were wired, and I had spent a few hours each week writing long, rambling missives that none of my working friends had time to write but did have time to read. Travelers are often ridiculed for making their way to distant reaches of the world only to spend hours in their virtual homeland. Pish. Everyone needs a lifeline home, and e-mail had become mine.

Nick was not homesick like I was, nor was he a prolific communicator, but he was a librarian and as such could not help himself when it came to offering reference advice. He had made the mistake of telling Bi that there were probably Web sites about lazy English. I sat down to read my e-mail, and Bi left me alone, but he hovered over Nick, who spent an hour showing Bi the marvels of Google.

The technical term for lazy English, it turned out, was *relaxed pronunciation*. Sure enough, there were a number of Web sites devoted to the phenomenon. None of these satisfied Bi. He wanted specific and prefab examples of lazy-English dialogue. Nick searched but came up empty. Bi requested a Web site on speeches. Nick found several classics—the Gettysburg Address, Kennedy's inaugural address, MLK's "I Have a Dream" speech—as well as sites offering step-by-step speech-writing instructions. Again, not good enough for Bi. He was after a corporate boilerplate snoozer, something that began with, "Good evening, ladies and gentleman . . . "

It had now been nearly three hours since the impromptu lesson had begun, and Bi showed no signs of letting up. In desperation, I invented some fictitious friends who were meeting us back at our hotel. Bi insisted on walking us back to our *binguan*, and, perhaps sensing that we were losing patience with him, began to impress upon us the importance of his quest: "I want to conquer the cancer, so I am writing book because Chinese doctors don't understand the efficiencies of English."

"The efficiencies of English? What do you actually mean by that?" I asked.

"I want teach people to talk like Americans. With the slogans of English."

"Do you mean conversational English, the idioms and slang?"

"Yes, yes, *eee-deee-ooms*," Bi said, testing the word out.

"Well, you've got your work cut out for you. English is so full of sayings, and the English have their own and so do the Americans. Even cities have their own speech. New Yorkers have some peculiar phrases."

"Say one."

" 'Waiting on line' instead of 'in line.' Or when someone says something to you that's just too incredible, you could say, 'Get out of town!' Of course, you have to do the 'Get out of town!' with the Elaine-from-*Seinfeld* push." I demonstrated by shoving Bi, maybe a little harder than I should have, below his left shoulder. He didn't seem to mind. He was delighted at this sudden burst of information, complete with examples—the mother lode for him.

"Or you could say, 'Are you kidding me?' or 'Are you shitting me?' which is kind of derived from the whole idea of bullshit, or BS. 'Are you BS-ing me?' Or you could say, 'Are you fucking with me?' " I paused. "We certainly do use a lot of swearwords, don't we?"

This, in turn, had prompted Bi to show off his vast knowledge of English obscenity, offering enough examples to last us the five escalators down. As I listened to him and hid from would-be offended parties, I surveyed the bookstore. The five floors were bursting with books, tapes, CD ROMs, and workbooks all dedicated to the studying, speaking, reading, understanding, pronouncing, and polishing of English. There was English for business, English for computers, English for medicine, English for police, English for the TOEFL, English for conversation. English for reading. Also: English for travel agents, English for travelers, and English for dealing with the annoying complaints of overbearing English-speaking travelers (not the actual title, but this was the crux of the dialogue being offered on one tape: a disgruntled American tourist bitching out a service worker and a polite and friendly service worker attempting to calm the pissy client). American English. British English. Aussie English. History of English. Future of English.

If all the world's an English school, China is the advanced class—and the remedial one. No other populace is so behind in adopting, or so rabid in learning, the global lingua franca, and nowhere is this more apparent than in Beijing, where legions of students attack their English studies with the hunger of a starving man at a Sizzler buffet. In Tonga, the shrinking world was encroaching slowly, but in China, globalization was on speed. Twenty years ago an English practicer like Bi was a novelty. English scholars were primarily a rarified cadre of engineers, economists, scientists, or doctors, and English was still exotic enough to be a secret language. But now the Bis of the world are multiplying. China's main cities, Beijing and Shanghai in particular, are in the throes of a full-court English-language press with more than three thousand new foreign language schools in operation.

At first I assumed that this English obsession was merely a symptom of Olympic fever. Beijing had won the bid for the 2008 Summer Games in 2001, and a few months later city planners were already designing new buildings, stadiums, hotels, highways; planting new trees; and devising elaborate antipollution measures to contain the city's infamous dust storms. Moreover, city officials were urging the entire populace to get with the Anglophone program, and pushing for four hundred thousand new English speakers—about 3 percent of the city's population—by 2008.

In reality, the Olympic Games are just a symbolic example of what China has to gain by learning English—inclusion, which brings honor and opportunity. More important, the winning of the Olympic bid was a potent example of what China had already gained by its Westerly movement thus far: again, inclusion, which brings honor and opportunity. Chinese people understood this even better than the government did, so exhorting anyone to learn English was a tad redundant. They were panting for their primers.

Such enthusiasm is often mistaken by foreigners as a desire by the Chinese to *become* like America—proof of the hegemony of McCulture. Hardly. Chinese nationalism is as strong as ever. There was the sense among many Chinese I met—a sense that was reinforced whenever I read the local English-language press—that Americans were a silly lot, far less evolved and sophisticated than the Chinese, who have enjoyed more than five thousand years of civilization. It just so happened that Americans spoke English, the neutral language of science, industry, finance, and the most common language of software programs. China is projected to become the world's largest economy this century, and as such the country can no longer ignore the English language or the people who speak it.

English also turned out to be my lucky charm in Beijing. After the isolation of Hong Kong, I had my doubts about coming to another

Chinese megalopolis. I wanted to head west to the smaller cities of Kunming and Lijang. It was Nick who lobbied for Beijing: How could we visit China and not see the elaborate imperial buildings of the Forbidden City that had been the center of Chinese power for nearly six hundred years? How could we not hear a dissonant Chinese opera at the Zheng-Yi Temple Theater? How could we *possibly* skip leaving flowers at Chairman Mao's Mausoleum, frolicking in the pagodas of the Summer Palace, paying a visit to Tiananmen Square, riding a bicycle with the masses, or clambering over the Great Wall?

He was right, and we did all those things, and were awed by the city's history, exuberance, and foreignness. Yet, for me, it was the "practicers," as Nick and I called them, who made our stay in Beijing lovely. Usually the relationships were casual. A student at Beijing University escorted us through the ancient Forbidden City, offering what turned out to be erroneous facts about the Ming Dynasty in exchange for a few hours of stilted conversation. A teenage girl guided us to the bank for the chance to work on her verb conjugation. We never saw either of these kids again.

But sometimes the friendships stuck. A pair of art students who called themselves Yanni and Alan adopted me for the duration of my stay, taking me for picnics in Beijing's parks and boat rides on serene Lake Holhai, where we floated candles on the water as offerings to our ancestors. They clued me in to the student cafeteria, where you could eat a bowl of fresh noodles with vegetables and broth for thirty-five cents. They took me to the Muslim neighborhoods, the student neighborhoods, and the vanishing hutong neighborhoods. They gave me Mandarin lessons, Yanni drilling me on words and tones until I could ask, "Do you speak English?" and say, "Nice weather," and actually be understood.

What did Yanni and Alan want? They knew I was married; they weren't looking for action. They knew I wasn't rich; they weren't looking for sugar mommies. They wanted me for my English. They just wanted to talk.

One afternoon Yanni sneaked me into his dorm room, where a half-dozen of his student friends approached me as though I were the Oracle of Delphi.

"What is good English name for me?" asked one guy.

"You read?" asked one girl, proffering a Dick-and-Jane era textbook.

"You just speak for us, OK?" begged another smiling girl.

Then Yanni and Alan sang me a serenade of "My Heart Will Go On" from *Titanic*. It is tradition to sing back, so I gave them my best Doris Day rendition of "Que Sera Sera."

And it wasn't just the students. One afternoon, Nick and I went to the Museum of the Chinese Revolution, only to find the block-long institution closed for a few years, presumably for some Olympic-inspired propaganda revision. Outside the museum loitered the usual gathering of trinket-sellers, many of them illegal migrants from the countryside. After attempting to sell us postcards and Mao cigarette lighters, one industrious peddler drafted Nick into teaching an impromptu language lesson. Sitting on the museum steps, Nick read to a group of rapt hawkers a chapter from an English study manual. The essay, a tribute to Lenin, covered the basic biographical details and went on to extol Lenin's unparalleled intelligence. So smart was Comrade Lenin, the author gushed, that he was able to see through the corrupt ways of capitalism and imagine for his countrymen a much better life. After the tutorial, one of the touts gave us a free pack of postcards and thanked Nick. "More tourists, more English, more money," he said through a grin of yellowing teeth. Across the street, Chairman Mao, architect of the People's Republic of China, no doubt flipped in his marble mausoleum.

The morning after I met Doctor Bi, the hotel operator called at 7:30 and ordered me to the front desk, where I was solemnly handed a package covered in Chinese characters. It was Bi's book. I shuffled through the 150-page manuscript, which had no title, no preamble, no author page. Bi had just launched into what he saw as the necessities of conversational English: a lot of small talk on how to accept a dinner invitation, how to chew out a not-up-to-par employee, how to seduce a woman. It was a hodgepodge of English and Chinese, graphs and tables, in a sprawl of fonts. It looked like a headache. I stuck the thing in a drawer. The following morning at 6:30 the phone rang.

"Hello, this is Bi," the doctor shouted into my ear.

"Oh, uh, good morning," I said.

"My book, you get my book? I leave for you."

"Yes, I got it yesterday."

"When you meet with me, to help me with it?"

"You want me to read it through, right?"

"Yes, you meet today, at ten o'clock?"

I told Doctor Bi that I hadn't read it yet, that I would certainly do so in plenty of time to meet with him before I left Beijing, but that sadly I would not be finished by this morning. He tried to impose a deadline. I refused to accept one and politely requested that he refrain from calling so early. After I hung up, Nick lifted his head from his narrow bed across the room. (Older Chinese hotels invariably define a double as a Lucy-and-Ricky-style set of twins, separated by an immovable console; though most nights we shared the twin, sometimes sleep demanded separation.) In a sleepy voice he asked who that was. When I told him it was Doctor Bi, he groaned. "That guy is going to be trouble," he said.

Two mornings later, trouble called back, this time at 7.

"Hello, this is Bi." Pause. "Have you finished my book yet?"

"Doctor Bi, I asked you before: Stop calling early. We sleep late."

"What time I call?"

"Never call before nine. And I haven't finished your book yet."

"You meet me at the Internet place? For more research?"

"No, I'm busy. I'm a tourist. I want to go sightseeing."

"When you finish my book?"

"Look, I'll have it to you by the end of next week, OK? I'll call you as soon as I finish and we'll arrange to go over the changes."

"When you read my book you write lots of speech for me. You write how things should be said."

"If you get the dialogue wrong, I'll correct it for you," I said.

"Tomorrow, you are done with book tomorrow?"

"No, I haven't started yet. By next week I will be done."

"It's important. I want to cure the cancer and I am writing this book to cure the cancer."

"Yes, yes, I know. But I am not going to do this overnight. Give me time."

"OK, you call me when you done."

"Yes. Goodbye. And please stop calling so early."

Nick rolled over in his bed and gave me a grumpy glare. At home I would have blown off Bi by now, his quirky charms quickly over-shadowed by his obnoxiousness. In fact, Nick was usually the un-selfishly helpful one, always getting roped in to digging up some obscure fact to help someone write a fanzine article or to settle a bet. But this was different. Nick valued his morning sleep and he'd had enough of Bi. I, on the other hand, was on a trip, meaning that though Bi *was* annoying, aggressive, dense, and difficult, I was open to him. It was my destiny to meet him.

Two mornings later, when the phone rang again at 7, I wasn't feeling so gracious. It was time to reassess strategy here. In China, in-deed all over East and Southeast Asia, one of the basic codes of conduct is the concept of face. In a conflict, you never lose your cool. To do so would cause not only you to lose face but might also result in the face-loss of whoever you're arguing with. This, for some reason, would be really bad and should be avoided at all costs. One evening, after a waiter charged us fifty yuan for a box of juice—that's six dollars, more than the rest of our meal—I didn't say *"Tai gui le,"* which means "That's too expensive," in part because beyond that first sentence I had no way of engaging in this debate but also because I didn't want to insult the guy. I'd already infuriated the waitress at the local dumpling house by questioning my order. It had been hard to enjoy my meal with her glowering. It was this respect for face that kept me from investigating Doctor Bi's legitimacy as a doctor. Between his phone calls and his seemingly wide-open schedule, though, I began to suspect that Bi was BS-ing me. I quizzed him on various medical facts and about his training. He seemed to know as much as I did, which proved nothing. I fished for an invitation to the Children's Hospital, and when Bi didn't bite I considered calling to see if they'd heard of him. Nick pointed out that whether I caught Bi in a lie or not, I would only cause him to lose face and suggested I back off.

Fair enough. But by Bi's third wake-up call I'd lost all sense of decorum. Before he could ask me about the book, I yelled at him, shouting that I had asked him repeatedly not to call early and that if he wanted to talk he should call back at a reasonable hour. I hung up before he could say a word.

At ten o'clock Bi called back, not apologetic or miffed, just dogged. Was I done with the book? When could we meet? I still had some days to go before my self-imposed deadline, but I realized that Bi wasn't going to let up. It would be better to finish the damn thing sooner rather than later, if only to get some sleep. To buy myself a few tranquil mornings, I told Bi that Nick and I were going to the Great Wall and would be gone for three days and would meet with him when we got back.

This was only partly a lie. We *were* going to the Great Wall with Matt, the American we'd met on the train from Hong Kong, but just for one day. Matt had done some research on wild Wall walks—the portions of the ruins that had not been restored or turned into a tourist attraction—and two mornings after my last conversation with Bi, Matt came to fetch Nick and me at our hotel. After a cab ride, a long-distance bus ride, and a bumpy trip in a *miande*, or "bread taxi" (so named because the vehicle is shaped like a bread loaf), we found ourselves in a tiny village. Matt pointed up a steep incline and, at the top, there it was.

We trudged up the side of the mountain until, panting and sweating under our fleece, we reached the ridge. The Wall stretched atop the rocky promontories as far as the eye could see in either direction, hugging every curve, valley, and peak. An icy, gritty Mongolian wind had turned the sky grayish brown. This, the barren trees, the putty shade of the crumbling wall with tufts of shrub growing through its cracks, bathed the tableau in a mute winter palette.

We walked along the Wall for five hours, a vertigo-inducing hike as the ground seemed to fall away beneath our feet. Nick insisted on walking behind me, even though I was slower, so worried was he that I'd fall off. After about six miles we arrived at a tourist section, where we caught a taxi and a bus back to Beijing. There, exhausted, wind-blown, and starving, we feasted on authentic Beijing duck in a fire-lit restaurant and that night rode our bikes back to the hotel through a cold wind, finally cuddling together in one of the twin beds and falling into a sleep as deep as the earth itself.

We slept late the next day, the phone kept quiet by my lie to Bi. But then it was time to face the music.

The book. It was like a car crash: twisted and bloody and not without its own perverse allure. The conversational section, covered a hundred times in already published books, was a strange mix of the most quotidian sayings, expressed in the most clunky and formal way. He would explain when to say "How do you do?" and "It is my pleasure to make your acquaintance," but leave out "Nice to meet you." Simple phrases like "Make yourself at home" had apparently been translated verbatim from a Chinese dictionary, resulting in "Please to make my home as yours while you are my guest." For an English book, there was an awful lot of Chinglish going on.

Bi devoted pages and pages to standard work-speak of the "Johnson, I need that report in the morning" ilk, but much of it was from the perspective of a despotic boss, flagellating inferiors in out-of-context slang:

A: If you don't get this account, you're toast.
B: Yes, I know. It is all very down to the wire.

Or

A: I'm going to take the Smith case.

B: In your dreams!

Or

A: Is this the file you desired?

B: Not that file, you retard.

Next to this last one I wrote: "No one would say this. Doing so could get you fired!"

There was a bewildering assortment of phrases that were either archaic, British, or not English at all. In some cases I couldn't tell. *That cuts up* was purported to mean that something was unappealing. As appropriate responses to someone sneezing, Bi included *Bless you*, but also *Sneeze me, kiss me*. A half page was spent on the various usages of *Oh bother*. I wasn't sure if he'd meant *Oh brother* and had left out the *r*. Nick noted in the margins that only Winnie-the-Pooh says *Oh bother*, which later on would require its own five-minute explanation. Then there were the pages of *fiddle-faddles, chop-chops, righty-oh, chaps*, and *oh rots*. Oh rot, indeed.

The lazy-English section—which in spite of Bi's obsessiveness only warranted a half-dozen pages—was illuminating. Once I actually read it, I understood why Bi thought English was littered with severed words. What Bi heard as lazy English was often just the way English sounds when spoken rapidly. Yes, *gotcha* and *betcha* and *gotta* were true adulterations of "got you," "bet you," and "got to," but Bi had conjured up an English-speaking world where such terms were the norm. When I said, "Will you go to the store for me? I have to shower if I'm going to be ready on time," running together the words in my typically American way, Bi heard: "Willya go to the store for me? I hafta shower if I'm gonna be ready on time."

By far the most amusing and disturbing chapter in Bi's encyclopedia was the extensive catalog of curses and epithets. He did indeed know lots of swearwords—more than ten pages of the various uses of *fuck, fucker, fucking A, fuck a duck, shit, bullshit, shit-eater*, etc., as well as a range of more creative terms and even a few neologisms. An awful lot of the terms were sexual, and it was hard to fathom how an understanding of *muff-diver* would lead to any oncological breakthroughs.

If the swear section displayed a real polish—no grammatical mistakes here—it also revealed an astonishing lack of sensitivity, or perhaps just cluelessness. Bi readily called women "prick-teasers" or "sexmongers," and gay men were "fudge-packers." He also included every racial slur under the sun. During the first of our hours-long edit sessions, I had the disquieting task of explaining to Bi why it wasn't OK to call a Chinese person a "Chink," and how "Chinaman," while not as offensive, would not win him any friends. I told him that no one but the most ignorant of people would use these terms. I tried to explain what seemed obvious to me: that it was just wrong to use these words. He seemed genuinely surprised, as though it had never occurred to him that calling a female manager a "bossy bitch" might ruffle feathers.

In his inability to grasp the vagaries of English, Bi is not alone. As the world shrinks, English is increasingly the global standard of communication, spreading kudzulike over the planet. It's becoming difficult to find a corner of the world—even the remote Malawian village or most rural Cambodian backwater—without some person who knows his or her way around the language. Yet in Beijing I often had the sense that almost no one *really* understood it, despite the hundreds of books and thousands of classes and plentiful tourists to practice on. For all their enthusiasm, it seemed many of the Chinese English speakers lacked a critical link that prevented them from getting the gist of English, no matter how much vocab they acquired.

This impression was only magnified by the multitude of supposedly English signs, banners, flyers, and notices that were posted around the city. A sign in a Beijing park read: LITTLE GRASS IS SMILING, SLIGHTLY, PLEASE WALK ON PAVEMENT. One plaque on the Great Wall warned: THE DANGEROS ROAD BECARFUL YOUR SAFE! In 2002, China was the fifth most popular tourist destination in the world, with more than 36 million visitors, the majority of them spending time in Beijing and along the Wall. How is it possible that the Ministry of Tourism bureaucrat charged with this important bit of translation—and that bureaucrat's superiors and the myriad other officials who must have seen the plaque before it was nailed onto the ancient monument—failed to understand that this prominent piece of signage made no sense?

The Chinese government has vowed to crack down on Chinglish, calling it a blight on China's hopes for modernizing, but the fact that the government is a key purveyor of Chinglish is testament to just how deep the English confusion goes. Which begs a question: Why do Chinese speakers have such troubles with English?

The reasons are linguistic, logistic, and historic. Mandarin and English are about as different as two languages get. Mandarin is a four-thousand-year-old system based on forty thousand pictographs, logographs, ideographs, and phonetic compounds. Slight graphic changes tweak meaning, and combinations of pictographs create entire new meanings. Direct phonetic translations between Mandarin and English are bogglingly complex in both directions. Mandarin's grammar and syntax, on the other hand, are simple and basic: There are no feminine or masculine words, no pesky changes in verb conjugation based on first or second or third person, and no distinction for singular or plural; there's not even a change for past tense. For Americans learning Chinese, the simplicity of the grammar is a sigh of relief. For the Chinese, all the ever-breakable English rules are the stuff of nightmares.

The greater challenge, however, is the scale of the endeavor. China is a massive nation of 1.3 billion people with more than a dozen distinct ethnic groups spread over 3.7 million square miles. The vast majority of Chinese have not only never studied English, they've never even heard it. Unlike their Japanese or Vietnamese neighbors, the majority of Chinese have never bumped into English on a TV, on a T-shirt, on a carton of juice. They have never had much opportunity to say "hello" or "welcome" or "moron." They've never adopted English words into the Chinese lexicon because for so long, China purposely kept English, and all outside cultural influences, at bay.

Although China began trading along the Silk Route in the second century B.C., entrenched nationalism and xenophobia created a buffer against other nations. Throughout the centuries, Imperial rulers made sure that while goods were exchanged, foreign cultures and ideas were not. After the fall of Imperial China in 1911, official xenophobia was tempered somewhat, and trade with the West flourished, but Western culture was still disparaged. When the communist People's Republic of China was established in 1949, that intermingling with the West ended as Western interests, which had been aligned with the now-exiled Kuomintang party, were expelled. China now looked to the USSR, and Russian became the foreign language of choice. In the 1960s, after the Sino-Soviet Split, there was a move toward internationalism, and English again became the dominant foreign tongue. That lasted until the decade-long Cultural Revolution from 1966 to 1976, during which the study of English was banned in schools, and foreign-language teachers were routinely accused of being spies. Since the 1980s, English has been reintroduced in various curricula in China, but it's been a touch-and-go process. Political struggles like the 1989 Tiananmen Square Massacre, and diplomatic rows like the United States' accidental bombing of the Chinese Embassy in Belgrade during the war in Kosovo, again created a squeamishness in the Communist Party about all things Western. Finally, in 2001 the government introduced a new national curriculum with mandatory English instruction starting in third grade.

The irony is, now that China is getting with the program, the program is changing. As David Graddol, a language expert at the UK consultancy firm The English Company writes in *The Future of English?*: "We may find the hegemony of English replaced by an oligarchy of languages, including Spanish and Chinese." As Western culture infiltrates China, casually immersing millions of people in English, and as English goes from being the province of the highly educated to the language of the masses, China will become an ever more wealthy world power, and Mandarin will become a more universal and dominant language. I expect that when I visit China in ten years, Doctor Bi won't be able to shout "Shit!" on a crowded escalator without causing a scene. Maybe in thirty years, New York City schoolkids will be grabbing little old ladies in Chinatown and begging for help with their Mandarin homework.

When I finished editing the manuscript, Bi met me outside my hotel at noon and ushered me to his office. Along the way, he spotted a young white couple enjoying the early spring sunshine on a patch of grass. He made a lunge for them, but then stopped abruptly like a dog on a choke chain.

"What?" I asked. "You want to draft them as tutors, too?"

Bi missed the sarcasm. "Yes, I ask every foreigner to help me with the book."

"Even ones who aren't native English speakers?"

"If they speak any English, is good enough," Bi said. Which explained a lot.

Bi's office turned out to be the lobby of the Novotel, where he staked out a leather couch in a side alcove. A small army of waiters descended on us to offer tea or cocktails. (This client-to-staff ratio was typical in Beijing. Want 100 percent employment? Hire ten people to do one man's job.) Bi shooed them away. I was sure someone would realize we were interlopers and kick us out, but Bi carried on with confidence, as if he owned the penthouse upstairs but liked to slum in the lobby. I was impressed. I still got nervous sneaking into luxury hotels to pee, but Bi, I was learning, was a virtuoso in the art of appropriation. It was a very American attitude: grab it now, manifest destiny, chutzpah is half the battle. If only his language skills were as sharp.

Alas, they weren't. It hadn't been too difficult to mark up Bi's manuscript, but trying to convey the idea of verb agreement, let alone the concept of political correctness, was an ordeal. For every note I had made on the manuscript, Bi demanded two or three clarifications and examples. I spent four hours on that leather couch, going over all of my notes. When I realized that Bi's English wasn't advanced enough to understand my edits, and that his worldview was nowhere near ready to grasp the more sophisticated concepts of cultural sensitivity, I made the case for simplicity.

"Less is more," I told Bi. "Just give your doctors the conversational basics, so they can make themselves understood. They'll pick up the subtleties once they are in America."

Eventually Bi gave in, but when we got to the profanity he put up a small fight. After doing my best to explain to Bi about the inappropriateness and offensiveness of "Wop" and all the other slurs, I drew black lines through much of his curse repertoire.

"It's one thing to understand what 'skanky slut' means. It's quite another to teach it."

"Why?"

"Here's the thing. If you don't want to get your friends sacked and sent back to China in shame, delete the profanity."

Doctor Bi frowned but nodded.

By five o'clock, Bi and I had finished running through the manuscript and now he was plumbing my ever-shallowing depths for idioms. So far, he'd managed to gather a dozen droopy clichés of the *if-life-gives-you-lemons-make-lemonade* variety—did he even know what lemonade was?—and he was convinced that the key to melanoma was hidden somewhere in the meaning of *the early bird gets the worm*. I was tapped out, so I struck a deal: my freedom now, and I would meet him later with idioms in tow. I had no intention of honoring this.

On the way back to the hotel I asked Bi if he had ever been to the United States. He had not. Nor had he been to any English-speaking country. Nor had he left China. He had not even been to Hong Kong. He explained that he was trying to apply for a grant to go to Ireland. I asked him why then he was so obsessed with learning and teaching American English.

"Because American English is English."

In Beijing, at least, Doctor Bi's pronouncement was true enough. Yankee-speak is the dialect of choice, as I found out when an American teacher named Richard invited me to sit in on his class at the OK! Language School, whose motto was "Learn American English. No Problem!" Richard's class consisted of six students who ranged in age from teens to thirties. That night was a very special class because the second half of it would be conducted in a bowling alley.

"There's a *bowling alley* here?" I'd asked.

"A few of them, actually," Richard said. (Further travels would reveal that bowling was experiencing a global renaissance.)

Richard had been teaching his class about the resurgence of all things 1950s—the whole swingers/martinis/bowling craze thing—and they were doing a vocab section around bowling, so he figured he'd cut out of class a bit early to show them the real thing. Richard had obviously been doing his job well because when I showed up at his class that Wednesday night, he asked the class how they would describe my shoes. Six pairs of eyes gave me the once-over, resting on my black-and-white Adidas Gazelles. "Retro chic," the students replied in unison. Richard beamed with pride.

Richard was a former New York City hipster boy who was now fast becoming a Beijing hipster boy. He was partial to certain elements of style (bowling shoes, at the moment), which sometimes determined what he taught. But Richard's quirky curriculum was not just an extension of his own conceit. The way his students ignored his grammar lessons—when Richard conjugated verbs, the younger girls sent text messages on their mobile phones and the older boys doodled—and sat rapt for his treatises on hepcat speak, it was clear that they came to school for a cultural education as much as a linguistic one. Richard was a popular teacher, not because of his skill at teaching irregular verbs (which was pretty bad) but because he was good at explaining American-ness. He embodied it: handsome, young, well-traveled, rich by his students' standards, cultured, cool. His students seemed to come to school to learn *him*.

Some of these kids, particularly the teenage girls, seemed to be learning the lessons too well. Cati, a fifteen-year-old ingénue with a trendy asymmetrical haircut, Hello Kitty paraphernalia, and an attitude from hell, had already surpassed her teacher both in her understanding of the world of cool and in perfecting the veneer of the in-the-know scenester. In class she chatted with her friends, took cell phone calls, flipped her hair with a practiced glamour, and sassed Richard with that same hauteur one sees in privileged kids from New York or London. Her English was abysmal, but she had the American attitude down. I wondered if it was as easy for Cati to be so, well, catty, in her mother tongue. Language is a child and a parent to culture. Mandarin has been as influenced by Confucianism, with its emphasis on honor and respect, as by Communism. (Mao Zedong simplified the complex traditional

Mandarin to make it more accessible to "the people.") English, on the other hand, is the idiom of the rugged individualist, the lingua franca of the Cosmo Girl.

As Cati pranced around, I thought of Bi and was flooded with a sudden sense of pathos. I had never believed that he was writing the tome to cure cancer, and increasingly I doubted that even *he* believed that. Bi's book, I now understood, was both his wish-ticket to America, and his badge of honor in China. Bi didn't have a passport or money, and if he was a real doctor, he was an unemployed one. Cati, on the other hand, was planning to study in the States; several other OK students had already done so. Bi was probably not catching a flight to the United States anytime soon, but his book gave him an excuse not only to meet Americans but to imagine himself a part of the shining city on the hill, the place where men determine their own destinies, where cancer gets cured. Maybe more important, Bi's book gave him an opportunity to show off his skill, which not so long ago was a novel and important one to have in China, one that elevated him above the pack. Now Bi was being ousted from his perch by a generation of Catis who not only spoke English but also understood American.

We met one more time for tea and editing, Doctor Bi and I. We finished the manuscript, and I handed over a list of fifty idioms and their translations. Nick and I were leaving Beijing in three days, so I assumed that this satisfied my duty. I figured Bi did, too, when he invited us to his apartment for lunch the following day. "It will be my treaty," he said.

He promised to make *jiaozi*, or dumplings, which I had become addicted to, and I accepted.

It's always a bonus to score a meal invitation in a foreign land. The feasts are often sumptuous, the treatment royal. I didn't suppose I'd get such pampering from Bi, but a visit to his apartment would be fun and, at the very least, offer some clues into his mysterious life: medical degrees on the wall, a wife, or if not a wife then photos of her, a wardrobe full of medical suits, a stethoscope, *anything* to verify his identity.

The flat itself couldn't have offered less of a clue to Bi's medical pedigree, and that lack of evidence seemed to tell the entire story. It was a bare and dirty place: a cramped kitchen, a bedroom with a mattress on the floor, a dining room with a card table and chairs, and an office with a computer and desk. There were no photos on the gray walls, no knickknacks on the empty shelves. The whole place felt like a squat, and knowing Bi's gift for appropriation, I wouldn't have been surprised if it was. Bi said that it belonged to a doctor friend of his who had offered it to Bi as a workspace to finish his opus. Then Bi explained that he was not actually working at the hospital; he was on leave. I asked where his wife was. Oh, she didn't live in Beijing, he said. She was back in Hebei Province, working as a nurse.

I'd given up any belief that Bi was a doctor when a friend of his, one Doctor Chang, arrived to join us for lunch. Doctor Chang wore a suit, carried a beeper, and had a mobile phone, which rang often. Bi explained that Doctor Chang was his partner, but when I pressed the men for clarification, I couldn't get an answer. Bi said they worked together at the hospital, even though he'd just said he didn't currently work at the hospital. Chang didn't say much; his English was not as evolved as Bi's. He gushed a bit about his friend's book, how important it was. Nick and I smiled and nodded.

We all sat down at the table. Bi pulled a package of paper cups and a dusty bottle of *ehr guo tou* off of the shelf. We drank a few shots, toasting in Chinese, *Gan Bei,* and in English: Cheers, Bottoms Up, Down the Hatch. Bi knew all the toasts. After four shots, Doctor Chang placed a hand over his cup. Bi explained that Chang had surgery that afternoon; good to know that the doctor was being temperate and all. Bi disappeared into the kitchen and returned with some to-go cartons, the tops torn off to make our plates.

There are certain rules to follow when you, as a foreigner, are invited for a meal. First, eat what's served to you, at least a little bit. To decline is impolite. The second rule is even more important: Never ask the identity of a dish, no matter how pig's-eye the morsel appears to be. Culinary cluelessness is essential in overcoming an ethnocentric aversion to, say, beetles (which taste a bit like shrimp). You may break rule two *only* after you've tried the mystery dish, but I find it better to dine and digest in ignorance. As such, I wasn't about to inquire by which process the eggs Bi served me had turned a putrid shade of green, or what exactly the shimmering trufflelike layers of yellow and pink fat were. Instead, I followed golden rule number three: When in doubt, or in fear, eat the least scary thing on the table first. In China, where meals are eaten communally, you can get away with eating *only* the least scary thing because the only person dumping food onto your plate is you. I went for the long strips of dried meat, white with flecks of fat, which tasted like leather and made me thirsty enough to down copious quantities of the *ehr guo tou*. Nick made a valorous attempt on the green eggs, and even skewered one of the truffles. Doctor Chang, meanwhile, tucked right in, nodding and smiling at us as we nodded and smiled at him.

"You like food?" Bi asked, after serving us something that, hallelujah, looked like spinach. We nodded. And then, breaking the fragile peace of mind established by rules one through three, Bi, like a waiter over a dessert tray, gave us detailed explanations of the fermented eggs, pig's ears, and jellied animal fat with skin; the latter was his favorite. I pushed my plate away.

"I don't want to get too full. We *are* having dumplings, right?"

"Oh, yes, dumplings."

Bi hopped back into the kitchen and emerged with the first batch of dumplings, which I inhaled, even the ones stuffed with tripe. (Bi seemed to be intentionally preventing me from sticking to my rules.) Bi spent most of the meal bustling around the kitchen, and Nick and I chitchatted with Doctor Chang. I asked him if they really used acupuncture needles for anesthesia. Indeed, they did and do. He, on the other hand, was fascinated to find out that Americans even knew of the ancient healing art, and that I had even been poked and cupped on a few occasions. This seemed to open a new realm of possibility for him.

Doctor Chang mused that perhaps he could practice overseas one day, after Bi's fame paved the way.

When we had polished off the five varieties of dumplings, Doctor Chang got up to leave, presumably sober enough now for surgery. He solemnly shook our hands and said that he hoped to see us in America. Following Chang's clue, Nick and I started to gather our belongings. Bi went into the office and booted up the computer, and Nick gave me a look. When Bi saw us preparing to leave, he protested.

"Oh, no. You no leave now. Chang go to hospital."

"We really should be going."

"I have computer here. Maybe you write your changes," he asked, pantomiming typing.

"I'm not inputting your edits for you, Doctor Bi. I wrote them on the paper. I told you what they meant. You can input them and I'll look over them afterwards. That's how it works."

"Oh, yes, yes," he said. "You look over them."

I looked at Nick and mouthed, "Help!" Forget it. He had predicted this. "You know he's going to make you work," he'd warned, and now that his prophecy had proven true, he was cheerfully gloating. But I think even he understood Bi's strange pull on me. There was something so un- believable about the doctor's tenacity, you couldn't help but admire it.

With that in mind, I followed Doctor Bi to the office, where he sat me down in front of the screen. I'd been expecting the manuscript I'd worked on, but this was an entirely new chapter of pages and pages of barely differing phrases: *in a while, after a while, for a while.*

"Please," he begged, "you write the speech for me. Show me how to use the words in speech."

I stared at the screen.

"Just this part," Bi said, bracketing the entire section. "Please, is very important." Bi wanted not only examples used in a sentence, but dialogue. My sense was that he didn't understand how the different prepositions affected meaning. In my drunken haze, I sat down and half-assedly wrote a few pages of dialogue.

A: Are you ready to go to the movies yet?
B: I'll be ready in a while.

A: When can we leave Grandma's house?
B: After a while. She's very lonely.

A: Do you want to go to the park for a while?
B: Yes, that would be very nice.

After a half-hour I'd gotten a significant amount of dialogue written, but my head was spinning from cheap booze and prepositions. It was time to go.

"But you have pages left. It no finished," Bi cried after looking at the incomplete section.

"That's all I can do."

"But only seven pages."

"Yep, not much for you to finish."

"Please. . . . "

"Doctor Bi!" I snapped. "You invited me to lunch as a friend, not as a worker. You'll have to find someone else."

"No problem. No write more. I finish it."

"Yes, you're the writer. So you can write it."

Nick and I gathered up our coats and wrote Bi our e-mail addresses. I winced, imagining the cyber onslaught, but I never heard from him. I shook his hand and thanked him for the experience. I was almost out the door when Bi made one last-ditch appeal.

"Wait, I have more question."

I knew he would. "Make it a fast one."

"Sarcasm. I don't understand sarcasm. Can you explain it me so I can put it in the book?"

I couldn't help but laugh. The whole notion of sarcasm and irony, which rules so much of American humor, is alien to most Chinese I met. It's one of the things I adore about China. Its people are so thoroughly without guile.

"Much as I would absolutely *love* to," I told Doctor Bi, "we really gotta go."

China to Cambodia—April

It took forty-four hours to travel by train from Beijing to Yunnan Province, and though the journey was as full of scenery and bonhomie as the jaunt from Hong Kong had been, Nick and I needed a break from the rails. After spending a few weeks in the mountains of Yunnan, we took a shortcut and flew from Kunming to Saigon, arriving on a muggy night in April. We stayed in Vietnam ten days, long enough to commemorate April 30th, the day that, in 1975, Saigon fell, abruptly ending what the Vietnamese call the American War. Young Vietnamese celebrated Western imperialism's ignominious defeat by tooling around on their motorbikes and listening to Asian boy bands sing "Livin' La Vida Loca."

It was also long enough for us to have our first big fight, which happened in the seaside resort of Mui Ne. I was feeling homesick again, and panicky about having left my career behind. Nick had already listened to a couple of diatribes on the subject, and when one night I launched into my spiel at a seafood restaurant, he sat there glaring at me, the expression on his face suggesting that he'd rather be swimming in a vat of burning oil. Back in New York it merely annoyed me when he iced my insecurity rants with silence. On the road, with no one else to talk to, it drove me nuts.

"You know, I took this trip for you, so the least you could do is be supportive."

"I am being supportive," he said.

"No, you're not."

"What am I supposed to do? Cry for you?" he said, wiping fake tears from his face. For the normally impassive Nick, this kind of sarcasm was a highly unusual display of nastiness, and for some reason it sent me over the edge. I responded by flinging a coconut shrimp at his face and stalking off to stay in a different hotel for the night. (With room rates at $8, I could afford such drama.)

We cooled down and met back in Saigon, and from there we joined a tour group to Cambodia via the waters of the low-lying Mekong River Delta. The last leg of our three-day river journey— on which we had seen everything from a river market to a floating village to a candy factory to a pig farm—took us from the Vietnamese river town of Chau Doc to the Cambodian border town of Kaom Samnar, where we cleared customs and, along with a dozen other Westerners, boarded a speedboat that was supposed to have us in Phnom Penh within two hours. About twenty-five miles from Phnom Penh, the engine began to sputter and soon it did the inevitable; it died. Our guide steered the boat to the Mekong's shore, where a path switchbacked up the steep bluff. He hiked to the top, testing for land mines as he went, and then waving for the rest of us to follow.

We climbed up the side of the cliff and, on the plateau, found ourselves in a village a million miles and years away from the *shrinking world. There was no electricity, no telephones, no cars, and no roads in or out of the place. Amid a cluster of stilted huts and a small shack selling drinks, a group of women wearing traditional Kharam scarves around their heads and babies papoosed on their backs, startled to look at us, inspecting us as one might scrutinize little green men exiting a spaceship. Within minutes, word of the interlopers rang through the village, and seventy-five men, women, and children approached to take a gander at us.*

Our guide addressed the village elder, explaining our dilemma to the weathered man, who nodded as if in emphatic agreement. The rest of us stood under a grove of trees examining the locals, who stood under a different grove of trees examining us. If one of us ventured closer to them, the women—all so stunningly beautiful that it felt as though we'd entered some Shangri-la—smiled shyly, but the children howled with fear, terrified by our white skin and our unfamiliar features, clothing, and smells.

An hour passed. We continued to survey one another. Finally, Jill, a schoolteacher who lived in Denmark, and I dispatched ourselves as emissaries, stepping out of the shadow of our tree into the sunny no-man's land. We looked toward the women, who gave us silent permission as we inched closer. The babies cowered behind their mothers' thighs but did not cry as much. One little girl let us play with her gold bangles. We stayed there, smiling and nodding and cooing, until our guide announced that a replacement boat was about to arrive. (Apparently there's cell phone service between Shangri-la and the shrinking world.) When our boat sped off, the villagers stood in a line atop the bluff and waved us farewell.

A few hours later, as Nick and I, and Jill and her husband, Peter, tucked into a meal of French food, we wondered at the lost village we'd drifted into, as if through some secret portal. But of course, the village was real and I was fairly certain—and oddly comforted by the thought—that on this night we were the dinnertime conversation for its inhabitants.

The Erudite Urchins

Hey, Mr. Monkey Man. Mr. Monkey Man, I am speaking to you. *Je te parle. Parlez vous francais? Deutsch?"*

Mr. Monkey Man, a standard-issue Western tourist bearing no particular resemblance to a primate, pivoted to face the little girl. She looked to be about nine and was already beautiful, with long black hair, almond eyes, and sweetheart lips. She stared at Mr. Monkey Man expectantly, her hands planted on her hips, her chin jutting forward, a pose as provocative as it was babyish.

"Meeester Monkey Man," the girl trilled.

"Are you talkin' to me?" he asked in a Cockney-flavored English accent.

The girl laughed, then set her mouth into a serious line and, in a not half-bad Cockney, said, "I'm talkin' to you," before dissolving into a fit of giggles. Her posse—two similarly outfitted little girls—scrambled over, and the trio now formed a semicircle around the beleaguered tourist, who, to his credit, was looking more bemused than annoyed.

Like Nick and I, he probably had set his alarm for four o'clock that morning to catch the sunrise over the twelfth-century temple of Angkor Wat. With its majestic lotus-bud towers, its thousands of eye-popping carved gods, goddesses, and bare-breasted celestial dancers, its steep stairways leading to hidden galleries and nooks and crannies, Angkor Wat is the crown jewel of Angkor, the ancient stone city that, before it was lost to the jungle, constituted the capital of a Khmer empire that stretched across what is now Thailand, Laos, Cambodia, and Vietnam. Angkor, and in particular Angkor Wat, is what pulls most visitors to Cambodia. Sunrise over the temple, which in spring takes place at the ungodly hour of 5 A.M., has become an obligatory stop on the Indochina tourist circuit.

For good reason. Dawn is a breathtaking shifting of the shadows as night's indigo mist gives way to day, bleeding violet to pink to blue until a golden light emerges, bathing the moats, causeways, staircases, lower towers, and, finally, the two-hundred-foot central tower in a celestial glow. At one point in this show, the sun casts a perfect reflection of the symmetrical temple onto the glassy waters of its moats. It's a postcard vision that occurs daily and then, as quickly as it arrives, vanishes. By six o'clock the tropical sun has captured the sky and the light has turned harsh, white, and blaringly hot. All of which can be a little much if you're not a morning person, and can be a lot much if you're not a morning person *and* you haven't had your coffee, which was the case with Nick and me.

So this was why we had instructed Samnang—"call me Sammy"— the young man who'd been ferrying us on his 50cc motorbike, to drive

toward Ta Keo, an eleventh-century temple known for its uncharacter-
istic lack of carved adornment. We had it on good authority from some
Dutch tourists that the makeshift café near the temple was not only
open early but also served a decent cup of brewed coffee.

Apparently Mr. Monkey Man was also in need of caffeine. He
shrugged his shoulders at the little girls, sidestepped them, and shuffled
over to the café. We followed him to a rectangular table covered in
plastic cloth and sat down next to him and a cheerful woman who
turned out to be his brand-new wife. We commenced with small talk
about the sunrise, weddings, and, the perennial favorite topic of the English tourist, how bloody hot it was. Nick was telling them about a
band of amputee musicians we'd met outside Ta Phrom—the eaten-by-
the-forest temple through which Angelina Jolie gallivanted in the first
Tomb Raider flick—when the little girl returned. The sardonic teasing,
it turned out, was merely the opening salvo of her sales pitch. She
spread out her inventory of wood-carved bangles, postcards, origami
Angkors, metal reproductions of the five-sided Bayon temple, charms,
and a few Jew's harps. "Cheap," she told us. "These bracelets, just five
dollar."

"No thank you," Mrs. Monkey Man said.

"One dollar, special price for you," she turned to me.

"I'm not really a wood-bangle kind of girl, but thanks."

She half-heartedly pointed to her greasy, creased package of postcards. "You buy postcards then?"

"Already did," I told her.

She shrugged again, then gave me a quick once-over. "What is that?" she asked, pointing to the angry circular welt on the inside of my right calf.

"I burned myself. On a motorcycle."

She peered closer, bringing her index finger perilously close to my flowering blister. "Whoa, there. Don't touch."

"When did you do this?"

"Just now, this morning."

This cracked the girls up. They nodded their heads knowingly. "On the pipe," she said.

I nodded.

"All tourists do that," she informed me.

"Not just the clumsy ones like Fragile Gayle?" Nick asked.

That made me laugh. Fragile Gayle was one of the early nicknames Nick had bestowed on me (the latest one was *Pukka Sahib*, which he explained was Hindi for excellent fellow). When we were first together I had told Nick how the mean girls at school had called me that: "Fragile Gayle, touch her and she'll break," they'd taunted, making fun of my gangly limbs. Nick had adopted the name as his own, though in his version I was Fragile Gayle, breakable on the outside, tough on the inside. I adored my pet name because it showed that Nick recognized my two dueling selves. I also kind of liked it when he teased me about my clumsiness because it came from the same place: a sincere worry that I could hurt myself and an understanding that I probably wouldn't. Nick gave me a lot of space and room to breathe, but such sweet teasings made me feel understood, taken care of, worried about, loved. A girl needs that.

"Some of us aren't used to waking up so early," I told Nick and the girl.

"Hey, I'm less of a morning person than you are," Nick teased.

"Yes, you are both lazy," the girl said, giving Mr. Monkey Man a good chuckle. At least he wasn't the only one getting guff.

"Who *are* you?" I asked the girl.

"My name is Leeda. You should buy my postcards. They are very nice. Only one dollar for ten."

"I don't need any postcards. I've got way too many. In fact . . ." I reached into my backpack and pulled out a brown bag full of cards that were as creased and greased as Leeda's. Mine highlighted various New York City sights: the Statue of Liberty, Central Park, Times Square, and the universal crowd-pleaser, the downtown skyline with the now destroyed Twin Towers, which children with no geographical concept of the United States, let alone New York, always seemed to recognize and refer to with some variation of "Osama." Leeda and her friends surged forward to look, Leeda grabbing one of the Brooklyn Bridge and giving it a quick appraisal.

"I have bridge. Do you have others?"

"Have the park. It's New York's Angkor Wat."

She gave the Central Park postcard a gander. "That is no Angkor," she said. "You have a pen for me?"

Pens: When I first started traveling to the developing world, I was always surprised by this request, but I soon understood it was not a grown-up need. Pens were the ideal tourist giveaway. Unlike money and candy—the other two in the triumvirate of child-requested treats—pens do not rot teeth or cause the giver to feel uncomfortably condescending. Pens seemed like a fine gift, except that I never managed to hold on to my own—a liability for a writer. So Nick and I had settled on postcards as our present of choice, buying five hundred before leaving New York. When I told Leeda I had no pens, she made a *pfff* noise through her lips. I was sinking fast, but thankfully our British friends rescued me.

"I've got pens. What d'you do with the Biros?" Mr. Monkey Man asked his wife, who pulled out a selection of three.

"Thank you," Leeda said as she took one and disappeared, her girls trailing after her. A few minutes later she returned with a thin stack of postcards bound with a rubber band. The cards offered snaps of familiar cityscapes from all over the world. There was the other Bridge, the Golden Gate, and on the back: "Leeda. What a mouth you have on you. But you're funny." Tokyo's flowering cherry trees: "Dear Lida: Don't Forget. Knock-Knock. Who's There. Japan. Japan who. Japan is hot; don't touch!" The Sydney skyline and on the flip side a hand-drawn map of Australia in relation to Asia, with Leeda's face sketched in Cambodia. There were also postcards with messages in German, Dutch, and French. She held out Central Park, offered me her newly acquired pen, and requested I sign.

"Where did you meet these people?" I asked, handing my card back.

Leeda shrugged, spun around, twirled some of my hair around her finger (curly hair is a big novelty in Asia). "Here. They are tourists. Like you and Mr. Monkey Man."

"Stop calling me that," MM said, but he was smiling.

"Can you read these?" I asked.

"Can *you* read these?" Leeda shot back.

I shuffled through the pack. "Not really. Maybe the French one a little, but not the Japanese. I don't speak Japanese."

"How many languages?" Leeda asked, and perhaps I was overly sensitive, but I swear I detected a hint of that deprecating tone foreigners take when inquiring about Americans' language abilities, or lack thereof.

"English, Spanish, and some Dutch. Why, how many do you speak?"

"*I* speak English, Khmer, French, German, and Japanese. And I am young."

"How young are you?'

"I am ten."

"Do you go to school?"

"Yes."

"Why aren't you in school now?"

"I go in the afternoon."

"You'll go this afternoon?"

Leeda shrugged.

"Do you go to school?" I asked her friends.

"Sometimes," Leeda explained. "When there is no work to do. But we learn from the people. *Ich liebe dich. Aishi teru wa. Je t'aime.* I love you. . . . "

"That's very impressive. You know lots of languages."

"What we know, you could write in a book."

Monkey Man sputtered on his drink. His wife patted him on the back. "Some cheek these girls have," he said, when he'd begun breathing again.

"Very cheeky, indeed," his wife replied.

"Bit different from other Asians we've met who are more, what would you say, quiet?"

"More gentle. More shy. But they are children."

"I don't know. I think 'Leeda' might be short for 'Lolita,' " I said, and pointed over to the little girl, who had gravitated, as children often do, toward Nick. He claims not to like kids, but something about his gentle spirit and unassuming ways makes them love him. Leeda was chirping away, hounding him to get a carving of the Bayon temple for me because "the wife likes the husband to buy things," and then pestering him about why he didn't wear a wedding ring. (I pestered him about the same thing.) Nick then attempted to give Leeda a dose of Dale Carnegie: "You should tell your customers they're handsome, not that they look like monkeys," he advised. She wasn't having any of it. "If customers look like monkeys, I say it," she retorted.

Eventually Nick wandered over to view the Ta Keo temple. I opted to stay behind, ostensibly to rest but really to hang out with this bizarrely precocious little girl. I chatted with her and her friends about home, theirs and mine. I showed a few snapshots. In return, and in bits and pieces over the next two hours, they told me as much as any ten-year-olds can about their lives. They drew me pictures of houses and rivers, all the while pressuring me to buy something. (I relented and got a Jew's harp that swam in the miasma of my suitcase for months.) When more customers came, I sat back and observed Leeda pulling her shtick. Her humor was not always well-aimed or successful. She miscalculated by using the old you-have-something-on-your-shirt-tweak-the-nose joke on a pair of stout middle-aged Germans, who were not amused. But when she tried the same gag on some Australians, it went over like a bowl of candy. They laughed heartily and bought several wood bangles and postcards, at the regular price, no less.

When I first became a reporter, I spent several years working at a popular magazine for teenage girls, writing about the range of adolescent experience around the world, from the depths (teenage prostitutes in Vermont) to the heights (feisty Taliban-rebelling Afghan refugees). Since then, I have had a soft spot for sassy girls, so it's not surprising that Leeda had me smitten. Here was a girl with such smarts that in two years of interacting with tourists she had absorbed not only several languages but also their culturally specific humorous nuances. While to some degree she was merely parroting jokes travelers had taught her, she seemed to intuitively understand that she could put native-nervous tourists at ease by presenting them with a kind of comedy they understood. Plus she was so punk rock. In one morning I saw her readily give shit to several adults who were as much as five times her age and thousands of times her wealth.

All of this would've impressed me even if Leeda were the ten-year-old daughter of fancy-pants intellectuals or an honor student at New York's toniest primary school. Leeda, however, was the ten-year-old daughter of a widowed mother from the Kampong Thom region of a country that until recently had been decimated by the most brutal of civil wars. Moreover, Leeda, like so many people in Cambodia, was homeless, having spent the last several years living at times alongside the Tonle Sap lake in nearby Siem Reap, and now sharing a small shack with her aunt, uncle, and cousins in one of the villages dotting the Angkor Wat area. Whatever basic schooling Leeda had enjoyed had been sporadic at best. She could make jokes in my language but, as she admitted to me later that morning, she could not read or write her own.

If Leeda's a paradox, she's a common one. Cambodia, indeed the world, is full of children as bright as diamonds whose sheen is dulled by the poverty and drudgery of daily life. Leeda is also emblematic of the crossroads at which her country stands. For two decades Cambodia kept the world out and smothered its Leedas in war and poverty. In the last ten years the world has returned with a vengeance, injecting Cambodia with a megadose of globalization—first under the guise of the United Nations and later under the guise of the United Nations of tourists. The return of the outside world has in turn lured many of these children out of the fields and into the cities, where they lack the basic necessities but come into daily contact with people like me; hence their language skills, selling strategies, and anachronistic sophistication. This preternatural erudition seems at odds with these kids' situations, but such is the limbo in which Leeda's generation, the first born of peace in more than thirty years, finds itself.

Cambodia's entry into the shrinking world is actually more of a reentry. For the last two hundred years this small nation, about the size of Oklahoma, has played unwilling host to the whims of its capricious neighbors—suffering frequent invasions and annexations from Thailand and Vietnam—and the French, who colonized the country from the 1800s until 1953. After independence from France, Cambodia enjoyed a brief period of calm, and during this time Phnom Penh took up the mantle of Paris of the Orient, as a decadent cast of expats, businessmen, journalists, and joyseekers took up residence, spending days sipping gin and tonics at the Hotel le Royal, trading gossip at the Café de Paris, or debauching in one of the city's many opium dens and brothels.

The party didn't last. In 1969 the U.S. military launched a four-year secret bombing campaign against North Vietnamese soldiers in Cambodia, dropping nearly 540,000 tons of explosives (three times the amount dropped over Japan in World War II) over the eastern half of the country, killing between one-quarter and one-half million people, and sending millions of refugees into the cities. Prior to this incursion, Cambodia's communist movement had been a marginalized affair, but resentment over the U.S. bombings, coupled with frustration over the inherent corruption in the Lon Nol government, helped to energize the radically socialist Khmer Rouge and its leader Saloth Sar, more commonly known by his *nom de guerre* of Pol Pot. By 1973, the KR army had swelled to 40,000 and by the end of that year it had captured the Cambodian countryside. On April 17, 1975, the Khmer Rouge took Phnom Penh.

Within days, the army evacuated three million urban-dwelling Cambodians on forced marches into the countryside. It was the start of one of the most drastic and violent social experiments in history, as the Khmer Rouge sought to turn Cambodia into a collective, agrarian, Maoist cooperative. To do this, all elements of the outside world—and the former Cambodia—had to be erased. The country was renamed the Democratic Republic of Kampuchea, the calendar was annulled, 1975 became Year Zero, currency was abolished, schools and post offices shut down, borders sealed, and all flights, except for a twice-monthly shuttle to Beijing, were cancelled.

With the country sealed shut, the purging began. Former government and military leaders, businessmen, teachers, intellectuals, urban dwellers, Vietnamese, and Westerners who had not managed to escape—anyone who was perceived to be working against the revolutionary regime—were killed. So were their families. "When you pull the grass, you have to pull the root," was the prevailing wisdom. Everyone else was sent to militarized farm communes where the work was back-breaking, the hours long, the food rations at starvation level. By the time the Vietnamese invaded Cambodia on Christmas Eve of 1978, eventually ousting the Khmer Rouge, more than one million Cambodians—one in seven—had died of malnutrition, overwork, or mistreatment, and at least a hundred thousand more had been executed by the state.

The next dozen years, while not as brutal, were no picnic. Cambodian factions emerged to fight one another, the occupying Vietnamese, and the still-lingering Khmer Rouge for control of the country. This continued until the United Nations secured a peace agreement in 1991. Once the fragile truce was established, the U.N. Transitional Authority in Cambodia, or UNTAC, was created with a mandate to rebuild the country from the bottom up. UNTAC soon deployed some sixteen thousand military personnel and five thousand civilians to do the job. Thousands more workers from an international brigade of nongovernmental organizations (NGOs) descended to support the reconstruction.

Just like that, the tatty streets of Phnom Penh were filled with soldiers and aid workers from Japan, the United States, France, the Philippines, and Holland, driving around in spanking new Landcruisers and looking for places to spend their seemingly endless hard currency. Good U.N. jobs not only brought foreign workers a sizeable (and tax-free) salary but also a per diem of up to $160. This in a country where the average daily income for Cambodians is less than $1.

To accommodate the gold rush, colonial buildings were hastily restored to make way for villas, stores, and garden bistros serving beef bourguignon and merlot to hungry expats. To make travel easier for the Landcruisers, roads were cleared of land mines and paved. (Some of them, anyhow; even today, it's common to find a tarred road adjacent to a red-clayed potholed mess.) To keep those SUVs humming, state-of-the-art petrol stations and 24/7 minimarts sprang up, selling gas, soda, and current editions of *Foreign Affairs*.

As soon as UNTAC set up shop, a swarm of reporters followed, and with journalists come bars, and with bars come a scene. Phnom Penh entrepreneurs quickly opened a host of watering holes—Sharky's, Heart of Darkness, the Foreign Correspondents Club—where parched expats could amuse themselves with endless beers, dirt-cheap Khmer weed, and equally inexpensive Khmer prostitutes. In her book *Gecko Tails*, journalist Carol Livingston describes those rowdy days in the capital as being like "the first term of college—lots of people who didn't know anyone, whose commitments were far away, and who partied." From war zone to MTV's *Spring Break* in a year.

If the expats were in hedonistic heaven, the locals were less enthused. Although a peace treaty had been signed and U.N. peacekeepers had been deployed to enforce it, the factions had yet to demobilize, and bloody clashes continued. The ongoing power-grabbing between the political parties—culminating, in 1997, in a period of heavy fighting, a coup, and the final collapse of the Khmer Rouge—shook the already unstable populace, weakened an already devastated economy, and stymied reconstruction throughout the country. This political and economic instability in the rural areas, combined with tales of Phnom Penh's foreign lucre, was a siren song, enticing thousands of impoverished farmers into the cities. Once again, Phnom Penh became home for the huddled masses, and a decade later there were between ten thousand and twenty thousand homeless kids and street-working youth on the city's streets. By conservative estimates at least five hundred families now call these sidewalks home.

At least a half-dozen of those families lived on the four-block stretch between our hotel and the riverfront, although it took me a while to figure out that we were neighbors. As soon as Nick and I rolled the Beast and Beastette off the boat and inland onto Street 118, we were rushed by a greeting committee of homeless kids. Many were practically naked, wearing only scraggly underwear and begging in that uniquely heart-breaking Southeast Asian style, palms together in front of their chests, heads bowed in prayer. We figured that the kids staked out the boats to take full advantage of new arrivals. That night, as Nick and I walked back from dinner with Jill and Peter, whom we'd met on the boat from Vietnam, the sidewalks, which earlier in the day had been abuzz with women doing their washing and cooking, men their dealing and dominoing, and children their playing and begging, had suddenly become dorm rooms. Those same families now sprawled on mats or lay in hammocks tied to street posts.

The next morning—and every morning thereafter—when we ventured out of our hotel, Nick and I faced a gauntlet of need, the intensity of which I had never encountered. At the sight of us, the kids on our street would flock and beg, following us several blocks before giving up, at which point another group of kids would take over. Meanwhile, a contingent of hungry-eyed motodoc drivers—young men, many of whom had invested what little capital their families had on motorbike taxis——trailed us, enquiring over and over again if we wanted a ride. As soon as one driver quit, another took up the cause. At the riverfront, the onslaught quintupled with old women, scamming teenagers, stump-waving amputees, gangs of child beggars, all asking for some money, some food, some help with living. Pimps sidled up to Nick, offering up the pretty ladies at the "boom-boom rooms." Armies of street kids rushed me, beseeching that I buy a magazine, a flower, a shoeshine. At the end of each day we would come back to the hotel, our local street kids waiting for us, the motodoc drivers asking again if we wanted a lift, even as we entered the lobby.

Nick and I felt overwhelmed.

"We need a system," he said.

"I know."

"We've got to help people, but we can't help everyone. We should give money to amputees because they can't work. And it's what the locals do."

"And we should give the local amount."

"We can also leave a donation with a charity here. We just have to figure out which one."

"Also, buy whatever crap we can from the kids."

"Even a shoeshine," Nick said. We'd already had our nylon sandals "shined" a few times, even though the black polish turned our feet gray.

But what about the child beggars? Many were pleading on behalf of their families, but many others were working as part of organized begging gangs. We decided to buy them food—bananas and baguettes being relatively easy to tote and divvy. For the first few days, this seemed like a swell idea. Our block party began to expect us, and when the kids saw us they put their hands in prayer pose until we gave them the goods. Then they smiled and whooped with joy. They were a little less hungry and we got to feel like Santa Claus.

One afternoon Nick and I ventured to the Lucky Supermarket, an expat grocery store that sold expensive goods like Snapple and brie. We stocked up on Corn Flakes and Yoplait and then went outside to buy a barbecued chicken from a vendor. While I was waiting for the bird to cook, a little girl in a ratty pair of sweats grabbed my leg. I looked down into the familiar wide-eyed stare. When the vendor handed over my chicken, I snuck her a thigh. Not thirty seconds later I was surrounded by more than a dozen children, miming eating, touching my face, my arms, my legs. I dropped the chicken into the crowd and watched as the kids pounced on it like a hungry dog with a hundred limbs. Nick and I started to walk away, but that first little girl blocked our path. Behind her cowered three tiny chicken-less boys, tears clearing paths down their dirty faces. The chickens cost $1.50 each. I could've easily bought ten more, but the gesture seemed Sisyphean: no matter how many kids I fed, there would be twenty more behind them. Donor fatigue on a small scale. I felt awful.

This wasn't the first time that Cambodian poverty had made an impact on me. One rainy Sunday afternoon when I was eight years old, my bored siblings and I had been burning Monopoly money in the fireplace. I'd wanted to up the ante, so I had asked my parents if I could have a real dollar bill to torch. They told me I shouldn't waste money when so many people were in need. To prove their point they directed me to the black-and-white TV set, which was broadcasting news of the famine in Cambodia. Image after image of swollen-bellied, starving children floated across the screen. Stricken, I went to my room and cried. The following Monday I organized a fund drive at school.

Twenty-some-odd years later I was still being affected. It wasn't just that I felt guilty—which I did—but that I felt angry and preyed upon whenever I stepped outside, which made me feel even guiltier. I began to understand why rich tourists who visit places like Brazil and Mexico keep themselves cosseted behind the walls of luxury hotels, and I hated that I was now sympathizing with them when I should have been empathizing with the poor kids. I didn't get why I was such a wuss all of a sudden. Hadn't I witnessed and reported on all manner of poverty-stricken Third World children in fucked-up situations? What I now realized was that in those journalistic jaunts I had parachuted into the mire but, like those rich tourists, had always retreated back to some relatively comfortable, expense-account hotel where I could decompress over a cold beer with my colleagues. In Phnom Penh, there was no escape.

The more I isolated myself, the more discontented I felt. I tried to reach out to my family and friends. I sent a weepy mass e-mail warning "Western-girl guilt to follow." I then admitted how hard I was finding it to "vacation" among so much poverty. "You learn things about yourself here that you'd rather not know," I wrote. "You are forced to acknowledge the limits of your selflessness." Well-traveled friends wrote back sympathetic e-mails, recounting their own harrowing experiences.

Those helped. A little. I even splurged and called my sister over the Internet from one of the new generation of cyber cafés. She patiently listened to me as I spent fifty cents a minute to cry from seven thousand miles away.

Nick also tried to comfort me. One afternoon, as we lay on the bed together watching CNN Asia, I told him how interminable the trip felt and how much I missed my family and friends. I put my head on his chest while he stroked my hair. He suggested I could go home for a visit or have someone from home meet us. And he kept urging me to leave Phnom Penh for somewhere less harsh. We probably should have, but something about that felt like quitting. Besides, as the days went on, I wondered if it was Phnom Penh that was really the problem.

"I don't know if I can hack this," I told Nick after another guilt-ridden foray into the city.

"We can leave here whenever we want to."

"It's not just Phnom Penh, Nick. It's the trip. I don't know if I can handle traveling for a year."

"Well, then," he said in measured tones, "maybe you should go home."

"You mean go home by myself?"

"Uh-huh."

"What about you?"

"I want to keep traveling."

"I'm not sure I do."

"I know. So you should go home."

I shouldn't have been surprised by Nick's proposal. Following our usual rules of engagement, the solution to our problem would be for me to do what I had to do to feel better. We have always done what's best for ourselves, so long as it didn't harm the other person or the relationship. The problem was, *I* thought that spending eight months apart definitely qualified as a potential marital deal breaker.

"Wait, so you're saying that being on this trip is more of a priority than being with me?"

"I'm not saying that at all," he countered. "But if you're so unhappy, you should do what you need to do to fix that. But I've always wanted to travel. This is my chance. I don't want to give up on it. If you need to, it's OK. I'll see you back in New York when the year's over. Or you can go home for a few months and we can meet back up later."

"So let me get this straight. I came on this trip with you, for you, but if it doesn't work, you want us to separate?'

"We wouldn't be *separating*, just I'd keep traveling," Nick replied.

I had just meant to float the idea out there: What would happen if I couldn't hack the full year? I hadn't expected Nick to send me packing. And thus did I begin to wonder whether this trip would wreck our marriage and whether either of us cared enough to do anything about it.

"Guilt stirs me, but only to self-pity." So quipped aphorist Mason Cooley. And so it was with me. Even *I* was growing sick of my whining, and it occurred to me one morning that the Phnom Penh "system" for dealing with the constant neediness was a failure. It had only served to keep the neediness, and the people behind it, at arm's length. Bearing in mind something a local photographer had told me—that the children were as hungry for attention as for food—one morning I decided to take a different approach.

That afternoon I went outside by myself. When the motodocs asked if I wanted a lift, I looked at them and said *"Adtay au kun,"* no thank you. When they asked again, I repeated, "No thanks." I found that twenty refusals felt far less unkind than a single empty stare. That night when the gaggle of homeless kids on our street ran after Nick and me, I took a breath, pushed past the instinct to duck, and, along with Nick, started playing with them. We grasped them by the wrists and twirled them around, and within minutes, five more kids joined in, each wanting a turn. It was easy; they were all so light. We spun and pattycaked until we were dizzy and our hands were red. Nick offered piggyback rides, and soon four kids were piled onto his back. We learned one another's names: Bourey, Luang, Chea, Neek, Girl (this last one being the easier-to-pronounce version of my name).

In the middle of the street, with amused adults looking on, something wondrous took over. I stopped seeing these kids as Social Issues and started engaging them as actual children. When that happened, all at once I stopped fearing them and my gloom lifted. I started to actually enjoy my final days in this chaotic, dynamic city, ending each one with a play session in the street, along with a food drop. Though it didn't fully register then, the playtime was a turning point in the trip, and an important, if counterintuitive, lesson that I would draw on for the rest of the year. The antidote to cultural discombobulation is never retreat; it is immersion.

If the UNTAC mission—which officially ended in 1993, although a heavy foreign contingent remained until 1998 and a significant presence remains today—changed the face of Phnom Penh, then the peace and stability the mission helped to establish radically altered Siem Reap. From the get-go, development experts saw the town of Siem Reap as a cash cow. Not only was it only eight miles from Angkor Wat, it was also bisected by a lake, with colonial architecture and tree-lined streets. It was also close to the Thai border, an easy in-and-out for Bangkok tourists. But the areas around Siem Reap and Angkor Wat remained in Khmer Rouge hands on and off until 1998, and the intermittent fighting, not to mention a countryside honeycombed with land mines, kept the temples off limits to all but the most intrepid travelers.

When the Khmer Rouge completely disbanded, Cambodia enjoyed a new stability that paved the way for infrastructure upgrades, including a massive demining and reconstruction effort around Siem Reap. This rendered most of the immediate surroundings of the Angkor temples safe, and so the floodgates opened, creating a Vegas-style boom in this once-sleepy town. The number of tourists shot up eightfold between 1993 and 2002 and is expected soon to reach one million annually. To accommodate the hordes, developers built and restored 57 hotels, 120 guesthouses, 27 resorts, and 59 restaurants. In 2003 there were more than 30 additional hotels under construction. Land that had recently been farm or mine territory—or both (many land mine accidents happen to farmers plowing the fields with oxen or to children minding the family cow)—now sported sprawling, Khmer-style hotels, with lush green lawns and sparkling sapphire swimming pools.

Just as the United Nations created a boom economy in Phnom Penh, the tourist trade has done likewise in Siem Reap. Thousands of rural Khmers left their country homes to seek crumbs from the table at which foreigners so sumptuously dined. Many of these migrants found work, officially or unofficially, in the exploding tourist trade, be it as guides or cooks or beggars, and many of them landed on the streets. As it happened, a large contingent of these homeless lived in a Hooverville, along the banks of the Tonle Sap, across the street from the hotel where Nick and I set up housekeeping. If they were to be our neighbors, I was determined to be neighborly this time around.

Not that Lon and Non would have let me be anything but. I met the devilish brothers, ages eight and twelve, within an hour of my arrival in Siem Reap. Nick and I were sitting outside our hotel, drinking a beer in an attempt to wash down all the dust we'd swallowed on the eight-hour, dirt-road drive from Batambang. Lon and Non came bounding up to me, hands in prayer pose, lips quivering like fishes, begging for food. They were short and tall mirror images of each other, with cropped black hair, torn T-shirts, and eyes glimmering a little too mirthfully to make them truly effective beggars. I told them, "Later," to which they mimicked, "Later, later." When I finished my drink I walked to the market and bought a bunch of bananas; upon returning to the hotel I held them up in the air to the boys as a greeting. They, along with their assembled crew of siblings and cousins, ran over to grab the loot. Only when they had skipped halfway down the block did they skitter around and offer a sloppy bow of thanks.

I bumped into them again not two hours later, as Nick and I strolled around the town's open-air market. They raced up to me, putting their hands in prayer, mouths in hungry Os. "I just gave you food," I told them. They continued begging. I turned to Nick. "They don't recognize me."

"You know how it is. All whiteybirds look the same to them."

That night, as Nick and I sat outside eating dinner, another of the tarp city's residents, a twelve-year-old girl named Sokha, strolled up and back along the terrace of the restaurant, giving me a little smile as she went. She did not seem to be begging, but rather flirting, and effectively, too. I could not take my eyes off of her; she was a hauntingly prepubescent beauty, with doe eyes, long wavy hair, and a Marilyn Monroe beauty mark over her lip.

At first I feared the worst—she was cruising for clients. The U.N. presence kick-started Cambodia's prostitution industry simply by importing thousands of lonely male soldiers into a country with thousands of destitute young girls. When the soldiers returned home, the tourists began to take their place, and sex tourism is now one of Cambodia's fastest growing industries.

Sokha didn't strike me as a girl of the night, not the least because her coquetry was for my benefit, not Nick's. When we left the restaurant I saw that she was hunting not for customers but for bugs. Spring is cricket season in Cambodia, and every evening biblical quantities of flying bugs blanket Siem Reap, much to the horror of travelers who awake in the middle of the night to find their hotel rooms crawling with pests. To the locals, however, this is less like plague, more like manna. Cambodians consider grilled crickets a delicacy, and the industrious street kids trawl the waterfront, collecting them in water bottles and plastic bags. Adults then grill and sell this bounty on the roadsides. Every night Sokha dutifully collected bottles of critters until long past my bedtime. Lon and Non also chased insects, although they were so easily distracted with their games that their jugs seldom held more than a handful.

Nick and I spent most mornings visiting the temples, as memorable for their architecture as for their squads of industrious sales kids and tour guides. There was the peerless Leeda of Ta Keo. At Angkor Thom we met Johnny, a ten-year-old rapscallion who hijacked Nick and me away from our guide and yanked us by the hands around the temples and walls, offering a running commentary with a few mix-ups in regard to dates, religions, and rulers. As he skipped through the grounds barefoot, with his little black trousers rolled up his legs, he would, on occasion, duck behind a Buddha statue to avoid being caught by the cops, the legit guides, or the other pirate guides on whose turf he was trespassing. At the rosy sandstone temple of Banteay Srei, I met Leab, fourteen, who'd lost her left leg in a land-mine accident and had been living by herself in a shack, until a charity caught wind of her and got her a prosthetic leg and some rehab.

We'd return to town in the afternoons to wait out the midday heat. When the sun began to dip I would take a solo stroll around town, where inevitably I would bump into Lon and Non. Every day I gave them food, but this never prevented them from begging for more as soon as they spotted me. I decided that I needed a distraction to pre-empt the beggars' greeting, so I taught the boys to high-five while uttering a dudely, "Hey." I know, a most odious cultural import, but I couldn't help it; like cigarette quitters, they needed something to occupy their hands and mouths to short-circuit the pleading instinct. They took to the high-fiving, taught it to their friends, and by the end of a few days I was slapping more skin than Shaq on a good night.

Occasionally I would tag along with Lon and Non on their daily jaunts. I'd sit with them outside the market in the shade next to the stalls selling incense and spices. I'd follow as they skittered through the market, sliding along the slime of the fish stalls and out to the street, past the cafés where they would beg and clown until the waiters chased them away. Then they might cut up to the banks of the river, where many food vendors and stray dogs loitered. I'd buy some chicken and we'd share it under a tree, at which point they'd scamper off again and I'd head back to my hotel.

In the evenings, nature turned off its furnace and turned on its fan, and the inhabitants of the tarp village emerged from under the trees. The proprietors of our hotel dragged chairs outside, and I often joined them, sharing the spiky, sweet rambutans and the deformed but plummy mangosteens that they generously offered. Other times I wandered out to the sidewalk to catch bugs with Lon, Non, and Sokha. Some nights I drafted the driver Sammy, who hung out nearby, into translating for me; it was a request that initially perplexed him. "Why you want to talk to these naughty childs?" he asked, after I explained that, no, I didn't want him to shoo the kids away; I wanted him to help me communicate with them. Like a lot of the locals, Sammy gave money, clothes, or food to the beggars—his Buddhist upbringing, if not his conscience, demanded it—but being in the tourist industry, he was acutely aware that the in-your-face poverty these kids represented upset foreigners and probably kept away business.

None of the kids spoke much English, for, as I learned with Sammy's help, they were recent arrivals to Siem Reap's touristy shores. Lon and Non had come from a village near Anlong Veng—an infamous Khmer Rouge stronghold and the place where, in 1998, Pol Pot died without ever having been tried for his crimes. Sokha hailed from the nearby Angkor Thom district, but she had never seen the city until her mother moved her and her three brothers here. Sammy beckoned over Lon and Non's uncle, who had fought with the Khmer Rouge (which did not necessarily mean much—many of his generation did; Pol Pot's Cambodia was a kill-or-be-killed world). He told me, as did Sokha's mother, that they had come to Siem Reap in hopes of finding not fortune but subsistence. They could not farm enough to eat, and it was so rich in the cities, he had heard. When I asked Sokha's mother how this wealth might benefit her family, she did not answer but spread her hands wide, as though all the riches from all the hotels and tourists would, through some sort of fiscal osmosis, automatically improve her family's lot.

Though Lon, Non, and Sokha were born long after the KR tyranny had ended, their mothers and fathers and uncles had lived through it. I met many Cambodians who would willingly, if numbingly, recount the litany of family members killed during those awful years, but when I broached the subject with Sokha's mom, she gave me a hard look and shook her head. "It's a bad story," Sammy said. "A hurt story." The journalist in me wanted to press on, but the human in me realized that in doing so I would only reopen painful wounds and pigeonhole this woman and her children, whom she would not allow to beg, as victims. I stopped asking questions and hung out with the kids on the sidewalk and charade-talked with Lon and Non, who were learning bits of useless English by rummaging through my bag and identifying the artifacts found within.

"This?"

"Wallet."

"This?"

"Knife."

"This?"

"Music," and I put the headphones over their ears and played them a selection of Stereolab. They crinkled their eyes and laughed.

One night I brought down my photo album of friends and family from home to show Lon and Non. I flipped through the pages, pointing out mother, father, sister, brother, cat, baby. On the last page was a shot of Nick and me, taken on our wedding. We are standing on a boat, the Manhattan lights twinkling behind us, the wind mussing my hair. We look so happy. I pointed to Nick. "Husband," I said.

"Husband," they repeated, and looked around for the human who bore that title. Nick had been absent from my sidewalk evenings, opting to go out boozing with a group of expat journalists we had met. Now that relative peace had come to Cambodia, the stories were drying up, but a few diehards were determined to stay. Many of them were broke and were happy to find someone to sponsor a few rounds. Nick, I suppose, was happy to find someone other than me with whom to drink a few rounds. I looked at his picture and sighed. The boys sat uncharacteristically still for a few seconds, watching me, and I had the distinct impression that they were pitying me. Then Non grabbed a cricket by the wing and waved it in my face until I shrieked.

The morning after I met Leeda—whom I would try, unsuccessfully, to find again—Mrs. Monkey Man had tutted what a shame it was that a child so smart and multilingual was illiterate and therefore bereft of any real future. Whether she had meant to or not, Mrs. MM had gotten to the heart of the debate about the good, the bad, or the neutral impact that tourism and internationalism (including, to my thinking, foreign aid organizations) have on the local populations they patronize. This in turn had got me thinking about Leeda, Lon, and Non. What has globalization done—what will it do—for them? Will it offer them better opportunities, such as an education, an income, maybe even a slot in the new hospitality school in Siem Reap that trains locals for service positions? Or will it simply ensure that they are more effective, multilingual beggars?

I have to admit that I am a fence-sitter when it comes to this larger issue. I have read Noreena Hertz's *The Silent Takeover*, the bible of the antiglobalists, and I agree with her thesis that multinational corporations have come to exert too much power over governments, and even possibly that "the pendulum of capitalism might have swung just a bit too far; that our love affair with free markets may have obscured some harsher truths; that too many are losing out." I have met with disenfranchised anarcho/enviro activists who share a profound belief that big business will pillage the earth and its peoples if there is a profit to be made. I have seen firsthand how our Western culture is becoming terminally consumerist as people attempt to buy their way into happiness only to dig themselves deeper into debt—the average American family carries nearly $9,000 worth of credit-card debt—and spiritual emptiness. I don't want that ethos exported. I don't want to see countries wind up like Thailand, where I had the impression that the nation had been swallowed by the West and regurgitated to the specifications of package tourists, an endless strip of monoculture: hotels, Internet cafés, clothing stores. I have also seen evidence of globalization's missteps—countries plunged into poverty while trying to conform to IMF and World Bank austerity measures. A 2003 study found that NAFTA, the benchmark North

American Free Trade Agreement, had a minuscule net effect on job creation in Mexico. Another study from the United Nations Development Programme reported that the first generation of Latin Americans to come of age in functioning democracies, those with globalized economic policies, had experienced virtually no per-capita income growth. At the same time the disparity between rich and poor in Latin America (and almost everywhere else) has grown larger than ever before. Not exactly ringing endorsements for globalization.

Yet I do believe that globalization is like democracy; the best system in theory, even if it's exceedingly tricky to put into good practice. And there are plenty of success stories that make the naysayers' black-and-white arguments tough to swallow. Global trade agreements have helped spawn a huge middle class in China. Maybe the Seattle protester doesn't think that's a good thing, but the Chinese merchant sure does. The World Bank, vilified though it is, has funded cultural restoration projects from Azerbaijan to Eritrea. Globalization has brought a certain amount of stability to a turbulent world. As Thomas L. Friedman, the guru of globalization, noted in *The Lexus and the Olive Tree*, no two countries that both had a McDonald's have gone to war with each other. And I have seen the successes up close. I've met a Filipino mother who found work in a textile factory at a wage that would make the antiglobalists and union workers shriek in dismay, but this mother sent her daughters to school with those earnings. I have seen the United Nations, for all its foibles, eradicate disease and create order out of chaos. I have seen women succeed with the help of corporate-sponsored microloans in a way they never could with mere government handouts.

I have also visited countries that, unlike what I saw in Thailand, manage to balance the desire to attract tourists with the need to maintain tradition. I'm not talking about Bhutan, which Noreena Hertz touts for its isolationist policies—stringent visa allotments keep out all but the richest of tourists who can afford to spend at least $165 a day while visiting the country. No, I'm talking about Bhutan's neighbor India, a country that seems able to integrate the modern world *and* multiculturalism while maintaining its own ancient identity.

In the end, it's not up to me anyhow. It's up to Sokha's mother and the Filipina factory worker. If, for now, they want Nike or Marriott in their backyards, if they believe that big business will improve their family's lot, who am I to tell them otherwise? To deny those in the Third World access to the global economy under the assumption that in their blinding poverty they don't know what's good for them or how much they're being exploited, is just as paternalistic and hegemonic as forcing Western culture upon them. Besides, the assumption that globalization is a one-way street is just plain ethnocentric. The currents run in *both* directions, even if much of that giveback is imperceptible from the financial pages. I'm guessing that the Dalai Lama has influenced more people than George Soros has.

I saw Lon and Non for the last time just before I left Cambodia. I was not in good shape. Once Nick and I started fighting, we got stuck in the habit, and now every little disagreement seemed to escalate. The evening before we were due to leave for Thailand, we had yet another fight. Though I had resolved my Cambodia-poverty angst, I was still stinging from the fact that Nick had been so ready to send me away. On top of that, we'd been spending way too much time together, and now arguments seemed to spring up out of nowhere and instead of dying down they escalated from an inconsequential fight—whether or not one of us had given the other of us a dirty look—to a screaming match. After an hour of arguing at the dinner table, Nick recommended not just the obvious but the sensible.

"I think it's time to travel apart for a while."

I gulped. He might as well have said that he planned to divorce me tomorrow. Which was strange, because solo traveling, which I've done plenty of, had always been part of the plan and had struck me as a fine idea back on the solid ground of New York. But now that I was feeling raw and unstable, and considering how acrimonious things had grown between us, Nick's suggestion had an end-of-the-affair air to it. It terrified me. So I threw a hissy fit.

"Fine. You want to travel separately? Let's start now. You move to a different room."

"I'm not moving to a different room. It's late. We're leaving in the morning."

"I don't want to travel to Bangkok with you. If we're going to separate, we have to do it *now*."

"Stop being such a drama queen," he scolded. This did not help.

Telling an actual drama queen *not* to be a drama queen has the same fuel-on-fire effect as admonishing an outraged person to "lighten up."

"Fuck you!" I screamed. "I'm not being a drama queen! If we're going to part, I don't want to wait another day. I want to do it right now. I can't bear to be around you anymore." And then I began to cry.

Nick softened. "C'mon. We'll go to Bangkok, spend your birthday there, and then split up for a week or two."

Split up? I wasn't having any of this kindness. "No, I want you to leave *now*."

"No."

"Then I'm going to stay an extra day so I don't have to go with you to Bangkok." To prove my point, I went through the Beast and Beastette and separated my clothes, my medicine, and my books from his. In my frenzy, I banged my leg against the bed, reopening the motorcycle burn.

That night, I couldn't sleep. When I finally dozed off, the sun was angling through the curtains. At 8 A.M., Nick's watch alarm bleeped; the minibus to the Thai border left in an hour. He again tried to reason with me, to talk me into coming. I refused, but as I watched Nick pack, I questioned why exactly I was playing the martyr when it was to no one's benefit, certainly not my own. If I were to stay another day, it would ensure a perfectly miserable birthday bumping along Cambodia's roads. (This hardly seemed fair; we'd spent Nick's birthday at a forest hotel off the coast of Auckland.) I was in a ridiculous self-dug hole, and there was nothing to do but swallow my pride and get out of it. Not that I'd be an adult about it. I got out of bed, dressed, downed a cup of coffee and juice, and within fifteen minutes I was out the door just behind Nick. Just to clarify, I announced: "We're on the same bus, but we're not together. Once we get to Bangkok, we'll go our own ways."

"Fine."

Outside, the heat already felt like midday. I looked across the street at the encampments by the river. All was quiet. It was just as well. I wasn't in any mood for high-fives or goodbyes. Nick and I walked to the market and located the red-dust-encrusted minibus, which was full of backpackers (the wealthier travelers fly right over Cambodia's potholed roads). Nick took a seat up front; I sat in the middle, next to the window. The blister from my reopened burn was leaking a trail of iodine and pus down my calf. My leg was throbbing, and the rest of me felt heavy with lack of sleep and heartache. I leaned my head on the open windowsill and closed my eyes. When I opened them, Lon and Non were approaching the bus. They spotted me, and as always, the Pavlovian begging instinct kicked in. I saw their eyes widen, their lips go into the O shape, their hands begin to reach out to make the imaginary meals they would mime eating. But then they came closer, looked at me, and stopped. The O-mouths broadened into smiles, the twittering, begging fingers raised into a farewell wave. I smiled and waved back. The boys skipped away, and the bus heaved off in the opposite direction.

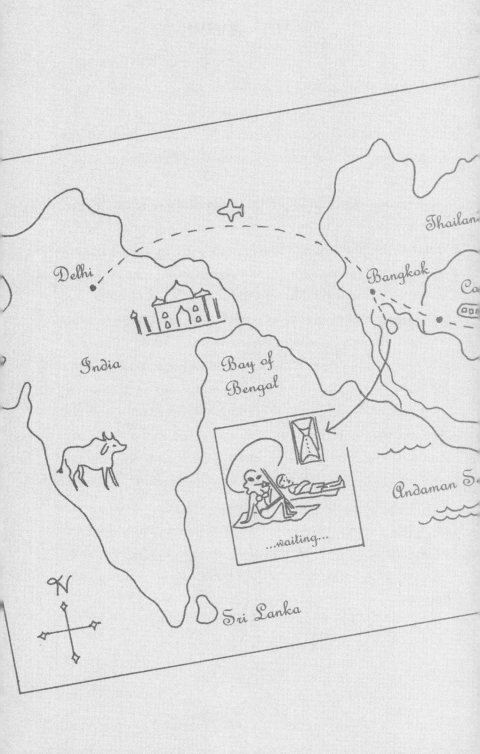

Cambodia to India—June–July

While traveling, there are certain important details to which you must pay attention, like cultural etiquette, lest you point with your feet and grievously offend a Buddhist; or health warnings, lest you find yourself in the middle of a dengue fever outbreak; and of course geopolitics, lest you land in the middle of a war.

Ever-changing geopolitics were of special concern to Nick and me, and we were constantly amending our itinerary to keep up with shifting events. After September 11th, Yemen no longer seemed edgy and adventurous, only dangerous. After Bush's infamous "axis of evil" speech, Iran dropped into the no-go column, not so much because we feared anti-Americanism—ironically, I've found that the more flag-burny the country, the more friendly its people are to actual Americans—but because the comment had made the difficult-to-get visa nearly impossible to get. Then, weeks before we were due to fly to Delhi, the long-simmering feud between India and Pakistan about the disputed region of Kashmir boiled over into what looked like imminent war.

If war did break out, it would be the third time since 1948 that these two countries had battled over Kashmir, a small but prized region nestled in the Himalaya. This time, however, things were different, because this time it was nuclear, with both Pakistan and India having acquired and tested nuclear bombs.

Nick and I watched the escalation from Cambodia. Both countries shot off a lot of hot rhetoric, but when it came to discussing the nukes—specifically, promising not to use them—Pakistani and Indian leaders played coy. Meanwhile, one million troops amassed at the border. Several governments, including the United States and the United Kingdom, evacuated all nonessential staff and issued travel warnings dissuading visitors from heading to South Asia.

At home, my writer friends eagerly asked me if I was going to cover the war. My family, generally rather nonhysterical about my trips to headliner locales, sent e-mails urging Nick and me to reconsider our travel plans. It was inconceivable to go around the world and not see India, I told them all, but even I entertained morbid scenarios of being trapped in a Cuban Missile Crisis–type showdown.

We struck a compromise. We had to go to Bangkok to catch our flight to India, so Nick and I would cool our heels—and our tempers—by spending some time apart in Thailand. Our tiff had ended after the minibus broke down a few kilometers from the Thai border, forcing Nick, me, the Beast, and the Beastette to make the last leg of the trek on motorbikes. On the luxury bus to Bangkok, we made up and then made a plan to spend my birthday together and then separate for a few days. Nick headed south in search of the perfect beach. I stayed on in Bangkok, seduced by the swimming pool at the perennially funky Atlanta Hotel and the multitude of multiplex theaters in Bangkok's malls, not to mention the guilty comforts of manicure salons and Baskin Robbins ice cream. A week later we reunited on the tropical beachy island of Koh Tao.

Time got lost in Thailand. Perhaps this was because Bangkok felt less like Asia than Los Angeles. Every second person walking in the Sukumvit district looked like me and talked, more or less, like me. There were shopping malls and traffic jams and freeways and TGI Friday's. On Koh Tao, the scenery changed—less pavement, more palm trees—but Thailand still didn't feel all that Thai. It was there, no doubt, underneath the massage parlors, hair-braiding salons, Internet cafés, dive shops, English pubs, and full-moon parties. But Nick and I did not do much exploring. We sat on the beach. We stared at the water. We read lots of books. We checked the BBC to see how the standoff was going. We killed time. We weren't really here. We were waiting to go there.

One day we looked up and saw that nearly a month had slipped by while we were hoping for things to change in South Asia. India and Pakistan seemed stuck in a high-stakes pissing contest. Though the Thai respite had done Nick and me good, we were in danger of stalling, and suddenly that seemed as perilous a prospect as the hypothetical war. Besides, things always seem more dangerous from a distance, which is what I told my fretting family.

We packed up our bathing suits, caught a bus back to Bangkok, and three days later were on a flight to India. We arrived in Delhi in the wee hours of the 4th of July, relieved to find no fireworks whatsoever.

Bhagwans and Born-Agains in Bollywood

I t was my Lana Turner moment. Except that instead of being discovered at the counter of a Schwab's drugstore in Hollywood, I was discovered while walking by the $3-a-night Salvation Army Red Shield Hostel in Bombay, India. A raggedy man with rotting teeth had emerged from behind the building's gothic pillars, hissing, "*Psst*, Madam . . ." I don't know how Lana initially responded to her discoverer, a writer for the *Hollywood Reporter*, but after four weeks in India I had learned that "*psst*" almost always preceded an entreaty: from a tout wanting you to stay at his hotel, or a salesman with a rug or suit or necklace or bag of spice to sell, from a rickshawallah offering you a ride. . . . I kept moving. Until I heard the magic words: "*Psst*, Madam . . . want to be in a Bollywood movie?"

As a matter of fact, I *did*. It was the reason I'd come to Bombay. So, two days later I found myself in the aptly named suburb of Film

City, where most of the seven hundred gloriously loopy films Bollywood produces each year are shot. My starring vehicle was a boy-meets-girl-boy-loses-girl-boy-gets-girl film called *Humko Tumse Pyaar Hai*, Hindi for "I Want to Love You." It starred Amisha Patel and Bobby Deol, the Bollywood equivalents of Renée Zellweger and Hugh Grant (though Bobby looked more along the lines of Robert Downey Jr.) and was directed by Vikram Baht, the handsome, gray-haired auteur behind the megasuccesful action-adventure blockbuster *Awara Pagal Diwana*.

This all seemed quite serendipitous; it was *Awara Pagal Diwana* that had started me on my Bollywood quest in the first place. A month earlier, Nick and I had been staying in the whitewashed lakeside city of Udaipur—itself made famous by the James Bond flick *Octopussy*, shot there in the 1980s—when we decided to inaugurate our Indian experience by going to a Bollywood musical. *Awara Pagal Diwana*, roughly translated as "Vagabond, Lazy Mad," was a pastiche of existing films— *The Whole Nine Yards*, *The Matrix*, *Face/Off*, *Crouching Tiger Hidden Dragon*—woven into a dizzying story line involving lust, greed, betrayal, murder, mistaken identity, and a lot of monster trucks. All this action was punctuated with the requisite Hindi-pop song-and-dance numbers. In other words, it was standard Bollywood fare, except for one curious thing: The film, which had clearly been shot for the most part in India, featured a sizeable cast of white Westerners mingling in the background as waiters, dancers, bouncers, and restaurant patrons. After watching two other films similarly peopled with white folk, I'd decided to come to Bollywood to investigate, and to see if I couldn't get myself cast.

Nick did not share my cinematic aspirations. He preferred to join the pilgrims, the bedraggled *sadhu* holy men, and the hippie tourists, all of whom who flocked to the holy city of Varanasi to bathe in the sacred water of the Ganges. Just as well. Nick and I had enjoyed a fight hiatus during our lazy month in Thailand. We'd also done fairly well traveling through Rajasthan. We'd read each other stories on the long train rides, pigged out on endless curry masalas, made puja together at a religious festival in Udaipur, befriended some kids in Orchha, and gone swimming every day in the Betwa River. And when I got sick, as inevitably happens in India, Nick had combed Jaisalmer for 7-Up and mashed potatoes and wet my forehead with cool washcloths. When he'd gotten sick in Jodhpur, I'd returned the favor.

But eventually all the togetherness and the crowds and heat and stomach bugs had reignited the tension. After three weeks in India we started bickering again, and in our compromised states a little disagreement about whether or not to placate touts or to ignore them almost always turned into a fight. Making matters worse, my perpetual career angst hit its zenith (or nadir) in the city of Jahnsi after I had received an e-mail from one of my best friends at home. She was coming to Pakistan and Afghanistan, she wrote, to do stories for one of the top magazines in the country. I, on the other hand, had just lost out on a story I didn't want to do for a magazine I didn't want to write for, to a writer who was a friend of mine.

"You see, I've totally screwed up my career," I told Nick.

"You're doing something else. Why can't you just be happy about that, and happy for your friend?"

In theory, I agreed with Nick's be-in-the-moment philosophy. It was just that on this trip I was having a hard time putting it into practice, and Nick's ability to do so, his general serenity . . . well, it annoyed me. "I *am* happy for her. I just think I'm going down the wrong road," I said. What I didn't articulate, though, was this silent accusation: *He* had led me down this road, and then abandoned me on it when I got freaked out.

Nick, now beyond sick of my whining, showed his sympathy by pretending to hang himself with the metal chain he used to lock up his bag. I in turn threw our 1,200-page guidebook at his chest. Yes, this seemed like a good time to give each other a little space.

After arriving at the studio on a sweltering afternoon in the midst of the August monsoon, I entered a giant hangar that housed the soundstage—a reproduction of a blue-tinted, Rainbow Room–like lounge with banquettes, tables, chairs, and a piano bar. Beyond the blue bar stood a pair of trailers where the stars hid between takes, and beyond those, the large waiting area where about a hundred Indian and Western extras milled about, gussied up in suits and gowns. I wandered through this alternate reality looking for Natasha, the woman supposedly in charge of extras, but found neither her nor anyone who knew what to do with me. I went back outside, where dozens more glammed-out extras sat on folding chairs. A woman with multicolored dreadlocks and yarn braids spilling out of her head beckoned me over.

"Hullo," she said.

"Hi there."

"You look nice. You want to smoke a joint with us?"

"Thanks, but no." The scene was surreal enough.

Lydia smiled a toothy grin and motioned for me to sit down. She introduced me to her friends: Pram, a fortyish blonde woman from Sweden, and Amrit, a fortyish black man from England. Lydia was from Israel. All three were devoted followers of the celebrity guru Bhagwan Shree Rajneesh, aka Osho, and had been living at his ashram in the city of Pune. Both the ashram, known by locals as Club Meditation, and its spiritual founder are objects of continuing skepticism and controversy both in India and the rest of the world. Osho amassed huge wealth—this was a guru who drove a fleet of Rolls Royces—by peddling his unique Eastern-mysticism meets-new-age-pop-psychology-meets-free-love philosophy to a following of mostly middle-class Westerners. He wrote dozens of books and set up his orgiastic ashram in Pune. Legions of acolytes flock there every year, even though Osho has been dead for more than a decade. To visit the ashram, these pilgrims pay up to $60 a day (in contrast to most Indian retreats, which are cheap or free). That's a chunk of change for a dharma bum, and the fees help explain why so many Osho-ites had left their spiritual haven to play partygoers in a Bollywood flick.

"How come you two aren't in costume?" I asked. Unlike Pram,

who was wearing a black spaghetti-strapped gown, Lydia and Amrit were dressed in the prototypical India hippie uniform: baggy genie pants, layered tank tops, and a harem's worth of scarves.

"I'm not white so they have no use for me. I came with her," Amrit said, stroking Pram's hand. "I couldn't bear to be without her."

"It's such a romantic story," Lydia said. "Amrit and Pram met fifteen years ago in Pune, back at Osho's ashram, but they did not see each other again until two days ago. Then it was love at first sight. I'm so glad. Before, Amrit was sad and drunk. Now, overnight, he's happy and drunk."

Amrit touched his hand to his heart and smiled. "It's true. I came here with her because they promised we could have our own hotel room, but they are making us all share the room and we can't make love. So I want to go back to Pune."

"You made love all night last night with me in the room anyway. I couldn't sleep," Lydia said, chuckling a husky smoker's chortle. "I'm going back, too. But I'm waiting for these bastards to give me my money. They want to cheat me. They asked me to come for the movie, but when I get here they tell me I have to hide my hair. I'm a hairstylist. This is good hair," she said, fingering her tresses, a Raggedy Ann meets Bob Marley kind of do.

"Can't you just cover it or put it back?"

"That's what I say. When Nash told me he wanted me, he told me to put my hair back. Yesterday I wrapped a scarf on like a turban and it looked very nice, but when I got on the set, one of the asshole producers had it in for me and kicked me off. I was so pissed," Lydia said, her voice rising. "Then last night at the hotel I got into trouble with the stinky-mouth Iranian bastard. He said it was not just my hair, but I was too skinny. He told me to leave today. But they have to pay me and now he hides. All day long they cheat me. The bastards can't cheat me!"

"Calm, Lydia, calm," Amrit, said, touching his hand to his heart. "Go have a smoke and get some food before we leave." Lydia got up, kicked her chair, and, muttering to herself, stalked off. Amrit smiled at me and touched his heart again. I asked him what it meant.

"When I get scared, I touch here. It means Osho is in my heart. It's like saying, 'Mommy, I need you,' and then I talk to Osho." He looked at me, then at Pram, who had not said a word since I'd sat down. "Are you OK, love?" he asked her.

"It's scary to be out here," she said in a faraway voice. "Inside, on the set, everyone has a role, but here I don't know what to do."

A half-hour later I got *my* role when Nash, the blond, curly-haired Iranian model coordinator, ran up to me. "Are you Gayle?" he asked. He apologized for the delay. Natasha had been in Bombay trying to scrounge up more extras and he hadn't realized I'd arrived. "It's crazy," he said. "They come, they go. Yesterday we lost ten. Today we have to find twelve more and now three more go home. No one wants to stay for the whole shoot. I have to go back to Pune tomorrow and find some others. Again, I am so sorry for your wait."

"That's OK. I met some interesting people."

"Oh, that one, she's crazy. What does she think with that hair? I was desperate and she seemed sweet, so I told her she could be in the film if she took it down. But on the set she refused. The producer called me over and said, 'Get this madwoman off my set.'"

I laughed and asked Nash how many extras came from the ashram. Usually it was about a 50-50 ashram/civilian ratio, but because of 9/11 and India's most recent skirmish with Pakistan, Bombay was suffering a dearth of tourists, so about 80 percent of the extras on this shoot were of the spiritual-seeker variety. "They're the craziest people," Nash said of the Osho-ites. "But I guess they like to take a break, see what Bollywood is like. And they all want money. OK, here's Natasha. See you later." He delivered me to an efficient and hip twenty-something Indian woman wearing jeans and high-heeled platform sandals.

Natasha started going through the racks for a costume and explained the setup: We were shooting the meet-cute moment of the film, in which Bobby's character spots Amisha's character at a posh NYC supper club and is so taken with love that he breaks into a serenade. Aside from the real actors, about a hundred extras—two-thirds of them Indian—played the club's patrons. All we had to do was to stand around and smile and clap while Bobby crooned his love to Amisha. "And you have to look upscale, of course. Here, try this." Natasha handed me a black number with giant poofs of pink taffeta circling the chest and hem. It was atrocious, but it fit.

"I look like a pastry. And I'll boil in all this polyester. What else have you got?"

This was how I ended up in an electric blue gown reminiscent of *Dynasty* circa 1982. The sequined bodice was so tight that it pushed my tits to my chin, and the chiffon skirt was slit so high that I had to wear bicycle shorts to avoid flashing the cast and crew. It was ironic, really. Since arriving in India I had stashed my characteristic knee-length skirts and sleeveless T-shirts—conservative enough at home but wildly revealing in these parts—and bought a new wardrobe of blousy peasant tops, long silk skirts, and a beautiful lavender *shalwar kameez*. The clothes were flowy, pretty, and so not me, but modesty trumped personal style. Now here I was prancing around in broad daylight in front of hundreds of people, for a film that would eventually be seen by hundreds of thousands of people, wearing what amounted to high-class-hooker regalia.

This dichotomy is an apt metaphor for the exceptional moral status Bollywood films occupy. Bollywood movies may be chaste—there's never any sex, not even a kiss; when lovers reach a passionate moment they consummate it with a song and dance—but the films' characters get away with the kinds of high jinks that would not be kosher in India, which at its core is still a very traditional, gender-divided society. Yet on the screen the girls dress like Christina Aguilera and switch boyfriends as readily as they switch outfits. Rebellious lovers marry out of caste, and heroes and villains engage in long, bloody shootouts that would make Jerry Bruckheimer wince. Some sociologists suggest that this over-the-top behavior is a form of national sublimation, a way for a conservative society to release its pent-up sexual energy: On-screen, anything goes, because off-screen, almost nothing goes.

In the Indian movie *Bollywood Calling*, Pat, a washed-up C-list American actor, comes to Bombay and, after a series of twists and turns, ends up famous. The film was made in 2000; the practice of packing films with Western extras began about five years earlier. It took less than half a decade for this trend to become common enough to be codified in a Bollywood film of its own. Strangely, though, this movement began outside the subcontinent. More than 1 billion Indians live in India, but some 20 million people of Indian descent live outside of the country (1.2 million in Great Britain; 1.7 million in the United States; 1 million in South Africa). Many of these nonresident Indians (NRIs) frequently travel back and forth between India and wherever else is home. Bollywood movies have always done brisk video business in expat communities, but the advent of DVD and cable satellite has broadened the potential international market for these films. NRI sales now comprise up to 65 percent of a Bollywood film's gross, and filmmakers increasingly make movies with an eye toward that demographic. Producer Raaja Bondela told me that NRIs are considered more worldly and well-traveled than the average Indian cineaste, so directors and producers began setting films abroad, in places like London, New York, and other iconic locales of the shrinking world.

Still, even though the bucks are coming from overseas, the bodies packing the theaters are still at home. The vast majority of Bollywood consumers are not sophisticates but uneducated men and women for whom the 20 to 40 rupee ticket (between 50 cents and a dollar) is a serious luxury that eats up the better part of a day's wages. As filmmakers attempt to lure more overseas viewers, they can't ignore the folks back home, which means they must retain the standard Bollywood template: a three-hour minimum running time, eight crowded song-and-dance numbers, deaths, marriages, and effects-laden action sequences. But, it turns out, the home audience's taste is evolving, too. The average Indian moviegoer is no longer content with what was once the mainstay of Indian film: period-piece dramas or stories depicting the lives of the rural poor. Rather, like his NRI counterpart, today's Indian wants a fast-paced tale about urban characters, and even though he has probably never left his country (let alone his town), he wants those tales to take place outside India. Even the poorest Indians crave a little international flair in their Bollywood experience, explained Mohit, the young and ambitious first assistant director on *Humko Tumse Pyaar Hai*. In other words, those Indians want to see *me* in a film—well, me standing off to the side in a blue sequined dress watching Amisha and Bobby falling in love, anyway. My presence satisfies the moviegoer's wanderlust. (Amisha and Bobby satisfy the other kind of lust.) Call it aspirational moviegoing: "Films set abroad look better but also patch into Indians' dreams of going overseas," Mohit said on a break between takes. "Most people know someone who does live abroad. Indians are curious, and they all have a concept of foreign lands even if they will never see them."

Problem is, shooting out of country isn't cheap. Most Hindi films are made for around $400,000; even the biggest budget Bollywood production, with all sorts of bells and whistles, costs less than $2 million. But when you set up shop in the United States—with all the necessary permits, SAG extras, and Teamsters—prices start to go the way of Tom Cruise's paycheck. The average American film costs around $40 million, four times more than the most expensive Indian film *ever* made, 2002's *Devdas*. So directors get creative. *Humko Tumse Pyaar Hai* was to have a short production stint in New York City, where much of the action was set. On an earlier film, the director Vikram Bhat had managed to grab exterior shots of New York City (as seen from New Jersey) and a quick scene in Central Park (filmed *sans* permit). For his climactic forty-five-minute New York City car chase, he fashioned NYPD cop cars and shot in the sand dunes of Dubai. Whether set in Rome or Paris, London or L.A., most Bollywood productions are usually made on Bombay backlots using fake scenery and Westerners like me plucked off the streets.

As the demand for Western extras has grown, a cottage industry of specialized model coordinators, including Nash and Natasha, has cropped up to supply them. These wranglers are contracted out by the production and given specifications—numbers, sex, race, special skills—and a modest budget. From that sum the coordinators must find, pay, feed, and house the extras, and also pay off the taxi drivers, hotel receptionists, and guides who help them recruit the warm, white bodies. It's a bit like human trafficking. Extras earn only about $10 a day, which explains the itinerant nature of the whole scene, with most extras being either cash-strapped travelers or tourists fashioning their own interactive Bollywood tour. But as the demand for white wallpaper continues, a handful of expat extras are digging in, betting that like *Bollywood Calling*'s hero, they might find fortune, fame, and happiness in the alternate universe that is India's film industry.

Bollywood moviemaking is notorious for its frenetic and chaotic production style: Scripts are written on the fly, actors learn lines as they go, many stars work swing shifts, shooting one film in the morning, another in the evening. Consequently, shoots can go on for months, even years. I knew filmmaking was a tedious business, but I still found it remarkable that our five-minute song scene, in which there were no lines, no dancing, just lip-synching, could take so long. For one week, we spent twelve-hour days smiling and clapping on set, eating and gossiping off it. On a typical day we arrived around 9 A.M. to a breakfast buffet (lentil dal, rice, nan bread, and tea). We changed into costume, then stood around, practicing, smiling, clapping, while Bobby sang to Amisha until 11, when it was time to break for a snack (dal, rice, nan bread, and tea), after which we did some more standing around and smiling and clapping until lunch at 2 (dal, rice, veggie curry, nan bread, and tea), and then back for more of the same until 6 and dinner (dal, rice, veggie curry, nan bread, and tea), and then yet more smiling and talking and waiting until around 9, when the director would break for the day and we'd shuffle across the lot for our last meal (dal, rice, salad, and tea) before boarding the bus for the hour-long ride to the hotel.

With all that spare time, it didn't take long for the social groups to ossify into high-school-like cliques. The Osho-ites splintered into two groups: the serious spiritualists, like Pram, who tended to stick to themselves, and the partyers. The partyer Osho-ites immediately hooked up with other like-minded folk, namely the twenty-something backpackers and the Persians, a trio of Iranian bad girls with lots of hair, lots of eyeliner, and lots of cleavage.

Then there were the adult tourists. Most of them were holiday-makers who tended to be a little less drug-oriented than the rest of the crew. Unlike the Osho-ites, who came to Bollywood for the cash, the tourists just wanted the experience. Consequently, many stayed only a day or two, after which a new batch would arrive to fill their costumes.

Finally, there were the regulars. Each day about sixty Indian regular extras sat inside the hangar, and five Western bachelors sat outside under a leafy tree. The bachelors were a funny, tuxedoed lot—being pros, they had invested in their own formal wear—and tended to keep to themselves. The regs took their work very seriously and could be competitive and proprietary, as I discovered on the second day of shooting. I had met Aubrey, a dapper goateed gentleman. He'd been all over India on film shoots, he told me, and had even gone on a ten-day cruise through the Persian Gulf to make the movie *Humraz*. As he bragged about the buffets and the swimming pools, Baman, an older Iranian gent—in the world of extras, Persian = Western—who worked both as an extra and a model coordinator, inched closer. "I was selected for *Humraz*, too," he boasted. "I have been acting for four years now, after being spotted in Pune." He pulled out a photo album of snaps of him posing with a variety of India's superstars. At this point, Tom and Simon, a British father-son team, joined the fray to list their film experience.

Then Shaboob strolled up. He was not a white extra but rather one of a handful of fair-skinned Indians who had gone to great lengths to Westernize himself, hoping to score the always-in-demand white roles. Shaboob had grown his brown curly hair long and dyed it blond and had made his brown eyes blue with colored contact lenses. He had also put together a portfolio, which he shoved in my direction. "I want to become a foreigner actor," he said, showing me a selection of come-hither shots of a bare-chested Shaboob in ripped jeans and a leather jacket. "But so far I am only an Indian extra."

When Shaboob pulled out his book, a jowly fifty-year-old fellow rushed over. He introduced himself as "Peter the German Actor" and thrust his own scrapbook under my nose. "Here is me with Karishma Kapoor. And here you can see me with Shah Rukh Khan. And here," he said, flipping pages, "are the numerous articles about me and my work. I was in all the Bhagat Singh movies, and from that I became famous." Bhagat Singh was a young Indian freedom fighter who was executed by the British in 1931 and deified by Bollywood some seventy years later. Four different production companies made four separate biopics about him, and Peter, previously a thespian novice, had had bit parts in all four films. This quadraperformance had caught the eye of the local press, and Peter had been written up in a number of Bombay papers.

For twenty minutes I sat amid this bundle of braggadocio. I had the distinct impression that the boys were jousting over me, and I can't say that I didn't enjoy it. In fact, since arriving on set I'd been engaging in a number of brief flirtations. Most of them were in my head, like the crushes I nursed for one of the producers and for Vikram Baht. I constantly tried to catch Vikram's eye, to wow him with my acting abilities. He ignored me. So I indulged in a coquetry with Fernando, a Spanish Osho-ite extra who spoke very little English and who looked like George Clooney when he wore his monochromatic suit-and-tie costume. We met the first time I came out of the dressing room in my blue va-va-voom dress. He'd swooped over to escort me to the set, and for the entire day, as we smiled and clapped, we'd engaged in some linguistically mangled repartee.

"You are sexy in that dress."

"You look pretty for a hippie," I replied in my rusty Spanish.

"Are you married?"

"Yes," I said, holding up my ring finger.

"Where is your husband?"

"Varanasi."

"Foolish man."

"This is true."

"You come for a walk with me?"

"Where?"

"Outside."

"To do what?" I asked. He grinned. "Give me a break. Only my clothing is of a prostitute."

"No, no. Not that," he said, and mimed smoking a joint.

"Marijuana makes me a hungry and tired person—and also boring."

"You cannot be boring."

"No, really, with marijuana I am a person who is boring. You're probably a boring person, too."

"No, I am very boring without grass."

"Do all of the people of Osho smoke marijuana all the time?"

"No, we don't smoke it when we are sleeping."

Unfortunately it was *really* difficult to flirt in a foreign language, and our banter soon petered out. That night on the bus back to the hotel, Fernando invited me to share his room. Right. As soon as he changed into his hippie clothes, the Clooney effect, and my attraction, vanished, and even if it hadn't, I wasn't *that* mad at Nick. The next day, Fernando ceased his seduction and employed me to help him snare a sexy Persian girl by translating his sweet nothings from Spanish into English.

After that interlude, I stuck with the regs, who looked after me like a kid sister. Aubrey alerted me when the buffet went up and escorted me to the set when shooting resumed. Baman kept me stocked in bottles of water. Tom and Simon kept me entertained with India stories. On-set, Peter advised me on how to position myself so I might be more prominent in the shot. He had quite the knack for it. Almost anytime Mohit or Vikram gave us direction, Peter furrowed his brow and peppered Mohit with detailed questions. Once the cameras rolled, however, Peter flouted those instructions and often positioned himself in the center of a shot, or kept moving to remain in the camera's line of focus. On day four we shot an integral part of the scene, when Amisha and Bobby lock eyes for the first time. Vikram had brought in fake smoke and turned the wind machine on Amisha, so that her waist-length hair billowed into a nimbus around her doll's face. Mohit had instructed us to stare, riveted, at this glorious love blossoming as the camera panned across our amazed reactions, and then on cue to break into applause. He did *not* tell us to pace alongside the camera to stay in the shot, which is precisely what Peter did. Mohit corrected him, and the rest of the extras groaned, but Peter carried on with the dignity of a Shakespearean actor being heckled by an audience of soccer hooligans.

Aubrey, who took great pride in his work ethic, did not approve of such antics. A bit of a lost mutt, Aubrey was English and Italian but had lived in the United States. He'd had a wife and daughter for a spell in England, but that hadn't panned out. In fact, life in general seemed not to have panned out for Aubrey. He hadn't spoken to his wife or daughter in years. He'd become estranged from his only brother and asked me if I could find him on the Internet. In the last few years Aubrey had been drifting around the world, picking up work where he could. Since landing in India in the mid-1990s, he had found steady work in Bollywood. He had appeared in seventy-five commercial and print ads and about fifteen movies, including one where he was an extra in a musical number. "I loved that. I love to dance," he said, doing a little soft-shoe. But at fifty-three, Aubrey's life was less than stable. He lived in a small room upstairs from his friend's store and didn't socialize much. He made just enough money to keep off the streets. "Acting does not make big money. It's enough to survive off of," he said. "I get such a big thrill out of the work when directors shake my hand, but I have no illusions of fame."

Peter, on the other hand, seemed to have plenty of illusions of fame. One evening, after dinner, while he, Aubrey, and I were sitting outside, I asked Peter how he wound up in India. "India was my dream as a child. *Magical, mystical India*," he intoned, as though speaking a re-hearsed monologue. "But it would take many years to realize that dream." Back in Germany he had lived a rather solitary existence as an insurance executive. Never married, no kids, very few relationships, just "superficial" friends. "Then I had an experience that changed my life completely. I was doing visualization and meditating—*Oohhhhmmm*." He stopped to make sure I understood what he meant. I ohhmed back.

"Yes. So, the ground started to vibrate it. The sun was coming through the cells in my body. You could not control it, you could not stop it or you would die. But I had no fear of death. I said yes to death. Implosion. Explosion. Now I was gone. I woke up totally surprised to find myself in this body."

Aubrey stared at Peter, perplexed by his typically nonlinear Osho-ian-type talk. I said, "That sounds very profound."

"It was. Friends came over but could not enter the room."

"Why not?" Aubrey asked.

"Because of the energy."

"The energy?"

"Yes, it was powerful."

"Like some kind of force field?" Aubrey asked.

"Yah. After that I knew I had to make my spiritual way, to find out what was beyond our belief system."

Thus did Peter's spiritual journey begin. He started studying hypnosis, nuerolinguistic programming, hatha yoga, and reiki massage. He also started reading the works of Osho. In 1998 he moved to Pune and rented a flat near the ashram and began what he thought would be a quiet life as a reiki master, spiritual student, and seeker of peace.

But then Bollywood came calling. The four Bhagat Singh movies. The newspaper articles. Peter pulled out one piece from *The Times of India*, and as I read it he recited it aloud. Aubrey frowned at this. Then Peter showed me (again) his special Bhagat Singh scrapbook, with snapshots from each shoot and pages from a children's book about Singh that Peter had highlighted and annotated with photos from his time on-set.

Now Peter actively pursued roles, was on familiar terms with the model coordinators, read the Bollywood magazines, and kept up with the industry gossip. He even put up a promotional Web site. It was a rather funny thing, with a photo of him in his yogi outfit and the following introduction: *A star was born 50 years ago who entertained German as well as Indian audiences. Acting since half a century on this planet as: Baby, Child, Taxidriver, Police Officer, Lawyer, Therapist, Reiki Master, Yoga Master, NLP-Master, Master Hypnotist, Cosmic Joke.* Down the side of the site ran a list of spiritual terms (Love, God, Shanti) bleeding into names of Hollywood and Bollywood luminaries (Arnold Schwarzenegger and Raj Kapoor).

"Where do you think all this will lead?" I asked, handing him back his scrapbook.

"Bigger roles will happen," he said. "I have no hope. I *know* this. Truth and fate bring me here. I go through so many stations, so much pain to bring me here."

"So your spiritual path has led you to Bollywood?"

"Not just to Bollywood, but wherever the movies are made."

"What about the reiki, the healing, the world peace?"

"For me, fame is a great opportunity. There is the possibility to make good money. Movies are healing. I want to play roles for the next twenty years so I can give healing for free."

"So you are making movies for the betterment of humankind?"

"Exactly."

Peter's healing-through-fame rationale was about as believable as Doctor Bi's curing-cancer-through-cursing book, and the two men's chances at success in their respective endeavors were equally dubious.

India's caste system rules much of daily life: where you will live, what job you will take, and who you will marry. The Sunday papers are filled with marriage ads that read something like "Brahmin doctor from good family seeks educated Brahmin wife . . . " A caste rules Bollywood, too. Many of the bigwigs these days are somehow connected to the dynastic families that rule Bollywood. Take the Kapoor family, with its four generations of fame: actor-turned-director Prithviraj Kapoor begat famous director/producer/actor Raj Kapoor who begat actor/producer Randhir Kapoor who begat daughters Karishma and Kareena Kapoor, currently two of Bollywood's hottest actresses. And these are just a few of the *really* famous Kapoors.

Once you are famous in Bollywood, you are royalty. I'd thought Americans went nuts over their stars, but Indians take it to a new extreme. Everyone, it seems, from the wealthy banker to the poor farmer, is up on the latest celeb news. Respected newspapers run daily sections of Bollygossip; countless fan magazines breathlessly report on Madhuri's new boyfriend or the love affair between Amisha and Vikram (regardless of whether such liaisons are actually true). Many Bollywood actors go on to become elected government ministers; it's hard to beat someone with such a built-in base. It's also difficult for an actor to break into this world, as so many stars are picked from this elite nepotistic stock. Rags-to-riches stories may be a mainstay of Bollywood film plots, but Bollywood itself is no fairy tale.

The Indian extras understood this reality, and few appeared to have illusions about their futures. Being an extra was a job, and a crappy, ill-paying one at that. It was not a stepping stone from the chorus to the spotlight. The most ambitious of the extras, like Shaboob, hoped for Western roles, but as long as actual Westerners were available, they didn't stand much of a chance. Aubrey seemed to understand that in Bollywood terms his status was fixed. But Peter still had hope of a ladder up, still stoked a burning ambition that drove him to kiss ass and do his damndest to get discovered, even though the reality is that if a movie has a speaking part for a Westerner, casting agents find some bona fide actor (albeit someone C-list or below) from England or the United States to fill the role—not an enlightened reiki master with delusions of an Oscar.

Then again, maybe the fame didn't matter as much as the pursuit of it. For in a way, Peter, like Aubrey, had already escaped one kind of strangling caste—the caste of social alienation and of life's limitations. Aubrey's life was, by his own reckoning, not a grand success. Peter's existence had been, from the sounds of it, terribly lonely. But in Bollywood these men could transcend their histories. Maybe for Aubrey and Peter the on-set camaraderie or the doses of recognition they received were already far and away more than they had ever imagined for themselves ten years earlier. Maybe Peter was rabid about his Bollywood career not simply because he wanted to be a celebrity, but because he yearned to be part of something larger than himself. In Bollywood, Peter and Aubrey had finally found a place in the world in which they fit.

I understood that. When I was younger I had been a total drama geek, entranced not so much by the glamour of theater but by the sense of community. It had been years since my play days, and I had forgotten how seductive that sense of belonging could be. I was reexperiencing it on this Bollywood set at a time when I badly needed it. The kind of traveling Nick and I had been doing, while uplifting and gratifying, was also lonely and isolating. We were always on our own, always drifting a little, *always* outsiders. On this set I had a part to play, I had a day full of structure. Here, all of the extras were outsiders, which made us insiders. It was a little bubble, shielded from my world, and I was happy in it. I found it worrisome that this period of well-being happened to coincide with Nick's absence, and more worrisome yet that I didn't seem to miss him. But I pushed such qualms to the back of my mind and basked in the comforts of being part of a group again.

It took about a week to get sick of that. The gossip, which had been juicy at first, now seemed juvenile. The extras' my-role-is-bigger-than-your-role competition had grown old. The sleeping arrangements—a mattress on the floor of a hotel room I shared with three other people— sucked. The skimpy dress had lost its irony value and now was just tacky and drafty. To top it all off, I had caught a cold. The shoot was running late, and Natasha urged me to stay on, but my friend Ruchira had invited me to bunk with her at the Bombay Yacht Club, a fabulous decaying Victorian relic, one of the many such landmarks that gives the city a humid, Miss Havisham feel. I loved the club, and I needed a rest, so when shooting wrapped that night I bade farewell to the cast and caught a train back to the city. I was exhausted, congested, and $60 the richer.

It turned out I was more like Peter than I had imagined. Bollywood had gotten into my blood, and I took to religiously reading the film section in the daily papers. One morning as Ruchira and I took our breakfast next to the open window overlooking the carved Gateway to India, I saw a blurb in the *Times of India* about an upcoming premiere for an English-language, Indian-themed film that was being buzzed about all over the world. The film's director, Gurinder Chadha, was in town to promote the film and seemed to be hitting a different party every night, based on what I could tell from the gossip pages. She would also be at the premiere. I called a friend of Ruchira's who got me in touch with a local production company and managed to score us tickets to *Bend It Like Beckham,* a sweet film that chronicles the trials of an Indian teenager in England who goes behind her parents' backs to fulfill her dream of playing soccer. The movie would go on to become an international sensation, grossing more than $75 million worldwide, but back then it was just starting to generate heat.

The premiere was decidedly low-key, so low-key that Ruchira and I were seated right next to Gurinder and her husband and writing partner, Paul Berges. During the intermission we chatted, and afterwards we all went out for coffee. Over cappuccinos we talked about why *Bend It Like Beckham* and *My Big Fat Greek Wedding,* another sleeper indie hit that dealt with culture clashes, were finding such audiences—and not just among the ethnic communities they chronicled.

Gurinder believed the two movies found easy resonance because of the shrinking world. "The films are about marrying tradition and modernity," she said. "Everyone understands that."

Modernity marrying tradition—in a way that's what seems to be happening with Hollywood and Bollywood. As the two industries edge closer to each other and begin to blend old traditions with new ideas, all kinds of synergy are beginning to flow. In the last few years, Hollywood money has started to pour into Bollywood. Twentieth Century Fox signed a deal with influential producer Ram Gopal Verma to market and distribute his next three films in India and possibly internationally. Hyperion Pictures put up $10 million for *Marigold*, a musical with Hindi and English musical numbers. The success of 2002's *Lagaan: Once Upon a Time in India*—a four-hour musical about cricket players in colonial times that became the first Bollywood musical to be nominated for an Academy Award—prompted distributor Columbia TriStar to distribute a dozen more Bollywood movies.

Even more telling, Hollywood has begun to share—or poach—ideas from Bollywood. Bollywood films have long recycled Hollywood plots and stunts, and even lifted entire story lines (like the recent *Kaante*, a musical remake of Quentin Tarantino's *Reservoir Dogs*). But the tide is turning. While Western directors have historically taken inspiration from seminal Indian filmmakers like Satyajit Ray, now they're starting to mimic the more mainstream Bollywood aesthetic. What was Baz Luhrmann's *Moulin Rouge!*—with its spazzy pacing, tragic love story, and anachronistic song-and-dance numbers—if not a Bollywood film? In 2002, Universal released *The Guru*, a screwball musical comedy with an Indian and American cast. In 2003 the Indian-born producer Ismail Merchant of the arthouse duo Merchant-Ivory started production on a musical about the goddess Shakti starring Tina Turner. And a few months after I met Gurinder she announced her next project: a remake of *Pride and Prejudice* called *Bride and Prejudice* that reimagines Austen's classic as an international cross-cultural Bollywood extravaganza. The film, which was set for release in 2004, was shot in India, America, and England and featured an international cast and Bollywood-style song and dance numbers.

In this shrinking cinematic world, the muse flows east *and* west.

I had not been back in Bombay two days before my cell phone began chiming continuously. Natasha, Nash, and Sanjeet, a model coordinator I'd never met but who had somehow gotten my number, were all offering me roles in various productions. I was getting ready to leave, so I turned them down. But I had one final set to visit.

I had been hearing about the Morel family since arriving in Bombay. All of the regular extras talked about them, as did the model coordinators. No one seemed to like them very much. Peggy and Paul Morel were described alternately as missionaries, social workers, and grifters who forced their extraordinarily large brood of kids to act in films and then used the kids' earnings to bring Hindus to the Christian light. Everyone expected someone from the family—there are nine of them—to show up on the set of *Humko Tumse Pyaar Hai*. None of them did, so I called them and got myself invited to lunch.

Most of the missionaries I had met on the trip were idealistic, earnest, hardworking people who seemed more consumed with helping the poor than converting them. Paul and Peggy sounded like the Bollywood version of Jim and Tammy Faye Bakker, and I was fully prepared to hate them. One Thursday, two days before I was to leave Bombay, I took a ninety-minute train/rickshaw ride out to the semi-swank suburb of Diamond Garden and found the Morel homestead, a rambling white stucco house with a big front yard. As soon as I swung open the gate, Paul bounded out the door wearing a Hawaiian shirt and a wide-open grin, bellowing "Welcome!"

I followed him into the kitchen, which felt comfortingly suburban. The walls were cluttered with family photos, flowcharts divvying up chores, a daily schedule laying out the times for (home) school, recess, meals, PE, and social time. There was also a smattering of ecumenically correct paraphernalia: a painting of the Virgin Mary and some fuzzy animal posters with Christian inspirational sayings on them. Peggy, a pretty blond woman, gave me a warm hello as her swarm of attractive kids zipped around, stirring enormous vats of lentils and setting a long wooden table for lunch. She quieted the kids and commenced with introductions. There was Ricky, nine, blond and moppety; David, eleven, blond and lanky; Jason, fourteen, blond and lankier; Jonathan, sixteen, blond with platinum streaks, and muscular; and Stephanie, nineteen, a brunette, poor thing. Two more—

Christopher, eighteen; and Paul, twenty-one—were currently living back in the States.

While Peggy and the kids got lunch together, Paul offered me a tour of the house, which belonged to a confederation of neohippie missionary groups called The Family. In the study, Paul pulled out a bunch of photo albums from various film productions. As we flipped through shots of teenagers in tuxes, he told me of his path to God. He'd been a hippie, a Scientologist, an acolyte of various Eastern religions. "I dabbled," he said. "And then one day I was tripping on acid, listening to the Moody Blues, and I just found Jesus. I said a prayer right there and then." The road from revelation to redemption was not straight, however. Paul fell off the faith wagon, experimenting again with drinking and drugs before meeting Peggy, also a believer. They fell in love, got married, and over the next twenty years sired seven kids; they traveled to Ecuador, Mexico, the Philippines, and India to do volunteer work— usually social work—for The Family. Unlike more structured missionary organizations, The Family offers little to no salary or stipend. Volunteers like Paul and Peggy never quite know how they're going to earn their keep and support their work. "If God's not in it, we're screwed," Paul told me. "But if there's a plan and a purpose, doors will open."

When the Morels arrived for their second missionary stint in India five years ago, they were, typically, broke. But soon enough, a door—a stage door—opened when a friend invited Paul to act in a commercial. Soon the entire Morel clan was getting roles in movies, commercials, and videos, as well as modeling in print ads and commanding daily rates of up to $100 per person. It's easy to see why they were in demand. When foreigners conjure up some ideal of American healthiness, they likely imagine the Morels: thin, blond, and, dare I say it, lit from within somehow. They were like a born-again Brady Bunch.

Downstairs, Peggy called us to lunch. We sat down at the rectangular table and, after grace, the kids passed around industrial-sized plastic bowls of lentil dal and rice and jugs of boiled water. I quizzed the kids on their filmographies. Jon had done more than fifteen movies. Jason had made only three movies but now was doing more modeling. Stephanie had been on more than twenty shoots and done countless commercials and videos. Paul had learned a bit of Hindi and had been getting speaking roles. I asked why none of them had been on the set of *Humko Tumse Pyaar Hai.*

"We don't work if it doesn't pay well," Peggy said. "We're not doing this for fame or experience."

"The tourists will do the shoots for any money," Paul said. "They'll sit for twelve hours for seven dollars."

"We can't do that," Peggy said.

"So you're being undercut by cheap foreign labor?" I joked.

Paul raised his eyebrows and laughed. "In India, if you're going to allow yourself to get screwed, you'll get screwed."

"So we're picky," Peggy said.

"Do you ever think it's ironic, you know, your family supporting your missionary work by acting in trashy Bollywood films?"

Peggy looked at me and chuckled. "We think it's God's way of showing us that he has a sense of humor."

After lunch, Peggy grabbed a pile of snapshots: There were pics of the family putting on performances and festivals for young Indian orphans (the social work), and more shots of the older kids dolled up in tuxedoes and evening gowns and colonial dress (the studio work). She also pulled out a stack of catalogs in which Ricky, David, and Jonathan posed in Nehru suits for the preteen set. "It used to be that we got free clothes when they did a brochure, but what use are these kinds of things for kids?" Peggy asked. Ricky grimaced and rolled his eyes. Peggy inspected her son, then the photos, then looked at me. "The kids are getting sick of this now, so we don't make them do it."

"How about you?"

"Not so much anymore. It was fun when we could do shoots as a family, but now it's getting old. Besides, I'm not so young but they still try to put me in tight stuff."

In the corner, Stephanie sat glowering. "I went on one shoot with a group of my friends," she said. "They told us we'd be princesses and we ended up being concubines. That about describes my Bollywood experience."

"What do you mean?"

"They tell you it'll be great but then you're treated like a dog. You sit on the floor and eat bad spicy Indian food. One person tells you what to do; another person tells you something different. It's totally disorganized."

"I got that sense. But that made it fun, like make-believe. And all the people. You must have made a lot of friends on the set."

"Not really. I go with my friends and we stay separate from the tourists. The Indians don't talk to us, especially the women. They are the worst. They have such temper tantrums. I was doing a crowd scene for a movie called *Love at Times Square* and the extras were supposed to reach up for a bouquet of flowers. Someone knocked over the leading actress and she started freaking out, screaming at us and the director. I hate acting now. I only do it for the money."

Stephanie possessed a world-weariness that belied her age, making me wonder if it was acting that she was so sick of. After all, she was nineteen years old and had lived a wandering life with her wacky family, spending the last five years in India, which can be the most vibrant, exhilarating, colorful, interesting country but which does not afford the average American a typical teenagehood. You often hear travelers talking about hitting their India wall—waking up one day and realizing that if they endure one more minute of mystics and sadhus and groping men and nagging peddlers and air-sucking crowds and steaming cowshit and piles of garbage stewing in the heat, they will go insane. I imagined that Stephanie had hit a bunch of walls: her India wall, her Family wall, her family wall. Like her two other brothers, she was preparing to fly the coop and return to America to experience what must have seemed very exotic: a normal secular life.

I never hit my India wall, but I did at times hanker for my normal life, some of which I'd recaptured in Bombay, where I had friends and, on-set, a daily grind. Now I was getting ready to throw myself back into uncertainty. Nick and I were to meet back in Delhi in two days. Nick, offering an olive branch, had promised to accompany me to a yoga retreat in the holy city of Rishikesh. I was no longer sure I wanted to go, but I knew I could not remain in this Bollybubble. Eventually the fun would wear off and I'd just be some lonely girl chasing parts in a hopeless attempt to feel like I belonged. And though I didn't feel it at the moment, I already *did* belong somewhere.

At four o'clock, Peggy and the kids went upstairs for the afternoon session of home school, so I said goodbye and walked to the town center to catch a rickshaw back to the train station. I'd turned my cell phone ringer off during lunch, but on the train I picked up my messages: one from Natasha, one from a model coordinator named Yunnus, and five text messages from Sanjeet, who was demanding I take a role in a music video. On the hour-long train ride home, Sanjeet sent me two more text messages. At first his attention had made me feel famous. Now it just made me feel stalked. I finally sent him a message to leave me alone, and he immediately called.

"You come to work tonight? I need you," Sanjeet asked.

"No. Stop calling me please."

"You don't want to be in a music video?"

"I already told you, I'm busy."

"How about a movie? I need someone for tomorrow."

"No."

"No?"

"That's right. No more movies."

"But why not, Miss?"

"Because, Sanjeet, I have retired."

India to Kazakhstan—
September

About an hour into the drive to Almaty, the Kazak driver we'd
hired at the Uzbek border began making a wild pawing gesture and
a grr grr noise. Nick and I had no idea what he meant, Murat
speaking no English, and Nick and I speaking no Russian or Kazak.
He pulled a screeching U and zoomed back down the empty road,
stopping in front of a lone adolescent boy who was holding a
sheepdog puppy in front of his chest as though it were a religious
offering. Murat got out and tickled the puppy, but when he found
out the price—$30 before bargaining—he returned to the car.

"Oh, grr grr," I said. "In America we say arf arf."

We all laughed. Nick called the scene a Surreal Central Asian
Moment. We'd had quite a few of those since flying from India to
Uzbekistan, where we had spent two weeks exploring the ancient
Silk Road cities. Two days ago we had started to make our way
from Bukhara to Almaty, Kazakhstan, a seven-hundred-mile over-
land journey that would take us from the skirts of Persia to the
edge of China.

After seven hours on the road, we pulled up to a row of restaurants that were literally in the middle of nowhere. We sat around a
low table, reclining on cushions, eating a manly meal of meat: a
mound of hot dog, chicken, horse sausage, beef cutlet, all topped

off with an egg. Around us groups of sunburned men knocked back $1 bottles of vodka. After dinner I went in search of a bathroom. The waitress guided me through the kitchen and out the back door, where the building gave way to wide-open steppe stretching all the way from Mongolia to Hungary. To the south I could see the snowcapped Tian Shan mountains lit amber by the setting sun. Between me and the mountains there was nothing but miles of emptiness—and a solitary cement shed where a woman sat behind a grated window collecting the six cents entry into a putrid pit toilet.

We were back on the road for another hour when we almost ran out of gas. We had paid Murat for the ride in dollars and had spent most of the tenge we'd changed at the border on all of our dinners. Murat was having trouble finding a gas station that would take greenbacks, and we passed three petrol stations without filling up. By the time Murat's gas gauge started flashing, there were no more to be found. "Benzin?" I said, pointing to the gauge. He shrugged, and twenty minutes later we found a station and Murat used the last of our tenge to fill the tank. Or so we thought.

We hurtled into the empty steppe, following the same path as the ancient traders who once ferried silk, spices, and other goods from China to Persia. The mountains jutted against the night sky, moonlight reflecting off of the snow. The Big Dipper rose before us. We entered an ethereal world inhabited not by humans but by specters: a ghostly shepherd on horseback, a farm field ringed by fire, plumes of smoke rising like a wall into the sky, a lone boy on a bicycle. It was hypnotic, so hypnotic that we feared it would put Murat to sleep. We took turns singing to keep him awake, Nick and I belting out "Hotel California"—the Esperanto of pop tunes—while Murat hollered some Kazak songs which we hummed along to. It was magical.

Not so magical, though, when the gas light started blinking again. It turned out that Murat had only filled up with $1.25 worth of gas and now the road, and our tank, had emptied. I thought of our Uzbek friends who'd warned Nick and me of bandits lurking along the highways and advised us to take a bus. We had waited four hours in the shithole border town of Chernevka for a bus that never departed before finally resorting to hiring a driver. We'd hoped to reach Almaty by midnight, but at 11 P.M. we were still 250 miles away—and about to be stranded. If that happened, Murat presumably would go hunting for gas, leaving Nick and me alone in the car in the dead of night in the middle of the steppe in a strange country whose language we did not speak and whose currency we did not carry. This was the kind of scenario I had nightmares about.

We pulled over to a group of soldiers on the side of the road who were tinkering under the hood of a broken-down Mercedes. How far till benzin? Murat asked. He wouldn't flash me fingers, which is how we'd communicated sums before, but I'd heard the soldiers answer tridtsat pyat, which means 35, as in 35 kilometers, or, as we say in my language, up shit's creek. Murat just tore on, pushing the little Lada to warp speed, as if by the time the tank realized it was empty we'd be somewhere, a strategy whose success surprised even Murat. When we spotted the lights of a distant town, he kissed the steering wheel.

By now it was midnight, so after filling up for real this time, I pantomimed that I thought we should sleep for a while before driving on. I was thinking of a two-hour catnap, but Murat reclined his chair and started snoring. His nasal racket, combined with the mountain chill, kept Nick and me wide awake. We huddled together, freezing, until 6 a.m., when I nudged Murat. "Sem," he said. Seven.

"No, now. You've slept plenty." Murat grumpily lit a cigarette and pulled back onto the road. A half-hour later he started twisting his hands in front of his face and gesturing at Nick to take the wheel. "He's still tired," Nick said. "He wants to sleep more."

"You've got to be kidding," I said. "He slept six hours. This isn't a road trip for kicks, you know. We're paying him."

Ever the reasonable one, Nick said, "What can you do? He's an amateur. We don't want him to crash."

So Murat went back to sleep until eight o'clock, when I kicked his chair to wake him. We descended through the Al Atu mountains in silence. At 11 he dropped us off at the Hotel Zerde, a decaying Soviet-era youth hostel where a stout babushka with hair the color and texture of red yarn delivered us to our room. Down the hall the prostitutes were beginning their early shift. It was an entirely different Surreal Central Asian Moment, but we would have to sleep before fully appreciating it.

Hobbits on the Silk Road

Hobbits are an unobtrusive but very ancient people, more numerous formerly than they are today, for they love peace and quiet and a good-tilled earth. . . . Even in ancient days they were, as a rule, shy of "the Big Folk," as they call us, and now they avoid us with dismay and are becoming hard to find.

—J. R. R. TOLKIEN, *THE LORD OF THE RINGS*

Tell me about it. I had been in Almaty, a cosmopolitan city in the Central Asian country of Kazakhstan, on a mission to find the mythical subculture of Tolkienists—Kazak kids who were so taken with the writer J. R. R. Tolkien's characters from *Lord of the Rings* that they frequently *became* hobbits, wizards, dwarves, and other Gandalfian creatures, dressing up in full regalia and parading through Almaty's tree-lined streets. In my search for them, I had prowled Zhibek Zholy and Tole Bi, the main pedestrian drags downtown. I'd witnessed plenty of long-haired metal kids hanging out and drinking beer. I'd also seen a fair number of ashen-faced babushkas, begging bowls before them, beseeching a spare few cents of *tenge*. (Their poverty is one of the unfortunate by-products of the demise of the Soviet Union; when state socialism collapsed, so did these grandmothers' pensions.) I had shopped among the nouveau riche as they spent their fresh cash on the latest electronic gadgets and imported French clothes at the TsUM department store. But so far I'd spotted no hobbits.

So I had tracked down a twenty-one-year-old writer named Erbol who worked for the Institute for War and Peace Reporting and who had written an article about the Tolkienists that I'd seen on the Web. Erbol spoke no English, but, using an Internet-based translation program and sign language, we had a conversation of sorts. He told me he knew a guy named Ilya, a punk rocker—this communicated via an outstretched hand run alongside the length of his head to denote a mohawk—who was down with the Tolkien scene and who also spoke good English. I had returned to my hostel armed with Ilya's telephone number and a Russian Language Beginner's Guide, a necessity in a city where few speak English. Under the bemused glances of the three matrons who guarded the front desk, I had practiced saying in broken Russian *"Mozhna pagavarit Ilya's telefonem?"* a few times before dialing. After three days I had finally gotten ahold of Ilya, who turned out to be a tall, lanky blond fellow with a buzz cut and a baritone voice. He'd informed me that he was no longer a Tolkienist but a writer and poet—one who'd recently received an award as Kazakhstan's best young author, it turned out—but that he was familiar enough with the movement to be able to track down some hobbits for me.

Which was why that Saturday I had met Ilya at the bus stop at the southern end of downtown Almaty, a few tram stops from my hotel. There, along with dozens of Almaty-ites all dressed up for weekend hiking trips, we'd boarded a packed bus to Butakovka, a wilderness getaway in the foothills of the snowcapped Zailiyski Alatau Mountains. Six miles later, Ilya and I had alighted at the end of the line and hiked along a cold mountain stream, passing a couple of half-built mansions—part of the upscale urban sprawl spurred by Almaty's new class of oil gazillionaires—before turning right and hiking straight up a steep mountainside. For the better part of an hour I'd trudged up the muddy path as best I could in flip-flops, pausing frequently to breathe deeply and drink water. Ilya had appraised my stumblings with a look of equal parts disgust and pity. At the top of the hill he'd guided us over the ridge and to a grassy clearing he'd kept referring to as the helicopter pad, where he'd promised me my hobbits.

When we finally arrived, we didn't find any hobbits. Or elves. Or dwarves. Or orcs. Not even a human. Ilya shrugged. I sat down to pant. Tolkien was right: These hobbits are a bitch to find.

There were a number of probable causes for the hobbits' elusiveness. It could be, as Tolkien instructed, the hobbitian temperament. It could also be the Kazak one. More than ten years after the collapse of the USSR, much of Kazakhstan had yet to shake its totalitarian character. Though its statues of Lenin and Marx have long been warehoused, Almaty still felt vaguely Soviet, and not merely because of the city's Stalinist apartment blocks and the ubiquitous Lada cars bucking for lane space with flashy new Mercedes. Politically, Kazakhstan, and indeed all of the former Central Asian Republics, which include Kyrgyzstan, Uzbekistan, Tajikistan, and Turkmenistan, have not exactly had great success in democratizing. All of these states are ruled by former Soviet officials who fell into power when the Union collapsed, and these men run their nations with iron fists—more Khrushchev than Kennedy.

Human rights, while not as bad as they were in Soviet days, ain't great. The Central Asian rulers retain a viselike grip over political expression and the media. Kazakhstan is the most progressive of the 'stans, but even here, journalists critical of the government are arrested or beaten. Religious and ethnic minorities are also tightly regulated to keep tabs on Islamists, Uighur Muslim separatists, and nascent Christian groups. But because a KGB-era cop does not really understand the subtle distinctions between Baptists, Scientologists, and Tolkienists, the hobbits, elves, and wizards have found themselves branded as members of an unregistered religion and have suffered a good deal of harassment at the hands of Kazak police. They have had their swords confiscated. They've been beaten. They've even been jailed for staging alfresco jousts on the mall. So the Tolkienists had taken to the hills. But Ilya and I were in the hills. Where were the Tolkienists?

Ilya was perplexed. "They come here every weekend in warm weather," he told me. "I just asked to make sure it still happens."

I stared at him, doing my best to replicate the disgust/pity look he'd given me on the trail up. Then I handed him my cell phone. "Why don't you call around?"

Ilya did that and discovered where all the hobbits were hiding: under the covers, nursing hangovers. The night before, one Tolkienist had thrown a wild Friday-the-13th party that had gone on till sunrise. But the hobbits would be back in form the next day, the voice on the phone told Ilya, who gave me a no-problem smile. I gave him a yes-problem frown. I'd have to hike this monster mountain again.

Before I left for the trek on Sunday—in appropriate footwear this time—I invited Nick to join me.

"You want me to meet the Dungeons and Dragons geeks?" he asked.

"They're not Dungeons and Dragons, they're Tolkienists. It's different. Besides, Ilya is a punk rocker, like you were, and it's a sunny Sunday afternoon. It'll be a beautiful day."

I really wanted him to come. Since arriving in Kazakhstan, things had been colder than ever between us, because before coming to Central Asia, things had gotten hotter than ever. Being in Bombay with my friend

Ruchira and all her journalist friends had made me miss my New York life even more. And though it was a cop-out to do so, part of me blamed Nick for instigating this trip, for taking me away from home. Home, where we didn't have to find a place to stay every few days, where we didn't have to consult maps to locate a post office, where we could eat a piece of fruit without contemplating dysentery, where we didn't have to wake up each morning and, again, figure out, What are we going to do *today*?

To make matters worse, while in Delhi we'd been in travel-hassle overdrive. We'd had to procure visas for Uzbekistan and Kazakhstan, which thanks to the countries' Soviet-era tourist policies had been a Herculean task replete with dizzying bureaucracy, bribery, and wild goose chases. Every day for a week we had fought with bureaucrats, civil servants, and wily rickshaw drivers, returning to the apartment exhausted and pissy. At this point we were both nearing our India walls. The night before we were due to leave Delhi for Uzbekistan, Nick and I were having another battle. I was angry at him for not being more open, not listening to me. It had become like a script I couldn't stop reciting. He said he was sick of hearing all this shit. I said I was sick of saying it. I told him that I liked myself better when I wasn't with him. And then I looked at his face. Instead of the vacant, angry look he usually wore during such lectures, his visage had crumpled. Tears were streaming down his cheeks, off his chin, and into his curry.

"I can't do this anymore," he said.

"What? What's wrong? What can't you do?"

"I can't be with you like this. You make me feel stupid. Worthless. Like I'm not good enough for you."

Before leaving on the trip, I'd been worried about how the daily stress and the constant togetherness would impact our relationship. Clearly, the answer to that was *not well*. The more time that went on, the more tired we both became and the more we forgot those little kindnesses: like holding hands (which we couldn't do in public in most of these conservative places anyhow) or buying each other treats or calling each other by pet names (it had been a while since Nick had called me Pukka or Fragile Gayle, and I'd stopped referring to him as Sweetie). Moreover, our yin-yang relationship balance had begun to disintegrate under the pressure of so many empty hours, and this only enhanced the less pleasant aspects of our personalities. All at once, with the kind of clarity wrought by a fist to the gut, I understood that I had been cruel to the person I claim to love the most and as a consequence had made him deeply unhappy.

"God, Nick. I'm sorry. I had no idea I was affecting you like this."

"You care about your career more than me."

"No I don't. I just obsess about it more."

"I don't want to travel like this anymore. Maybe you're right. We are too different to be together."

That scared me. I'd pondered the same thing, but to hear *Nick* say it. . . . Even if it were true, how could I live without the guy who made me construction paper cutout birthday cards, who calmed me down with his reassuring presence, who was smarter than anyone I knew but never showed off, who was the sexiest, sweetest man, and indeed the only person I had ever been in love with? Suddenly I was ashamed of myself. Travel can bring out the best and worst in a person, and that night in the restaurant I knew that my worst side had been attacking the best thing in my life. I apologized as much as I could. We decided to continue on to Central Asia, but a chill settled between us. We were polite now, not fighting. In Almaty we spent the chunk of our days separate, Nick writing an essay about his sitar-learning experiences in India. At night he didn't spoon me, and we'd stopped having sex. I didn't bring it up. I hoped our unspoken armistice would eventually take us back to peace. It was something of a victory that Nick agreed to come to the mountain.

In the bus up to the mountains, Nick and Ilya started talking about music and continued gabbing all the way up the trail, where we were passed by gangs of sneery kids and a fellow in army fatigues. At the summit, the helipad was, again, empty, but in the surrounding thickets we could see streams of campfire smoke.

We followed the smoke and found ourselves in an encampment full of elves, who except for the swords, daggers, and axes pretty much resembled your typical jeans-and-T-shirt-clad teenagers. They were all busy practicing for today's game, a battle against the Slavinians, the denizens of the mythical land of Gaia. A pair of older women—the elf moms—were breaking down tents and roasting hot dogs. I sauntered over to one young man of about sixteen who had delicate features, piercing blue eyes, and long hair. He was wearing a purple smock and leggings.

"You look like an elf," I told him through Ilya.

"I *am* an elf," he replied, raising his sword before turning on his heel.

"Well," Nick said. "Looks like he told you."

By one o'clock the elves had decamped to the battlefield. A crowd had gathered to watch the proceedings, and we took a seat on the sidelines and chatted with a few of the players. Many of the kids identified themselves as anything from Wiccan to wizard to Viking—the Elven and Slavinian thing was just a guidepost, I guess—and were dressed in jeans, heavy boots, and varying medieval accessories: smock, chain-link belts, and the like. Everyone, including the girl players, carried some serious weaponry—spears, swords, knives, scythes—except for one forlorn, runty kid with long black hair and an Ozzy T-shirt.

"What are you?" I asked Ozzy.

"I'm a hobbit," he said.

At last. "Oh, you're a hobbit. I'm so glad to meet you," I said, pumping his hand.

Hobbit Boy frowned.

"What's the matter?"

"I don't want to be a hobbit."

"Why not?"

"Hobbit is no good. It's what you have to be when you first start playing the games."

"But Frodo was the most important character in *The Lord of the Rings*. He's the one who has to bring the ring back to Mordor. I would think everyone wants to be the hobbit."

Hobbit Boy just stared at me.

"Have you read *Lord of the Rings*?" I asked.

"No," he said.

"You should. I read it when I was sixteen. It took a month and scared the shit out of me. But then you'll realize how important hobbits are."

"I don't care. No one wants to be the hobbits because the hobbits don't fight with weaponry and if you can't have a sword, what good is it? I want to be an elf."

The Great Battle of the Elves and Slavinians began like a schoolyard game of Red Rover. The two sides lined up on either end of the field, and someone sounded an alert. Then they charged, running full speed, weapons held aloft, hurling themselves into a giant communal slam. The warriors disappeared into a heap and then scattered like leaves back to their sides of the field, wiping the grass and mud from their backsides. Again, charge. And again, *blam!* By the end of three rounds, a half-dozen kids had limped off with injuries, including one valiant Elven girl who had twisted her ankle and the guy in fatigues who had sliced open his finger, leaving a stream of blood on the green grass.

"These are the Tolkienists?" Nick asked, appraising the carnage.

"I guess so," I said.

"It just seems like an excuse to beat each other up."

The warriors took a break to catch their breath and treat their wounds. One of them, an older fellow around my age, wearing chain-link body armor and a rubber orc face mask, introduced himself.

"I am *Voyevoda*," he said.

"What does that mean?"

"It means I am sheriff."

"I don't remember Tolkien writing about any sheriffs."

"It means I am the keeper of rule. I am the oldest one here. I am one of the original members of The Club."

"What club?"

"This. Our group. It started six years ago, to play Tolkien games. I was one of the first ones, and now I'm the only one left."

"What happened to the rest?"

"I don't know. This is my first time on the mountain in two years. I was in Chechnya. Fighting. I was injured when a bomb exploded and I got shrapnel in my back," he said.

"Why were you in Chechnya?" I asked. What I really wanted to know was who he had been fighting for. Kazakhstan had a sizeable population of Russians and of Muslims, so he could have been rebel or Russian army. As it turned out, he was mercenary.

"I fought for the Russian Army, for money," he said. "What do you do here?"

"I'm just a tourist. And a journalist. I'm curious about the games."

"Have you ever played? Do you know how to fight?"

"Hardly."

"More women should battle. Here, you take this," he said, as he pulled off his armor and placed it over my head. I staggered under the weight of it. Then he handed me his sword, which I needed both hands to hold. He borrowed a sword off a Slavinian and tried to teach me the basics, showing me how to flick and fleche and do a nice, neat balestra (a little hop forward before an attack). I did the best I could, thwacking myself in the leg once, causing my shin to bruise and my husband to admonish me to be careful. "Remember, you're a klutz," he said.

At three o'clock the sky clouded over and the air turned chilly. I took a cue from the Slavinians and Elves who were fleeing the pending storm, and herded up Nick and Ilya, who were chattering away about indie rock bands. When Voyevoda saw us getting ready to go, he came over.

"Will I see you at the closed meeting?" he asked.

"What closed meeting?"

"At Calypso. Every week the Tolkienists meet there. The real Tolkienists, the ones who live the fantasy."

"So these *aren't* the real ones?" I asked.

"Not so many. But they will be at the closed meeting. These kids will not."

"Can I come?"

"If you come with me."

"Then I'll be there. With Ilya."

"Do you promise?"

"Yes, of course." I offered my hand to shake on it, but Voyevoda kissed my fingers and swept his arm into a gallant bow. "Until Wednesday," he said.

Calypso, with its turrets and arches and low-ceilinged nooks and crannies, seemed straight out of the Shire. It was the perfect clubhouse for the Tolkienists, except for one thing: There weren't any there. When Ilya and I arrived the place was empty, save for Voyevoda, who was drinking a beer and feeding coins into a video poker machine. He'd cleaned up for the occasion, his dirty blond hair stiff with gel and his mustache trimmed. He greeted me with a wide-eyed look of anticipation and then he started talking to Ilya. My Russian had come far enough for me to recognize the word *muzh*—husband—and my insides lurched in an unpleasant melee of guilt and mixed signals.

"I think he came here for you," Ilya said, confirming my fears.

"I introduced him to Nick on the helipad. Does he not understand I'm married?" I wondered if my troubled relationship was *that* obvious.

"I think he knows you are married," Ilya said, "but he still came for you."

"Great, so is this an ambush for a date or something?"

Ilya shrugged. Voyevoda was staring with his hangdog expression. I sighed, sat down in a booth, and motioned for the Sheriff to join me. He was eager to talk, and after a few minutes I was happy to listen. He knew a lot about the brief history of the local Tolkienist scene, which began in 1995, after Voyevoda and a group of other Kazak students met a Russian Tolkienist who told them about the thriving fantasy movement back in Russia.

The Russian Tolkienist movement had been burbling since the Soviet era. Though the full *Lord of the Rings* trilogy was not officially released in Russian translation until 1991, anonymously translated copies had been disseminated via *samizdat*, or underground press, since the 1960s. In 1976 the Soviet government released an officially translated version of *The Hobbit* (whose greed-is-bad message fit nicely into the Communist ideology). The book was groundbreaking: There had been no tradition of literary fantasy writing in pre- or post-Soviet Russia, and the richness of Tolkien's imaginary landscape captivated thousands of readers.

The Hobbit was followed, in 1982, by an official translation of *The Fellowship of the Ring*. Rabid fans, many of them students, formed underground book clubs to discuss Middle-Earth mythology and to eagerly predict the plots of the trilogy's next two installments. The Tolkienist movement had begun. Alas, it would be a while before it could come out of the closet. In 1983, Ronald Reagan began ratcheting up his Cold War rhetoric, referring to the Soviet Union as an "evil empire" in one infamous speech. In September of that year, a Soviet fighter plane downed a Korean Airlines civilian jet, killing 269 people and bringing the Cold War to a boiling point. Reagan called the incident "an act of barbarism, born of a society which wantonly disregards individual rights and . . . seeks constantly to expand and dominate other nations."

That such rhetoric echoed Tolkien's depiction of Mordor and of Sauron's quest to dominate Middle-Earth was not lost on the Soviet apparatchiks, explained Nikolai Perumov, one of the pioneering Russian Tolkienists, who went on to write his own series of popular fantasy books about Middle-Earth. "After that, the publication of *Lord of the Rings* was abolished," Nikolai told me. The Soviet press ran a series of articles demonizing Tolkien for leading readers into fantasyland and away from the all-important class struggle. Frantic fans were forced back underground for several years.

By 1989 *perestroika* was in the air, bootlegged *Rings* copies were in the markets, and the Tolkienists came out of their holes for the first ever large-scale Hobbit Games. Hundreds of Soviet students, artists, and dissidents gathered in Siberia. There they dressed up as Gandalf and Frodo and Aragorn and spent a few idyllic days acting out the great battles of the *Rings*. In 1991, of course, the Soviet Union collapsed, and within a year the official translation of all three *Lord of the Rings* installments was released. Tolkienist role-playing festivals cropped up throughout the former USSR, pulling in hundreds of players in the larger cities of Moscow and St. Petersburg. For the first time in their lives, many of these would-be wizards could now experience the goofy joy of doing something as innocent as dressing up in a cape and pointy hat while parading around a public field. Of course, there *was* something deeper going on behind the games. While for Westerners the tearing down of the Iron Curtain was seen as a grand victory for democracy and a cause for celebration, for young Soviets (or former Soviets), even for those who had hated the Communist regime, its collapse bred a more complex set of feelings: relief and hope, to be sure, but also sadness and shame at the disintegration of their state—and anxiety about a now murky future.

By the mid-1990s the Tolkienist scene in Kazakhstan began to flourish. Small informal gatherings gave way to weekly meetings in houses, bars, and the mountains. As the group expanded, so did the material: Arthurian legend, Celtic myth, Viking stories, and Nikolai Perumov's tales all became fodder. Players began taking the ever more elaborate games to the streets, spending weekends dressed up in fairemaiden and elf garb, battling each other with homemade swords.

This may seem harmless enough, but the Kazak police didn't think so. They began confiscating swords, beating the kids (calling them dangerous weapon-wielding thieves), and zealously targeting not just the Tolkienists but anyone out of the norm (punk rockers and metal kids also caught a lot of heat). So the Tolkienists headed to the hills, but the cops didn't give up. They began staking out the trailhead at Butakovka, hassling kids as they went up and even arresting them as they climbed back down.

Such intimidation tactics, however, were hardly novel in Kazakhstan, and police brutality couldn't extinguish the Tolkienist flame. The weekly games continued, albeit with more discretion—no more public jousts—and the daily games thrived via computer chat rooms and informal role-playing groups. Every summer, Tolkienists from all over Kazakhstan continued to stage elaborate role-playing extravaganzas in the mountains between Almaty and Kyrgyzstan. The planning took months; there were plots to write, sets to build, weapons to forge, and costumes to sew.

For many Tolkienists, these two-week festivals—the latest of which I had just missed—were the stuff of magic. In the bar, Voyevoda told me about one particular game in 1997 when he was playing a Golem whose duty it was to protect a mistress magician. Halfway through the games, a handful of players veered from the preordained plot and "attacked" the magic woman. Voyevoda improvised a ragtag army and (figuratively) beat back the renegades. For those few days the game had transcended its earthly boundaries and alchemized into something otherworldly.

"That was the best game," Voyevoda told me. "I thought of it many times when I was fighting in Chechnya, and many more times when I was in the hospital recovering from my injury, and again more after my wife left me and took away my daughters."

As Voyevoda had been talking, the bar had filled up with Tolkienists. A few were circulating papers, outlining potential plots for future games. One ponytailed guy was sitting with a girl in a corner reading from Tolkien's *The Silmarillion*. Two young men were even practicing Elvish. Voyevoda stood up to get a beer, and I introduced myself, via Ilya, to Vjard, an Elvis-looking elf in a black leather vest and spurred cowboy boots.

"Tolkien, Tolkien, Tolkien. Tolkien is not a god for us," Vjard declared. He spoke fluent English, as did many club members, the majority of whom were college students. This left Ilya free to slink to the bar, which he promptly did. "We love so many fantasy writers," Vjard continued, and then contradicted himself by bragging about playing the heroic elf lord Glorfindel in a recent tournament. He even recited some Elvish.

"If you speak Elvish, you must like Tolkien a little bit," I said.

"I am not saying we don't like Tolkien. It is just that he is one of many. Even the name 'Tolkienist' is wrong. We are role-playing game players."

"Why do you play the games?"

"They are fun action. And I like to learn. I have studied the Middle-Earth bible, *The Silmarillion*. Have you read that?" I admitted I hadn't but that I had heard rumors that Kazak Tolkienists comb the text for evidence that the mountains, meadows, and steppes of Central Asia constitute the real Middle-Earth.

I continued to ask the other Tolkienists why they played the games. The guys mostly said they dug the action, the swordplay, the running around in the hills, whereas the girls were drawn to the psychological element. Anja, a pretty eighteen-year-old student, called it therapy, a place where "I can play a part, have different roles, have interaction with people that I don't get in my daily life." Her friend Jana, twenty-one, also a student, likened it to research and had even come up with her thesis topic on Scandinavian folklore during the games. Both women had played everything from shamans to magicians to Druids, and both had been warriors. Anja's face lit up as she told me about learning to fence. "That's another special part of this club," she said. "Both Russian and Kazak culture are very traditional. Girls are supposed to be pretty, demure. But in the club you can be anything you want: warrior, witch, queen."

"Not king," Jana interrupted.

"This is true, maybe not king. At first boys did not want us to play warriors. It was equally hard for them to fight stereotypes as it was to fight women. But they got used to it."

"Girls are good warriors. We are very good archers," Jana said.

"Also good with short swords and big knives," Anja added. "Jula is handy with a knife. You should meet her," she said, squeezing out of the booth. She returned with a beer and a melancholy young woman with a red bob and full, pouty lips. Anja introduced her as the group's most senior female member; she'd been a Tolkienist since she was fifteen. Jula was on her way out of the bar but said she would meet me later in the week.

"And of course you both will come to the festival?" Jana asked.

"What festival?"

"Next Saturday on the equinox. We will have a Celtic festival and feast, and the next day a big market in the Butakovka Hills. We will camp there. It will be beautiful. You must come," she said. "You have not yet met Vika. She makes all the costumes and is very important to the club. You cannot know the Tolkienists until you have met her."

"Will there be any actual games? I'd love to play." I was dismayed that I'd missed the summer tournament by a matter of weeks, even though a steady August rain had washed out this year's games.

"Not this time," Jana said. "This is just a festival, with a tournament and a market. We have one more big game before winter. We are writing the script now, but it won't happen until October."

I did some mental math. The festival was to be on the 21st. Nick and I were due to be in Uzbekistan on the 23rd in time to catch a flight back to India and then onward to Africa. If we took an overnight train back to Uzbekistan on the 22nd, we would make our flight and I would make the festival, if only by the skin of my teeth.

"I'll be there. Will you go, Jula?"

"I don't know. I don't play much anymore. Come meet me next week and I will decide."

After Jula left, I got up to take a taxi home. A group of Tolkienists followed me outside to ensure that I caught a ride with a reputable driver. "Otherwise they will cheat you," Jana warned. (In Almaty, every car is a potential cab; when in need of a ride you simply raise a hand and someone usually stops. When you get out, you offer some change.) The group settled on a bona fide taxi driver, an older man in a Lada sedan with curtains. He and I spent the fifteen-minute trip attempting to chatter in Russian and sign language, and when he let me out in front of my hotel, not only did he not overcharge me, but he refused any fare whatsoever.

I met Jula later that week on a damp, cool day with wisps of fog clinging to the pine trees. We walked together to the helipad in the Butakovka Hills and had a picnic of Russian bread and inky cabbage salad. As she and I ate, we watched a small group of youngsters play Elephant, the name of the charging game. Jula sighed at the spectacle. It had been years since she'd been to a meeting, although that was partly because she had been in St. Petersburg studying and then in Moscow working as a sound engineer. It seemed almost painful for her to be back.

"It is so difficult to explain why the games mean so much to me," she said, fingering the sunburst amulet around her neck. "Even when I don't play, the games are never far from my head. Maybe it has to do with reincarnation. Sometimes I think maybe I was one of these things in a past life."

"If you feel so strongly, why don't you come anymore?"

"It's like a fan club now. I don't like to be in a crowd. When I come, I'm just wanting someone to talk to. I want to do something strong, like a Druid ritual. That makes me feel alive. These fight tournaments with the men, it gets so chaotic. In Moscow the society is very strong; people believe in something. I want to live like that, to be part of a community."

"I can understand that. Back home in New York I'm always trying to create a sense of community. It's hard when everyone works all the time and lives such disjointed lives."

"Yes, you feel very disconnected."

"I think it's universal, that people all over yearn for that sense of connection."

"Here, everyone only wants to make money. There's no spirituality. There's no sense of history. In Soviet times, all of us—European or Asian—were Kazak. We came here to build something new. But that's gone," she said, throwing up her arms in resignation. "And I think that is why so many people like these games. By playing, we recapture part of our history and connect with other Europeans."

As I listened to Jula, a lightbulb switched on. While Kazakhstan's population was a mix of Kazak peoples, who are of Asian descent and look Mongolian, and of Russians, who are of European background, almost all of the warriors I'd met were Russian. I began to fathom why.

I had been asking the Tolkienists *why* they played these games, but I had neglected to ask why they played *these* games. Why were they attracted to *these* stories? What was the allure of Tolkien's tales, Celtic myth, Norse folklore, and Arthurian legend?

The answer to that question has as much to do with changing geopolitics as the thrill of swordplay. The country of Kazakhstan, indeed all of the 'stans, never really existed in any kind of organic way. After the

Russian Revolution, Stalin carved up the broad area of Turkistan into the Central Asian Republics, intentionally gerrymandering borders to contain pockets of different nationalities and thus discourage ethnic nationalism. Because it borders Russia and had such a large Russian population, Kazakhstan was always considered the most European and Russian of the 'stans. When it became an independent state in 1991, Kazakhstan's population was 40 percent Russian and 39 percent Kazak. Those numbers soon seesawed as millions of ethnic Russians and Ukrainians repatriated to their newly independent home countries. By 2003, ethnic Kazaks accounted for more than 53 percent of the population, while the Russian majority had dwindled to 30 percent and falling. With this demographic shift also came a cultural one: Previously ignored Kazak culture began to emerge as the national identity.

Though in Almaty, Russians and Kazaks seemed to mix seamlessly, many Russian Kazaks I met found all these changes unsettling. They wondered how an increasingly Asian nation might treat its Russian minority. Moreover, their egos were bruised: Russian culture had always been the golden rule, and now it was being consigned to the low end of the totem pole. These insecurities, combined with the perception of greater economic opportunity in the West, had spurred the Russian flight.

The Tolkienists weren't ready to desert their homeland anytime soon. Most proudly proclaimed themselves Kazak, regardless of their heritage. But many felt a strong need to reconnect with the European roots from which they, and their parents and grandparents, had been intentionally estranged. Asian Kazaks, on the other hand, have their own heritage to explore, one that taps into the nomadic tradition of the Turkic peoples, not the mystical ways of witches and warlocks. But for the Russian players, the stories of C. S. Lewis, Perumov, Celtic folklore, Tolkien—these were their keys to the shrinking world.

This need to reconnect wasn't so different from Tolkien's motivation in inventing his Middle-Earth legends in the first place. For his world of hobbits and dwarves and wizards he drew on a wide array of European folklore and history, from Roman tales to Norse mythology, and, arguably, the two World Wars he lived through. (Though Tolkien insisted the *Rings* was not allegorical, Sauron's quest for Middle-Earth is often compared to Hitler's dark march across Europe.) Like the young people he inspired in Kazakhstan some sixty years after the publication of his first book, Tolkien had looked to the past to find solace in a present he found daunting.

The morning of the equinox dawned sunny and warm. I packed up my suitcase so I'd be ready to leave the following day and planted a goodbye kiss on Nick. He wasn't coming camping. The ice between us was melting—the be-nice-and-give-space strategy was proving to be a success—but even on our best of days there was no way Nick would've accompanied me on this kind of adventure. I met Ilya at the bus stop and we made our way to the hills. By now I was used to the strenuous vertical climb; even the extra weight of tents, sleeping bag, and food didn't throw me. By four o'clock we were at the helipad, which was empty save for a pyramid of wood for tonight's bonfire. Down a small slope, several Tolkienists had already set up camp under a patch of trees.

Ilya and I got started on the ancient canvas tent that I'd rented from a local mountaineering company. (Nick and I, being the most casual of backpackers, carried neither sleeping bags nor tents.) Like many Almaty residents, Ilya was an avid outdoorsman, but this tent proved too much for even him. He stood over it, looking at the various parts and scratching his head.

"Hmm, this does not look like a tent."

"Of course it's a tent. You just snap these together," I said, pulling out the rods.

"I don't think so. Also, it doesn't have any spikes to hold it down."

"I'll make some," Jula offered from behind me. After much coaxing she had decided to come, but now that she was here she isolated herself from the group. While the rest of the women were busy putting on makeup, Jula pulled her dagger out of its holster and set about finding lumber to carve.

Ilya's struggle over the construction of our temporary home soon attracted an audience. Roma, a red-bearded fellow wearing a gray cloak over a black smock, circled the tent like an engineer appraising a bridge and began consulting with Ilya. Mikhail, a long-haired brunette guy wearing a plaid kilt, joined in, and soon Vjard, more Elvis than ever in medieval black leather, also jumped into the action. By the time Voyevoda showed up in his fur vest and chain link, six warriors and Jula were occupied with my tent. Twenty minutes later, when they finally triumphed, Roma announced, "OK, now it's time to get ready. You better change into costume. You have one, right?"

"Oh, sure."

A few minutes later, as we collected firewood, I confessed to Jula—who had an adorable hippie-Christ look going, with a fringed suede vest and a wreath of flowers in her hair—that I really didn't have a costume.

"Make something up," she said, thwacking off a thick branch with her knife.

I checked out the gathering of fifty or so Tolkienists for fashion inspiration. The women tended toward figure-flattering Edwardian dresses, while the men opted for a wider range of getups, from Celtic smocks to knight wear to peasant blouses. It all looked vaguely Ye Olde Renaissance Faire, and I figured I was safe as long as I looked *somewhat* dressed up. I wrapped my wool pashmina shawl into a sarong around my drawstring pants and set about making a daisy chain for my hair, which ended up looking like a ratty string of weeds. It would have to do. The tournament was starting.

As I made my way to the helipad, I spotted Jana and Anja, both looking pretty in homemade dresses and amulets.

"I don't have much of a costume," I said.

"Yes you do," Anja replied.

"You think this is OK?" I asked, pointing to my getup.

"No. We told Vika about you, and she made you a dress. She'll be here later. She's at her sister's wedding."

"She's coming to the festival on her sister's wedding day?"

"Nothing keeps Vika away."

"And she made me a costume? No one except my mother has ever sewed me anything."

"Vika does this for all of us, and while you're here you're one of us."

The tournament began at six o'clock. Mikhail, playing emcee for the evening, introduced various warriors who each took a turn demonstrating their fighting techniques with their weapons of choice. Then the competitions began: Pairs of fighters jousted, fenced, and showed off their blade mastery. Victors were determined by the gusto of audience applause. Unlike the weekend mosh players I'd seen—all brawn, no brain—Mikhail, Vjard, Roma, and Voyevoda had obviously studied the art of warfare. At times the proceedings were almost balletic; at others, they were comical, like when one warrior's cell phone rang midway through a battle, or when Voyevoda's wooden sword broke clean through during his fight. About forty-five minutes into the tournament, Vika arrived, bringing the games to a chaotic pause.

"Vika! Vika!" came the chant as the crowd jumped up to embrace the moonfaced eighteen-year-old. She was wearing a luscious gown with red and mauve panels and a tight bodice. I wondered if she'd worn it to her sister's wedding. I stayed back with Ilya, but Vika soon sought me out.

"So you are Gayle, our guest?" she asked.

"I'm so glad to meet you. I've heard all about you."

"That's nice. I made you something. It's not special. Next time, if you let me know you are coming, I will have more time." She pulled out a long brown cotton dress and a white braided belt, which I put on over my sad ensemble.

The tournament resumed. Each winner from the original matchup was paired with another fighter until, at the end, Vjard was the last man standing. Then we had the girly element: first an archery exhibition, and then a Lord of the Dance–type jig performed by two girls in black minidresses. It made me cringe to watch, but everyone else loved it. "Isn't it wonderful?" Vika gushed. "They choreographed it themselves." After the jig, Roma and Voyevoda lit the bonfire and the girls pulled the crowd into a circle. Arms twined, we danced around the flames, twirling into the dusk as the moon rose behind the mountain.

By nine o'clock, the sun had set and the air had taken on a pale blue chill. The dancers started to trickle down the hillside path to another smaller clearing where a feast had been set up. A circle of votive candles illuminated the bounty: whole roasted chickens, crusts of dense, dark Russian bread, boiled potatoes, braids of fat red grapes, and piles of fragrant tomatoes. My stomach gurgled at the sight.

"Is this food for everyone?" I asked Jana.

"Everybody who paid," she said.

"Can I give some money for me and Ilya?"

"We bought just the amount that people ordered. Don't you have food?"

I did. A loaf of bread and some salami. I kicked myself for not visiting the Zelyony Bazaar before coming up the mountain. The market was like fetish porn for foodies: rows of cured meats; piles of fresh peaches, pears, grapes, and melons; stacks of cheeses glistening in their gourds; mountains of breads, dark and moist or white and crusty; and, to top it off, stall after stall selling cheap Osetra caviar.

The Tolkienists tore into their dinners. I, meanwhile, chewed on a heel of dry bread and tested the salami, which turned out to be a nasty-tasting wurst. When people finished their meals, I snuck around, casually grabbing pieces of leftover chicken. Roma peered at me through the darkness and laughed at my scavenging-dog ways. "Eat. You are hungry," he said, proffering a chicken leg. After I'd foraged myself full, I found Vika and sat down beside her.

"Thanks again for the dress. It was so nice of you."

"Of course. It makes me happy. Did you have enough to eat?" she asked.

"I'm so full I could burst."

"Yes. Me as well," Vika said. She stood up and brushed her hands on her skirt. "Do you want to walk?"

We strolled back through the clearing to the empty helipad and lay down on the dewy grass. The moon was full and bright, the white of it reflecting off the snowy peaks. The bonfire was crackling, giving the air a delicious smoky smell. Vika took a deep breath and let out a long, slow exhale. "It is so special here," she said.

"It certainly is a very welcoming place. Like the way they greeted you today. That warmed my heart."

Vika smiled. "When you love someone, and they love you too, it is something that supports you, that gives you a second breath. It's amazing for me to have close friends. Before I had no one, just my family." She stared hard at me, as if to gauge my reaction. "I wasn't always so firm like this, you know," she said.

I could tell. Though she obviously loved, and was loved by, her friends, Vika radiated an ineffable sadness, much like the melancholy I'd felt in Jula and Voyevoda. As Vika told me her story, I could picture her as a schoolgirl, sitting quietly and alone and yearning for something more.

"So what happened?"

"Everything changed when I found my friends, my world, my mountain."

"How?"

"It started five years ago. I used to just sit home and sew or read. At first I read Charlotte Brontë and Jane Austen. And then I found Tolkien. As I read, I began to imagine his world, those people. I knew it was my world, that I could live there. I started to hear about the clubs in Russia, big clubs with thousands of people, not like ours here. I wanted to know these people. They weren't like everybody. They were something strange. I wanted to understand them. I wanted to be like them. My brother told me that he knew a man who knew about a club here in Almaty. I was so excited. I asked him to introduce me to this man, but he said no."

Then one Sunday while hiking in Butakovka, Vika happened across a group of Tolkienists playing Elephant. She found out about the club, its weekly meetings, and the fantasy games in the mountains. She went home that night elated, something in her already changing. She immediately wanted to do something for these people, but what could she do? She could sew. She asked her mother, who was a professional seamstress, for help, and soon Vika began showing up at the weekly meetings bearing maiden's finery and whimsical suits befitting an elf. She threw herself into the group, and they embraced her back. For the first time in her life she belonged.

"Can you imagine many, many colors, all the colors you like?" she asked me. "That is my world in the club."

I *could* imagine. After all, I was a Weird Girl, too, the kind of kid who didn't crawl but scooted on her ass, who didn't want to be a princess but hoped to become the sun. My family was strange: I had a New Age mom who meditated and lectured my suburban carpool mates on the joys of self-love; a father who thought that travel was more important than material possessions; a rock-nerd brother who turned me on to bands like X and the B-52s; and a fashionista sister who encouraged me to dress in vintage sweaters and skirts made from pillowcases.

My household was anti-TV, anti-McDonald's, anti-Jordache. My parents were the type who pulled us out of school to go to peace marches, dragged us on weekend hiking trips, and took the whole family on six-week backpacking jaunts through Europe. It was loads of fun, but we were not exactly your typical suburban clan.

Until I was seven I figured I was as normal as anyone. The other female students at my tiny Jewish elementary school—standard-issue princesses with names like Amy and Jenny and Susie—wasted no time in letting me know that I was anything but. Starting in the third grade, I was teased about my name (it had the word *gay* in it), my family (we lacked a microwave oven), my clothing (for example, the vintage silver lamé slippers I pinched from my grandma's closet), the way I talked (apparently with too much animation), the music I listened to (New Wave and punk—*the horror*), and the music I didn't listen to (Kenny Loggins—*please*).

What these Jenny Girls had sensed with that killer instinct known only to preteen females was not just that I *did* things differently, but that I somehow *was* different. They smelled it, and buying their jeans or copying their hairstyles did nothing to close the chasm between us, or prevent their cruelty. The Jenny Girls picked on me daily, and after a while I just figured this was life.

Then, the summer before junior high, my mother enrolled me in the Teenage Drama Workshop, a performing arts camp in Los Angeles's San Fernando Valley. I still remember the way the place smelled: mimeographed paper, freshly ironed clothing, stale cigarette smoke, and mold. When I walked in that first day, the hallway was packed. A blond boy with long hair and a leather jacket was reciting a monologue; a spiky-haired girl in army fatigues was singing scales; another girl wearing a John Lennon T-shirt was strumming a guitar and humming with friends. Everyone was gabbing or vocalizing or doing pliés. I felt like I'd entered a weird, alternate reality, a place where I might actually exist.

That summer, in the company of these strange and accepting drama freaks, I changed. The pendulum, for years tilted toward inhibition, swung the other way—too far initially. I became a spazzy blabbermouth. But I had friends. I belonged. I was happy. When drama camp ended, I wept, certain that the community and the sense of self I'd found there were never to be repeated. Luckily, I was wrong. From that summer on I always found a place among the freaks and geeks and punks and artists, until I passed into adulthood and such distinctions no longer mattered—and what *did* matter was kindness, intelligence, honesty, and generosity. I surrounded myself with people who had those qualities. Maybe it's not such a coincidence that many of them turned out to be weirdos, too.

As I told all this to Vika, to my horror, I began to cry. I have no idea why. I'm not a scab-picker by nature, and I certainly don't feel damaged by my childhood. If anything, I'm grateful. Were it not for my weird family and for challenges like the Jenny Girls, I might have become an insurance adjuster. "God, I don't know what's wrong with me," I said, wiping my tears and snot with the belt of my robe.

But Vika understood that my tears were not of sorrow. She reached out and touched my shoulder. "There's nothing wrong. You are just happy because you met people who see the world differently."

The night grew late. The Tolkienists grew drunk on vodka and the local Tian Shan beer. I found Jula and we walked through the dark woods before returning to the tent. Ilya, now stoned on some fine Central Asian weed, was sitting by a campfire, singing folk songs in his deep baritone. I offered Jula his spot in the tent and we drifted off, the moonlight reflecting through the trees, Ilya's voice floating over the forest.

The market the next day got off to a late start while the warriors and maidens slept off the long night of debauchery. By noon a few managed to stagger to the helipad to offer their wares: hand-carved axes and clubs, realistic-looking plastic daggers and swords, amulets and bracelets. Voyevoda laid out his metal armor.

"You're not selling that, are you?" I asked.

"If someone wants it. I can make another one. But people prefer to buy from the back of a magazine," he said.

"That's too bad. Homemade is better."

"I can make you one," he offered.

"That would be great, but I'm leaving tonight."

Voyevoda's face clouded over. "You want to take this one?"

"I couldn't. It's yours. And it's too heavy for me. I'm not much of a warrior," I said, laughing.

"You could be."

We browsed the market a while longer, and soon it was time to pack up and go. The market and tournament were to continue all day, but Jula and Voyevoda insisted on walking down with Ilya and me. I hugged Vika, Roma, Anja, and Jana and received a hearty handshake from Vjard. Jula, Voyevoda, Ilya, and I loped down the hill. The air was thick with pine needles and the mulchy aroma of rotting leaves—the scent of fall. I stopped, letting the trio disappear into a curve in the trail, and took a deep breath, trying to record the air's fresh tang, the forest's spongy fecundity, the mountains' hidden magic. Then I exhaled and scurried down the mountain to where the real world was, again, waiting.

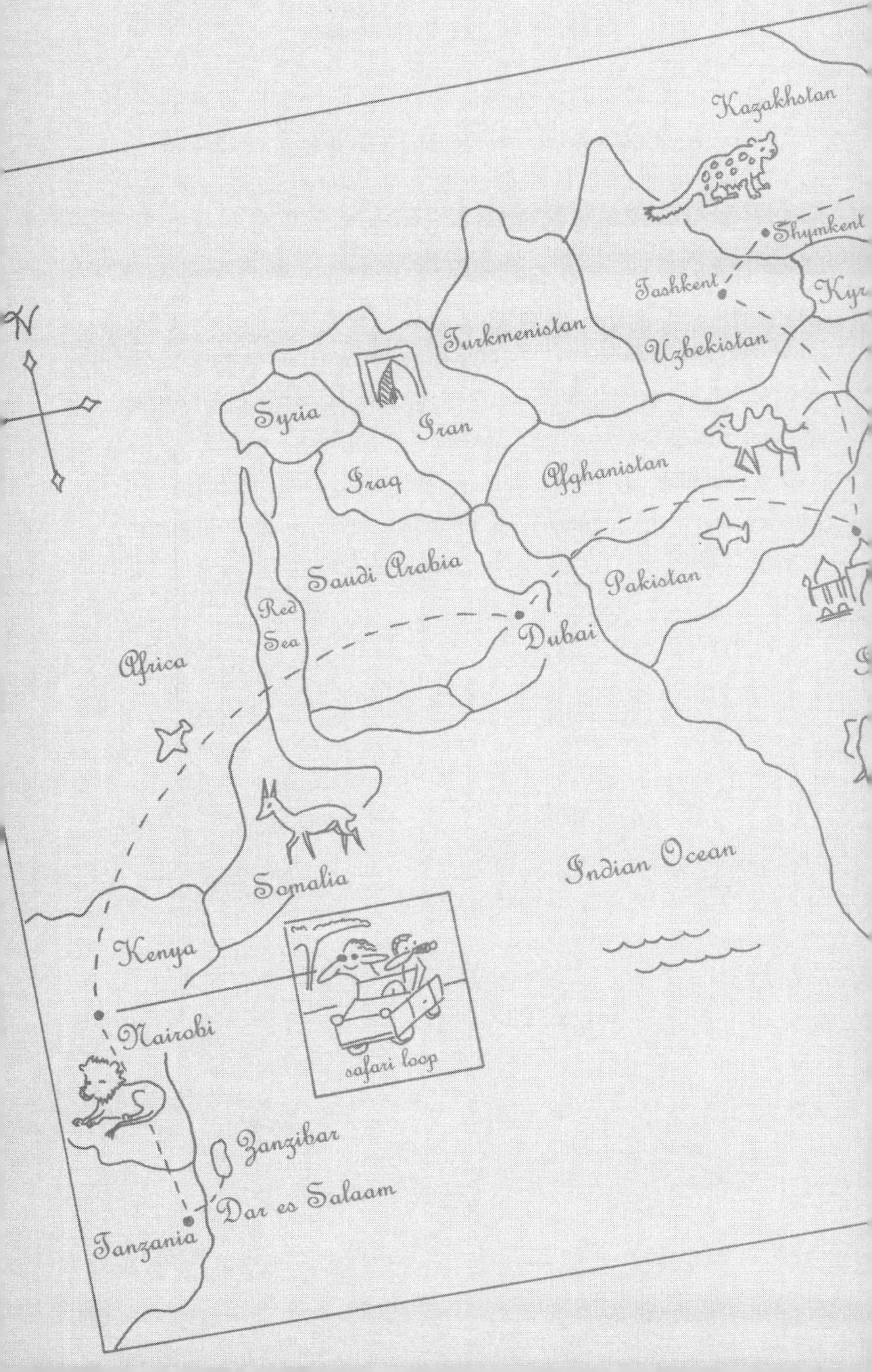

Kazakhstan
Shymkent
Tashkent
Kyr
Turkmenistan
Uzbekistan
Syria
Iran
Iraq
Afghanistan
Saudi Arabia
Pakistan
Red Sea
Dubai
Africa
Somalia
Indian Ocean
Kenya
Nairobi
safari loop
Zanzibar
Dar es Salaam
Tanzania

Kazakhstan to Tanzania—
October

The trip from Almaty to Zanzibar was about as smooth as can be expected, considering. . . .

Nick and I left Almaty on an overnight train for Shymkent at around six o'clock in the evening, arriving early the next morning. From there we caught a minibus to the Uzbek border. Unlike our entry into Kazakhstan—when border guards questioned us for an hour and tried to solicit a "gift," until I finally forfeited half a pack of soggy Marlboros—leaving was a breeze. We walked straight through the frontier, waving and calling out "Do svidaniya!" to the guards. We negotiated a taxi to what had become our Uzbek base camp, the wonderful Sambuh Hotel, where we stayed for the day.

That night we caught a 1 A.M. flight back to Delhi. When our plane pulled up to the gate at four o'clock and I caught sight of the turbaned Sikh airport personnel, it felt as though I had come home. Well, home for six hours. We rented an air-conditioned room in an airport dorm. It was chilled to typical Indian-AC frigidness, but at least the gang of resident mosquitoes was refrigerated into slow motion. Nick and I went on a bug massacre, decorating the wall with splattered parasites, and then drifted off for a few hours' sleep.

At 10 a.m. we caught our flight from Delhi to Dubai, where we spent our one-day layover gaping at skyscrapers and shopping malls in this Arabic Las Vegas. We watched mustached sheiks walk by in white kandouras, and chatted with migrant workers and tourists from all over the Middle East: fellow hotel guests from Iran, taxi drivers from Iraq, janitors from Palestine. We were relieved that no one seemed to hold it against us that our country was preparing to launch a war against Iraq.

The next morning, after replacing my crusty mascara and stolen cell phone at the excellent duty-free shops in the Dubai airport, we hopped another plane to yet another reality: Kenya. Cruising in from the airport, the driver pointed out the zebras at a local game reserve and showed us Nairobi's decaying colonial landmarks. Now our heads were truly spinning. We had been in five different countries in three days. Disoriented much?

We had two weeks to catch our bearings in Kenya but didn't really manage to, what with zipping from one end of the country to the other on a safari. Our guide was a genius named Isaac who instructed us in, among other things, how to distinguish between a Thompson's and Grant's gazelle, how to survive a Kikuyu circumcision rite without crying, and how to fix a broken axle while in the midst of the bush, using nothing more than logs, rope, and cherry-flavored fruit punch.

The safari left us back in Nairobi, and two days later we boarded a packed bus to Tanzania. The coach careened along the single-lane roads at dizzying speeds, blurring past Mount Kilimanjaro—the snows of which are mostly melted, thanks to global warming—and following a trail of humidity to the coastal city of Dar es Salaam. There we bedded down in a bug-infested hotel and the next morning dragged our bags to the pier where we attempted to purchase boat passage to Zanzibar. This proved trickier than expected. Tanzania's currency is the shilling, which we had, but Zanzibar, which only became a part of Tanzania in 1964, likes to be different. U.S. dollars are the main currency on the island—but in cash, no traveler's checks. Nick and I spent the morning haggling with the boat companies, finally having to change our traveler's checks into schillings and then back to greenbacks, losing about 15 percent of the value in the process.

At one o'clock our ferry edged out into the warm waters of the Indian Ocean, running along the shoreline before cutting eastward. We pulled into the dock at Stone Town, the harbor full of ancient dhow sailboats silhouetted in the afternoon sun. After going through laborious Zanzibari customs—a strange formality considering the island is part of Tanzania—we got lost in the winding alleys of Stone Town before finally arriving at the Garden Lodge. A clerk showed us to a room with a tall carved wooden bed and a window facing a quiet garden.

"Will you be staying long?" he asked.

Nick and I looked at each other. We weren't going anywhere for a while. The clerk left, and we plopped down onto the bed, falling asleep to the drones of a muezzin from a nearby mosque announcing the call to evening prayer.

Raparound

A couple of facts about East African rap: One, it was born on the sleepy island of Zanzibar, off the coast of Tanzania; and two, the artist credited with spawning it is none other than . . . Vanilla Ice. Legend has it that in the early 1990s a Zanzibari DJ started playing around with "Ice Ice Baby," Vanilla's only real hit. At the time, local musicians often rapped over American songs in English. But as DJ Saleh Jabir sampled Ice—who himself had sampled the song "Under Pressure" from David Bowie and Queen (whose lead singer, Freddie Mercury, was born in Zanzibar, bringing things even more strangely full circle)—he used Swahili lyrics. And so, Bongo-flavor hip-hop was born.

Not that I knew any of this as Nick and I made our post-dinner stroll through the winding alleys and bazaars of Stone Town, Zanzibar's main city. We walked to the waterfront and passed the Arab Fort, a seventeenth-century walled citadel. As usual, a huge crowd loitered out front. The Fort had concerts almost nightly, but they were usually attended by sunburned European tourists wearing HAKUNA

MATATA T-shirts. This night, however, it was the youth of Zanzibar crowding the entrance. Naturally I dragged Nick over to find out what was going on.

"*Jambo*," said a man in line next to us. He was tall with long, skinny legs, wearing the traditional Masai red-and-purple-checked blanket and sporting decorative stretched earlobes. He carried a staff for herding cows.

"*Sopa*," I replied in Masai.

"*Epa*," he replied. Then, in English, "How do you speak Masai?"

"I don't," I said. "Just that. What's going on here?"

"Music," he said. He bent his elbows and shimmied a bit.

"What kind of music?"

"Bongo-flavor. East Coast hip-hop."

East Coast? Did he mean New York rap versus LA rap? Or East Coast of Zanzibar, though we were on its West Coast? Or East Coast of Africa, where Tanzania lies?

"You mean it's hip-hop musicians tonight?"

"Yah." He grinned. "King Crazy GK. Tanzania hip-hop. Best in the world. *Karibu*," he said, and hopped off into the crowd.

We'd already been to a couple of shows at the Fort—to see a Senegalese band, and some local ensemble that had sounded like new jazz—and both times the amphitheater had been half-filled at best. Tonight the stone seats were packed with Zanzibaris, many of them adolescent boys in various states of Nike-swooshed dress, and girls whose stylie platform shoes peeked out from the hems of their long black veils. There was also a good showing of parental types: men in casual clothes, full-figured women in robes, their brows shining with sweat.

Everyone was ignoring the current act, which was supposed to be Tarob, the traditional music of Zanzibar, but really was one petrified teenage boy singing shaky tunes over a distorted synthesizer. The Kenyan dancers who took the stage next didn't fare much better. While the men gyrated, holding carved shields in front of them, and the women thrust their saronged hips, the audience caught up on gossip. When the dancers finished, a tall fellow with a white skinny tie and a quasi-pompadour stepped onto the stage, headed to a turntable, and started scratching. At once, the audience shut up. An emcee bounded out, waving his mike in the air and shouting "Hey, Mr. DJ!" over and over until a handsome, smiling boy waltzed onto the stage, and the audience surged forward.

This was the legendary King Crazy GK, one of Tanzania's most famous hip-hop stars. Dressed in his baggy jeans, emergency-orange tank top, and heavy work boots, he looked like a standard-issue rap artist to me, but his countenance seemed somehow . . . polite—more Jason Priestley than Jay-Z. He was soon joined on stage by one of the local up-and-comers, Mwanafalsafa, who with his surly pout, hip-sliding jeans, and braided hair looked like a petite, sweet Snoop Dogg. The two jumped around rapping in Swahili to a backbeat of Afro-influenced electronica. There was lots of grunting, crotch grabbing, armpit pulling, and tons of energy. The young men moshed in a little pit at the front of the stage, and every so often a brave soul would jump up and take a few moments at the mike. Meanwhile, older men, many holding children on their laps, bounced and boogied, some silently mouthing GK's lyrics while their wives swayed and smiled. My Masai friend with the cattle staff pogoed up and down like a jumping bean, and when he caught my eye, I jumped up and down with him.

It all seemed incongruous. Zanzibar is a fairly conservative place. Known as the Spice Island because it was once the world's largest producer of cloves (it was also once the world's largest colony of slaves, thanks to its central location between Africa and Arabia), Zanzibar was ruled by Omani Arabs for more than two hundred years. Today, the predominantly Muslim island—99 percent of the population is Islamic— feels as Arab as it does African. Along Stone Town's twisting, narrow streets, ornate doors hide courtyard homes more reminiscent of Marrakech than of Nairobi. The men wear decorative *kikoi* blouses and embroidered *kofia* hats, and most women cover their colorful *kanga* dresses with long black chadorlike robes called *bui buis*. Mosques dot the town, and daily calls to prayer echo through the streets.

The coastal regions of East Africa have long been melting pots of African and Arab cultures; in fact, the Swahili language is a fusion of Bantu and Arabic. Still, while there's nothing about Swahili or Arab culture that necessarily prevents a love of pop tunes, hip-hop is defined by defiance of tradition. Why, in this most traditional of places, was it not only accepted but loved? And the kind of rap music that brings parents and teens *together*?

It's always hard to pinpoint the exact birth of an art form, but with hip-hop, the general consensus is that it debuted in 1979, when the Sugar Hill Gang took the Chic disco tune "Good Times" and pasted over it these lyrics: "I said a hip hop the hippie the hippie to the hip hip hop, a you don't stop the rock it to the bang bang boogie say up jumped the boogie to the rhythm of the boogie the beat . . . " But though rap was born in the United States, it, like most Americans, isn't really from there. Its roots trail back through the public parks of the South Bronx—where visionaries like DJ Kool Herc began scratching, sampling, and mixing break beats—down into the Mississippi Delta blues bars and Southern Baptist choirs, past the Caribbean reggae joints, back to its origins in African villages, where the rhythms and beats that informed rap and so many of its musical predecessors originated. Today, hip-hop is coming home as artists from Angola to Zimbabwe redefine the music and, in doing so, make it their own.

I was curious to know more, so I talked to the guy who organized the Fort's concerts, and he put me in touch with DJ Saleh, a radio disc jockey, TV commentator, show promoter, and general bigwig about town. Saleh invited me out to his family's house for a tutorial, so one sunny afternoon, while Nick explored Stone Town's bookstalls, I hopped a *dala dala* pickup-truck taxi to the town of Mtoni. Saleh, tall and wiry, wearing baggy Sean John clothes and chunky silver jewelry, was an enthusiastic teacher. As he translated songs into English and lectured me on the complexities of Bongo-flavor, he punctuated his explanations with the frequent, throaty drawl, "I think you get my point."

From his tiny room filled with tapes, CDs, and two-year-old copies of *Vibe*, Saleh lectured me on the provenance of Bongo-flavor, including Vanilla Ice's role in it.

"Vanilla Ice—*really?*" I asked.

"Yes, really," Saleh responded, apparently unaware of the irony. (I still didn't quite believe it, but every rapper I asked confirmed it.)

Saleh told me how DJ Saleh Jabir quickly moved on and began transposing Swahili lyrics over other early hip-hop acts—Naughty By Nature, N.W.A., Run-D.M.C.—and soon artists on the mainland were layering Swahili lyrics and a Tanzanian sensibility on a modern hip-hop sound. Kwaanza Unit, or KU Krew, was an early breakthrough group, and when its star, D-Rob, died young, he became an icon akin to Tupac Shakur. Within a few years an industry of sorts had developed in Tanzania, and a handful of record labels began to record, produce, and distribute local hip-hop acts.

Unlike in the United States, however, where hip-hop lingered in the margins for years before exploding into mainstream youth culture, Bongo-flavor found a broad audience from the get-go. The moms and dads I'd witnessed rocking out at the Fort were no anomaly. When I told DJ Saleh that this surprised me, he said of course it did.

"You have to understand the idea of *mipasho,* which is a conflict-resolution ritual in Tanzanian music. In our culture you don't have an argument face to face. You use music. When you go see a Tarob band, it's a competition. Tarob bands sing about problems, about a man stealing another man's wife, about money tension. If you feel the musicians are representing what you feel, you tip them money on the stage. That tells your enemy that this is what you feel. He fights back by tipping another song that represents his point of view. You argue with your enemy using the music," he said, looking at me. "I think you get my point."

As Tanzanian rap evolved, it didn't follow that exact model, but like Tarob, and early American hip-hop, the musical form proved a good vehicle for social activism and dialogue. Eventually three styles of hip-hop emerged: *critical rap*, which attacks some element of societal wrongs, like government corruption or war; *educational rap*, essentially public service announcements about AIDS, drugs, and the like; and finally, *commercial rap*, the party songs about dancing and girls and boys and, well, partying.

One famous critical song is "N'dio Mzee" by local legend Profesa J. The track mocks a famous politician: "I promise to increase your salary, to hire more police officers and teachers. In fact, I will buy a helicopter for each new police officer." Each false promise is met with a sycophantic chant of "*N'dio Mzee!*" which means "Yes, sir!" The song tapped into Tanzanians' long-simmering frustration with their government. It also had a really catchy tune and was a massive hit.

King Crazy GK, the handsome artist I'd seen at the Fort, was one of the main purveyors of educational rap. One of his latest tunes, the national hit "Sister, Sister," offered this admonition to girls: "If you take water and spill it, it's not in the glass any longer. You just play with your life. Now what you gonna do? You spoil everything." The teenage sister in question had gotten pregnant and brought shame upon her family.

Mwanafalsafa, whom I'd also seen play that night, was making a name for himself as a commercial rapper. His first big hit, being played over Dar es Salaam radio, was the track "Mini Na Mabintini," which means "Me and Girls" and whose lyrics basically repeat, "I'm with the girls, girls, girls . . ."—a fairly blatant rip-off of Jay-Z's hit song "Girls, Girls, Girls."

The word *Bongo* means "brain" in Swahili, and so, girls songs notwithstanding, Bongo-flavor is meant to be intellectually stimulating and socially cathartic. It can also be powerful. Politicians listen to these songs, DJ Saleh explained, to gauge public sentiment. In the late 1990s the rapper Johnny Walker, so named because he raps in a faux drunk slur, released a track called "Walim" that criticized the government for not giving teachers their promised pay raise. The lyrics chastised politicians, "You've risen to the top because you were educated, but now that you have found success you won't support education for others." Johnny Walker even exhorted listeners to complain to the Minister of Education. Listeners did, DJ Saleh told me. And the teachers got their raise.

Of course, not all the music is quite so influential or even tuneful. I went to another show at the Fort featuring three Zanzibari groups I'd met that afternoon at DJ Saleh's weekly TV show. I didn't know what they were rapping about, but these acts were pretty rough, like kids rapping into a hairbrush in front of a mirror. Afterward, I went with Saleh and one of the only female DJs on Zanzibar to the disco at the Bwawani Hotel. As they sipped on brandy and Cokes, we watched tourists in cornrows get down with the locals to Christina Aguilera tunes. Saleh leaned over and somewhat mournfully said, "Bongo-flavor was born here, but it has not grown up here. We have no record labels, no industry to support us. It's all over the water in Dar. You should go there."

So, after joining Nick at the seaside town of Kendwa for a few relatively peaceful days in a bungalow on a beach so perfect it felt clichéd—pink coral sand, translucent turquoise water, swaying palm trees—I packed the Beastette for Dar es Salaam. I'd be going alone.

This was a good thing. Somewhere along the Silk Road I'd stopped blaming Nick for dragging me on this trip, stopped obsessing about what I was missing at home, and started to enjoy myself. I was happiest, I realized, when I was connecting with people in the places we visited. Nick didn't need these same connections, but fortunately he let me go with an open heart. He understood that we're different, even if I didn't sometimes. (Besides, he was quite content to spend days on the beach and nights at the bar knocking back Safari beers with the twenty-something backpacking soul-searchers, while that kind of thing left me antsy and alienated.) He has never balked when I went abroad for a month to work on a story, even when this meant missing our first wedding anniversary. On the other hand, he rarely asked me about my trips, which irks me. I suppose it's just the flip side of his laissez-faire attitude. Buy one, get one free.

A few days later I was in Dar es Salaam, driving around with some of Tanzania's hottest rappers in a souped-up Land Cruiser with leopard-print interior and a kicking sound system. You know you're in a different world when you can get this kind of access from a few phone calls. DJ Saleh had surprised me by riding back to the mainland on the same ferry as I did. As we pitched along the waves while grown men pitched their stomachs into the sea, Saleh worked the phone. "Ahh, hey, Crazy GK. Hey man. This is DJ Saleh from Zaaaanzibaaaar," he said. He called GK, Mwanafalsafa, and Bongo Records headquarters, and within two hours of my arrival in Dar I was driving with GK, his cohort Musa, and Profesa J to Mwanafalsafa's home. From there we traveled to a squat cement house in another part of town, where in the back room a bunch of guys huddled around a new iMac, editing the video for "Hii Leo," a track on GK's latest record that featured Mwanafalsafa. "Hii Leo" is a party song, and the video reflected that, alternating between quick cuts of the duo dancing—at a restaurant, at a gym, in the backseat of a convertible sports car—surrounded by a coterie of cute girls. The video had cost $500, expensive by local standards.

King Crazy GK, twenty-six, and Mwanafalsafa, twenty-two, seemed an unlikely team, a rapper's version of Felix and Oscar. Though Mwanafalsafa's name means "the philosopher"—"because in my first song I asked, 'What if Jesus came back?' and my producer started calling me that," he explained—he's more Tom Sawyer than Socrates. "Music is a pleasure fest. It's about good times, girls and all that," he said with a wicked grin at the cavernous Club Bilicanas in downtown Dar. He'd invited me to watch him shoot his video for "Mini Na Mabitini." When I arrived, there were more than twenty girls ranging in age from thirteen to twenty-five dressed in miniskirts and crop tops and crammed into banquettes applying makeup. After checking me out for a while, a handful of fifteen-year-olds approached. "Auntie, are you going to be in the video?" one asked. "Auntie" in these parts is an honorific denoting age, which I thought answered the question.

Mwanafalsafa arrived carrying an adorable little girl in a yellow halter top and a head full of braids. It was his friend's daughter and she was to be the youngest girl in the video. I asked him if that wasn't a little weird for a song about loving girls.

"Oh no," he said. "This is not a sex song. It's a girl-power song." He surveyed the room and turned to me. "You don't think the ladies here are wearing too much cosmetics, do you?"

The video itself was much like "Hii Leo," with Mwanafalsafa dancing around with a boogie harem. Between takes, he checked up on me and tried to get me to dance in the video, a request I deflected with standard rock-journalist questions like, Who are your influences? "Nas is the greatest of all time," he said, referring to the NYC rapper. "But Eminem, now he's a revolution. He's white but he makes hip-hop. Sometimes my brother says he is really black on the inside." He stopped. "Oh, I'm sorry. I don't mean to be rude," he added with a devilish grin.

Raparound

I only wished that the chisel-faced GK, on whom I was nursing a bit of an innocent rock-star crush, were more playful. He was a quiet man with a princely bearing who made it clear that he wasn't into any of that rap-star funny business: no girls, no groupies, no drugs, no drinks. GK invited me to his house to meet his mother, who served Cokes while his brothers and sisters and cousins giggled from behind the sofa. I tried to engage him about the music, his influences, his past. He told me his father had been a government minister who had gone to jail for two years for corruption before being exonerated and reinstated to his post.

During those two years GK's privileged life was turned upside down as his family struggled to stay afloat. He believed it was his father's honesty, his tendency to be a whistle-blower on other politicians' corrupt behavior, that sent him to prison, and GK's bitterness about that system lingered. "My father is a saved man," he said. "He would never do things like this, and they almost destroyed my family with lies." I asked why he didn't rap about this—the corrupt "they"—and he shrugged. "If I do the educational rap, the adults buy my records but the young people come to the shows and they like party songs, so I have to do some commercial rap, too. There's not time for everything." Then he turned and asked me if I'd been saved and had accepted Jesus as my lord and savior. I told him I had not, and asked if it was tough reconciling his faith with the partying music world. "It is. And my family does not really like it with me out late at the shows, with the girls and the drink. But they know I am strong and maybe I can have an influence over the others." This reminded me of what Saleh had told me about GK, that he was the "moral voice" of the hip-hop scene.

It turned out that GK would have to use that willpower in a few days, when he headed out of town for the weekend to a hip-hop extravaganza in Morogoro. More than a dozen big-name acts, including Profesa J and J. Mo, were scheduled to play the event, which was both an AIDS benefit and a record-release show for another well-known rapper, Afande Sele, who was from Morogoro. I finagled myself an invitation.

Morogoro is a peaceful town cradled in a valley between the lush green Uluguru Mountains. It took about four hours to drive the 120 miles along the sometimes paved, sometimes not, highway. While bouncing on the bus I met a dreadlocked Dutchwoman named Saane and invited her to join me at the show. When we arrived in town we made our way to the hotel where GK was staying. It was a restful place, with cool stucco rooms, a sprawling garden, and, of all things, a Chinese restaurant.

After checking in and saying hello to GK, Saane and I went to grab some chow mein. As we ate, the place filled up with rappers, mostly guys in their late teens or early twenties, giddy with that first-day-of-summer-camp high. A trio of these boys—Black Rhyno, Addo Boy, and Sajo—introduced themselves and promptly decided I needed a rap name, so Black Rhyno christened me Sister G. When the time came to drive to the show, Sajo grabbed my hand. "I take care of you," he said.

"Thanks, Sajo, but I'm waiting for GK," who along with Musa was collecting stragglers. We eventually piled into a decrepit van, and after a few false starts the engine backfired to life and we sputtered over to the stadium. As soon as we arrived, we were flagged down by one of the show's organizers, a white Canadian woman named Leanne who was married to a Tanzanian and lived in Dar. She eyed me and Saane, then looked right through us, asking GK, "Who are the *mzungu*?" Although I'd long since grown accustomed to Africans greeting me as mzungu, or "white person," I hated it when Westerners referred to other Westerners that way.

We situated ourselves in the VIP boxes as the other acts filtered in. Sajo stuck close and declared himself my chaperone, ordering me to stay with him between his sets so he could tell me who was who and translate the Swahili lyrics. The bleachers filled with kids, who started to grow restless. The show couldn't start until Afande Sele arrived, so while we waited, GK, Profesa J, and dozens of other artists were herded down to a holding room.

"Let me tell you about all these niggaz. These are my mother-fucking boys," Sajo said.

"Who are your boys?" I asked.

"All these motherfuckers are my crew. Fuckin' Black Rhyno. Addo Boy. GK. . . ."

"Why do you talk like that?"

"All the gangsta niggaz talk like this."

He prattled on, channeling some out-of-Compton gangsta, even though it didn't mesh with his actual personality, which was more along the lines of an annoying little brother. Finally, a motorcade pulled into the stadium and cruised down the middle of the field to the stage. Afande Sele sat high on the backseat of a convertible, waving like the Grand Marshal at the Macy's Parade. When he reached the stage, he, his DJ, and the emcee jumped out. By now the crowd was ravenous.

Unfortunately, things got off to a rough start. The problem was not the artists, who rotated on stage for a song or two, but rather the stage itself. It had been planted in the middle of the field, at least fifty yards away from the nearest audience member. This, along with a weak PA system, made it feel as though the proceedings were being broadcast through an ancient television set. The audience, not able to hear well, started talking, and the din drowned out the music even more. The rappers were having trouble sustaining any kind of energy, playing, as they were, to people who were a block away. The normally crowd-pleasing Masai rapper, who performed while bouncing around with a staff in his hand, tanked, as did sexy Vivien, the sole female artist I'd encountered in this musical boys' club. Even GK's "Hii Leo" flopped. The crowd grew frustrated and began pushing against the security staff ringing the field. Around 9 P.M., Profesa J went on, and as the first notes of his party song "Piga Makofii"—a tune so catchy it stayed in my head for months—blasted over the PA, several thousand hyper adolescents stormed past security and danced onto the field. At last, the show had begun.

When the bow broke, Sajo came to fetch me. "Come, I take you to the backstage." We wove through the throng of dancing, jumping, laughing, singing young men (the adults and girls stayed in the bleachers) to the "backstage," a square area of grass cordoned off with knee-length stakes and rope. Anyone could hop over this barrier, but the kids kept a reverent distance, only crowding around GK, Profesa J, or Afande Sele once the stars had stepped out of this boundary. Between sets I hung next to GK, with Sajo standing nearby, or went out front to take pictures for Sajo. GK was as relaxed as I'd seen him, smiling and joshing with the other artists, and though we didn't have much to talk about, we stood next to each other bouncing to the beat. After a few hours I went to fetch Saane, who'd taken a break in the bleachers. "I will come with you," Sajo offered, trying to hold my hand.

I pulled away. "No, it's fine. I'll be right back."

I took the long way around, wandering through the crowds, drinking in their energy. Kids smiled and waved and called out "Mzungu!" They seemed excited at the novelty of having a Westerner present. I was probably one of three white people in a crowd of five thousand, and it occurred to me that back in the United States this dynamic would've made me uncomfortable.

As I walked around, I thought back to a night in Memphis ten years earlier. I'd been Greyhounding by myself through the South, pining for my brand new boyfriend Nick, who had stayed in Eugene, Oregon, while I went traveling (thus setting a well-worn precedent). In Memphis I met a Danish girl named Prunella. We did all the touristy things together: Graceland, Sun Records, Beale Street, and were told by a couple of hipsters that if we wanted to experience the *real* Memphis, we had to go to Green's Lounge. If we could hack it, that was. Green's was an authentic blues bar in a run-down, all-black neighborhood, where some of the city's best musicians often let rip. When we gave Willy, our taxi driver, the address of the bar, he asked, "What do a couple of white girls like you want with goin' to a neighborhood like that?" We assured Willy, a balding black man, that we'd be fine. We wanted to hear some music, that's all. He reluctantly drove us, and before we got out he pressed the taxi dispatch number into my palm. "Call if you have a lick of trouble."

Green's Lounge was a dilapidated juke joint, and sure enough we were the only white people in it. Prunella and I smiled shyly and ordered two bottles of forty-ounce malt liquor, which is what the locals were drinking, and sat ourselves in a corner. After a while, the ladies with the fancy bouffants and marcel waves and the men with the silky button-down shirts stopped staring and eventually started to meet our timid glances with a slight nod of the head. We took this as acceptance. We drank. We got drunk. We got up to dance. Now the crowd smiled at us, cute little tourist attractions. We got drunker. We got comfortable. Some of the men wanted to dance with us, and we did, swaying wildly, caught up by the Blues and the booze. I was feeling very love-see-no-color.

Then all of a sudden, something changed. Prunella and I felt it as clear as a splash of cold water. Most of the women and a good number of the men were eyeing us with hard looks, and we felt the steely glint of violence in the air. One kindly lady shepherded us into her booth and demanded that we get ourselves a taxi before some kind of trouble broke out. We gave her Willy's card and she went to the bar to make the call. We sat huddled in the booth under the protection of our patron, both of us now stone sober, scared, and unsure as to why. Willy arrived not fifteen minutes later. He'd been loitering in the neighborhood, waiting to hear from us.

Neither Prunella nor I could sleep that night. We lay in our bunk beds, silent until we realized the other was awake, then tried to piece together what had happened, what line we had crossed. That night was probably the first time I understood in a visceral way the true depth of our race chasm in this country. To this day, every time I think of it I feel unsettled.

But this night in Africa, with this music playing—it was all so different. I didn't feel any gulf, any concealed animosity. Tanzania has its own bitter history, one fraught with racism, colonialism, and slavery, but my Westerness and whiteness did not seem to elicit resentment. Maybe here the past didn't matter so much. I went to grab Saane, and we boogied our way back to the staging area, where we danced and danced and danced.

After midnight, GK told me that he and his crew were hungry and leaving. Saane and I tagged into town with them and we all feasted on *nyama choma*, platters of grilled beef and lamb, mopping up the greasy grilled meat with *ugali* corn porridge. At 2 A.M. Saane and I staggered back to our hotel room and flopped into bed, falling asleep immediately.

At 4:30 I awoke to a pounding on my door. I buried my head under the pillow, but the knocking persisted. Finally I clambered out of bed, put on pants, opened the door, and sighed. It was Sajo.

"Hey, Sajo . . ."

"How come you leave me tonight?"

"Huh? I didn't leave you. . . ."

"After my boys came off stage I searched for you. You were gone."

"Yeah, well, it was getting late."

"Hey, listen Gayle, can I sleep here?"

"Why? You have a room."

"But my niggaz, they locked the door of the room. I knock and knock but nobody let me in."

Why didn't I think of that? "Hang on a minute." I closed the door and looked over at Saane. "It's Sajo. Do you care if he sleeps here?" Saane assented. "OK, Sajo," I said, opening the door.

I got back into the bed while Sajo stripped down to his boxers. I scooted over to leave him some room. He got under the covers, stretched his legs, wiggled around, and then reached out to spoon me. I'm so accustomed to Nick doing this that it took me a second to respond with a quick elbow to the rib cage.

"Ahh, fuck. Why you do that?"

"What do you think you're doing?" I said, trying not to laugh.

"Ah, Gayle. I just want to hold you in the night. I mean you no disrespect."

"Sajo, I'm letting you sleep here because you have nowhere else to go, but if you touch me again, you're out."

"But why? . . ." he whined. "Why don't you want to be with me? I'm in love with you."

Now I couldn't help but crack up. Boys. "Sweetheart, you are nineteen and I am married, that's why."

"I mean no disrespect to your husband, but I just want to be with you. And when we get back to Dar, I can take you to meet my family."

I looked over at Saane, whose body was shaking from laughter under her covers. "Sajo, you can sleep here, but if you touch me again, I'm kicking your ass out."

I awoke the next morning to Sajo's wheezy snores. Saane was already up, prepping for a hike around town. I ambled into the hotel restaurant and ordered some toast and Africafe powdered coffee. (It's a terrible tragedy that in the part of the world where coffee originates, so many restaurants serve *instant*.) Over the next hour the restaurant filled with rappers ordering hair of the dog. Around noon I set off in search of Profesa J and found him in what had become the party room, a large octagonal space with diamond-shaped windows where about a dozen hip-hoppers and their female companions were drinking, smoking, and playing pool. From the red eyes all around it was clear this party had been going on all night. I found a bleary Profesa J, and we went outside to sit on a bench in the shade.

"Did you see the show?"

"I did. You were rockin'. I loved the 'Piga Makofii' song."

"It's a party song. Everyone likes those."

"Yeah, but you're famous because of the political songs."

"True."

Profesa J's first group, the ensemble Hardwire Criminal, rapped in English about more prosaic matters. "Back then, there were no straight-up messages in our songs. We were rapping about love and things," he said. In 1999 he joined the Hardblasters, and in 2000 they released an album that included a track called "Chemshe Bongo," which translates to "Use Your Brain." The song was about a rich kid who had squandered his money and ignored the will of his family. Now his father had died and the money had dried up and the son was lost. The song and its themes struck a chord, especially with elders who appreciated the respect message. "This was the real rap revolution," J said. "Before this, elders didn't listen to rap. It was just for kids. But when elders heard this track, they understood that rap had something to say, and that's when people of all ages started listening." A year later, Profesa released a solo album with the "Yes, Sir!" song. "Even President Mkapa has repeated lyrics from that song," he said. "Even the leaders are listening to my music."

As Profesa talked about his success, it was as though he were describing someone else. Like all the rappers I'd met in Tanzania, he had zero attitude. Perhaps this was because even though he is one of the most successful rappers in the country, Profesa J is no mogul. He's never made money from his recordings. What little cash he does earn comes from live shows. "I'm a superstar here but I'm not rich," he said. "Most Tanzanian rappers don't rap about cash, girls, clubbing. All we can talk about is the complaints of the people, the problems in the economy, because we know them so well."

To make a living, Profesa works full time at the phone company. Crazy GK and Mwanafalsafa, both students, had jobs and lived at home with their parents. Bongo-flavor hip-hop may appeal to the masses, but its performers are almost always middle-class. Those who don't have a base of support from family or good jobs simply cannot afford to be in this business.

Part of the reason for this is that artists must pay their own costs. There is no model for signing a rapper and fronting his expenses to produce a record; consequently, the Cinderella stories that catapult South Central boys into millionaires don't happen here. Back in Zanzibar I met a guy who called himself Charlie. He sold curios at the market at Jamituri Gardens, the waterside park where tourists congregate nightly to munch on fresh seafood and bask in the cool air. When Charlie found out I was interested in rap, he spent hours talking to me about the relative merits of Gangwe Mob and Umoja Crew, Profesa J and 2Proud. He also rapped for me, pouring song after song into my tape recorder, and taught me rap lyrics, including one that translated as "I can't get the police off my back," which I parroted to every musician I met. Charlie obviously had a gift for rap, and it was his fantasy to become a Sean Combs. He also knew that wasn't going to happen. "Joblessness is a huge problem here," he told me. "Back home in

Tanga, I could not find work. My parents cannot afford to keep me if I don't make money. So I come to Zanzibar to try to make some money, and most times I make enough to get by—enough to eat, send some home, and if I'm lucky to take a prostitute out once in a while. But I don't have enough money to find a wife. How can I become a rapper?"

The irony is, even in Tanzania, hip-hop makes money. In Dar es Salaam, street corner music stalls sold cassette tapes by GK, Profesa J, and the lot. Their live shows sell out. So why aren't they rich? For the same reason that some of Africa's most resource-wealthy countries are its poorest: corruption. Somewhere along the cash chain, money is being skimmed away, so that by the time the bag reaches a rapper like GK, it's empty. There are no lawyers or managers to protect these guys. There is little competition among labels to ensure fair treatment of artists. Even when there are royalty agreements, the dearth of copyright laws (or the lack of enforcement of them) means that bootlegging runs rife.

But *someone* is making money off these guys. The night of the Morogoro show, I met the owner of one of the big Dar labels, whom I'll call Master D. Master D arrived with an entourage, including several beautiful women. He stayed at Morogoro's poshest hotel while the bands stayed in more modest digs, flashed cash around, and ordered cocktail after cocktail for his crew. The rappers kowtowed to him, like serfs to a lord, even though *they* were the talent, and even though, in private, a few had complained about his scooping profits. I asked Master D if we could talk, but in direct contrast to all the artists I'd met,

he pulled a diva act, refusing to speak to a lowly journalist. It's not unusual for record producers to be richer than their artists, and maybe D
had other financial sources, but he sure seemed to be infinitely better
off than the acts he produced. DJ Saleh had told me that there were
plenty of producers and show promoters profiting nicely off the hip-
hop biz even as the artists they supported did not. This is why, GK told
me, he planned to leave the music business and become an economist.
Even Saleh Jabir had to abandon the hip-hop scene he helped create and
move to Oman to find work.

Earlier that morning GK had gone out to get some noodle soup for
breakfast. When he hadn't returned by one o'clock, I called him on
his cell.

"I'm at the Morogoro Hotel. We have a situation here. I can't
leave. I'll call soon," he said cryptically.

A group of guys were going over to the Morogoro Hotel and I
tagged along. We took a shortcut through town, wading across a
muddy stream and up a green slope of lawn, past a golf course, and
onto the rolling grounds of the hotel. Inside the Frank Lloyd Wright-
esque lobby a bunch of hip-hoppers were hanging about, including
Master D and his cohorts. Gossip was flying. Apparently the artists had
been promised a fee of about $300 each. This morning, after the money
had been tallied and the promoter reimbursed, there'd been nothing left
over to pay anyone, let alone the AIDS charities the show was supposedly for. In true African tradition, a caucus of about thirty artists, in-

cluding GK, had been elected to meet with Leanne, the Canadian woman who'd co-organized the event. They were all sitting in a ring of folding chairs underneath the shade of a large tree.

I wandered down to the meeting, taking a seat on the fringe of the crowd. A rapper named AY was demanding to know how, with a head count of at least five thousand, there was no money left over. Leanne claimed not to know. She apologized profusely but then reminded them that she hadn't made any money either. This did not sit well. Some of the artists, like GK, had turned down a gig in Arusha that would have paid $500.

As the hours ticked by, the crowd rehashed the same questions, as if enough interrogation would produce the missing cash. GK played the quiet ambassador, calming people who got riled and asking a lot of specific questions. As the deliberations dragged on, he would catch my eye and give me a look as if to say, "Should I believe this woman?" I shrugged. Leanne had annoyed me the night before, and it was tempting to buy into the guys' assertion that the nasty white chick had ripped them off, but I was starting to wonder: Where was the promoter? Where was Afande Sele, the rapper who'd organized this show and who had personally asked all these men to perform?

Leanne said that she and her husband would go inside to try to figure out what to do. As soon as she left, the crowd erupted, everyone chattering over each other, trying to unravel the mystery. A group gathered around me.

"I can't believe this shit," Black Rhyno told me. "If Tanzanian people cheat, they cheat their own. Why do mzungu come here to cheat us? Why don't they go somewhere else, like Ecuador or Afghanistan?"

"I'm surprised," Addo Boy said. "I didn't know mzungu could cheat people and do such bad things."

"Are you kidding?" I said. "Have you heard about slavery?"

I turned to GK. He was sitting alone under the tree, and artists kept walking up to him asking his counsel. He answered in Swahili, in slow, measured terms while his questioners nodded intently. Meanwhile, the afternoon grew hotter and the artists kept nipping inside to buy beers. Many were still drunk from the night before, and those who weren't were getting there all over again. I sat down next to GK.

"What's going on?" I asked.

"We just try to figure out where the money went."

"So who was involved with organizing the show?"

"The backer, Afande Sele, and the woman, Leanne," he said.

"What about the backer and Afande Sele? Has anyone called them?"

"We don't have the number for the promoter in Dar. And no one knows where Afande Sele is."

"He's not here?"

"No. Someone said he left early this morning."

"Isn't he from Morogoro?"

"Yes."

"And his family's here?"

"Yes."

"But he left. Did someone call him on his mobile?"

"It doesn't answer. He has it turned off."

"Don't you think that's a little weird? The guy who organized the show has disappeared."

GK shrugged. Another rapper listening nearby interjected that Tanzanians would not cheat one another, but a short while later Misa, a half-American hip-hop producer who lived in Nairobi, sat down next to me and whispered that this kind of thing happened all the time. "Promoters disappear or pay half or a quarter of what they promise," he said. "They lie about the door take. There's just corruption everywhere."

"So you don't think Leanne stole the money?" I asked Misa.

"Nah. She's holding the empty bag. And Afande's gone. Put it together."

"So you think *he* stole it?"

"Maybe. Or the money came up short and Afande took off to avoid a confrontation."

"These guys don't want to believe that," I said. "They want to peg it on Leanne." After all, who made a more appealing scapegoat, their friend and colleague or a foreign white chick? For her part, Leanne was desperately trying to exonerate herself, and in doing so she had prolonged this meeting for hours. By now the combination of heat and frustration and booze was agitating the normally affable guys. "She'd better do something soon and get these guys out of here before things get out of control," Misa warned.

At four o'clock a red-faced Leanne returned with her husband. Choking back tears, she began by telling the group how proud she was of them. How much she loved her adopted country of Tanzania. What a great job they did. How fantastic the night was. Then she broke the bad news: After all the hotel and transportation expenses had been paid, there was about 300,000 shilling, or about $300, left over. Divvied up between everyone, it amounted to about $10 apiece. "I know this money is not enough, but it's just to help you get home," she said.

"We are not here to be helped. We are here to be paid," sneered one rapper.

"Yeah, bitch! You need to pay us."

"Yeah, mzungu, we know you have the money . . ."

By now I'd been called that dozens of times, but in this situation the tenor of it changed. It no longer meant "white person." It meant something harsher, the equivalent of "nigger." I looked over to catch GK's eye but he was staring straight ahead, refusing to return my gaze. Suddenly I saw that I, too, was a mzungu and everything that implied: colonist, slave trader, exploiter.

"The past is not dead. In fact, it's not even past." William Faulkner said that about the American South more than fifty years ago, but it felt just as true here. It's comforting to think that after a few generations, enough time had passed to expunge the anger over how Europeans and Americans treated Africa and its people. Unfortunately, that isn't any more realistic in Tanzania than it is in the United States. I had bought into my idealistic musings and once again had become tangled in the delusions of my naiveté.

Leanne kept lamely apologizing, as though the depth of her regret would win them over, but no amount of remorse could assuage their anger. Leanne stood up and began to back away toward the hotel to get what little money was left.

"No, mzungu. We want *all* our money," one of the men said and stood up to face her. A crowd surrounded her until all I could see was the white of her ankles and the brown leather of her sandals. One of the men lunged at her. I jumped up in my chair, my heart throbbing in my head. Misa surged toward the crowd. "Stop it!" I screamed. "You guys, stop it. This isn't helping!" I turned to GK, who was standing statue-still. "Don't you think it's suspicious that Afande Sele isn't here?" I yelled. "Do you think if Leanne had stolen the money she would've stayed here all day? Do something!" GK snapped out of whatever trance he'd been in and stepped into the fray. He reached for Leanne, separated her from the mob, and in a forceful voice he calmed people down and announced a plan of action. They would take the money for now and deal with the promoter once they got back to Dar. No one ever did mention Afande Sele, but the following day the story was all over the radio, with the implication being that he *was* at fault, if not for stealing the money then for running away like a coward when the coffers turned up empty.

Leanne went to the hotel to collect the money, and when she returned, GK took charge, coming up with a list of who was to represent each group, figuring out how much of a share each would get, and then calling out names to dispense the cash. Once the money envelope was empty, the crowd drifted back to the hotel and Leanne collapsed into a chair, sobbing. A group of boys walked up to her. They were sorry, one said. They knew she didn't have the money. Another couple of boys nodded. Thank you, Leanne said, crying harder. Thank you.

I glanced at GK, and once again he would look me in the eye.

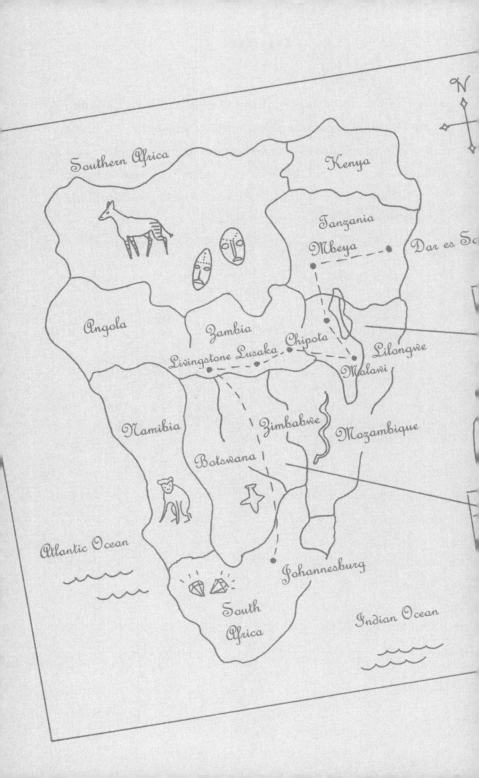

Tanzania to South Africa—
November

If the dining car had served coffee, Nick and I might never have gone to Malawi. But the café on the train didn't even have instant, and the thought of two caffeine-less days traveling from Dar es Salaam to the Zambian city of Kapiri Mposhi seemed interminable. Besides, we actually did want to go to the tiny central African country, and for once we didn't need a visa to do it, so we jumped off the train in Mbeya and caught a minibus or three to Nkhata Bay.

We stayed at a screened-in bungalow perched on a hillside above the translucent waters of Lake Malawi. It was beautiful, relaxing—and a mistake. I had long since learned that I could handle exactly four days of this kind of nothingness before I started to go crazy. And crazy I went. Nick and I spent long days lolling on the beach and tense nights arguing. The hotel was flypaper for lost souls, full of young backpackers who were "searching, man, just trying to figure out what to do in this life." In the meantime they were hooking up with other travelers pondering those same deep thoughts. Everyone drank a lot, got stoned a lot. Nick joined right in. I sat on the sidelines, feeling ever more at odds with my husband. I had the creeping sense that Nick was regressing into adolescence. He drank. He mouthed off to me. And most worrying, he started backpedaling on his promise that we could start a family when we got home. Before we'd left, he thought he would feel ready by the end of the trip, but now he didn't. Of course you don't, I told him. You've become a seventeen-year-old.

Maybe it was my resentment over the baby issue, or maybe just too many months together, but when I saw Nick drunk night after night, I felt disgusted. In all the years and in all the fights, I'd never lost respect for him. Until now. And this started me worrying about how things would be when we got home. What if Nick was like this from now on? Did I still want to be married to him?

He was probably wondering the same thing. The morning after one nighttime skirmish, we lay in hammocks above the water and described each other's next spouse: Nick conjured me a high-powered journalist; I crafted him a low-key party girl massage therapist. We pretended it was in good fun, but we were flirting with fire.

One night, ten months of stupid fights came to a head. After a crazy drunken bar hop, we came back to our bungalow at one o'-clock. The most screwed up of the misfits we befriended had just broken up with his girlfriend and wanted to continue his alcoholic binge by driving into town. Nick, whom I had left at the bar every night that week, wanted to go along. I asked him not to. He was drunk, and therefore belligerent, and he told me to stop acting like

*his mom, that he'd do what he wanted. I told him that he had
spoken like the adolescent he was becoming. He called me a nag.
It escalated until I locked him out of the bungalow, sobbing "I
want a divorce" through the screen window. Behind us, the waves
of Lake Malawi crashed against the rocky shore.*

*The next afternoon, Nick saw me off at the bus station. In the
morning we'd decided to travel apart for the next month, re-
uniting in South Africa in time to meet with my parents who were
coming for a visit. Nick's eyes teared as I got on the minibus, and
I started to cry again. "I can stay if you want me to," I said. Nick
shook his head. We'd tried staying. It wasn't working anymore.*

*On the packed minibus to Lilongwe, I was, for once, grateful
for the bodies jammed into mine, the forced intimacy. I wished
one of the rotund ladies would cradle me in her arms. I spent a
few weepy days in the boring capital hanging around with aid
workers who'd been kicked out of Zimbabwe and sending Nick
long, soul-searching missives about the future of our relationship—missives he wouldn't read for almost a week because he
didn't have access to a computer, let alone an Internet server.
From Lilongwe it was one final packed minibus to the border of
Zambia and then a shared taxi to Chipata, where I spent the
night in a guesthouse, trading tales and gifts with a wild-haired
woman named Yolanda. From there, a real bus took me to
Lusaka, and then another one jostled me onward to Livingstone,
the Zambian side of Victoria Falls. I arrived dusty, exhausted,
heartsick, and scared.*

My plan was to see the Falls and then hightail it down to South Africa to lick my wounds among friends. I booked a flight to Johannesburg for Saturday. Friday night I finally received an e-mail from Nick. It was brief, but it was what I needed to hear. Our marriage wasn't over, he wrote. We were just tired. It wasn't us causing all the fighting; it was the trip, and things would be easier at home. He wrote that he was taking the train down to Livingstone, arriving the following day. Would I still be there? The next morning I listened for the sound of the locomotive, racing out of bed and down to the station at 7 a.m., only to meet a freighter. A few hours later I heard the whistle of the passenger train arriving just before I was to leave for the airport. I ran down the main road, catching Nick walking toward me.

I postponed my flight until Monday. We spent the weekend together, swimming, reading, talking, lazing, being the couple we used to be. It felt like a honeymoon, a renewal, a second chance.

Welcome
to the Family

didn't know that there was such a thing as a white Jew," the teenage girl trilled. She was looking straight at me, a wide smile on her face. She was not being ironic.

"Yes," I replied. "There are white Jews. Lots of them."

"How long have you been Jewish?"

"All my life."

"How long have you known that you were Jewish?"

It was an odd line of questioning, but this whole afternoon had a tinge of the surreal. I had come to the South African township of Soweto to attend the marriage of a couple I'd never met. I was the only American present, the only white person present, and therefore the only white Jew present. But I wasn't the only Jew here. This was a Lemba ceremony, and the Lemba claim to be descended from one of the lost tribes of Israel. Our common heritage is why I had been invited to witness the wedding, a beautiful, meandering affair with the attendees crowded under a red-and-white tent as they listened to elders and relatives offer the newlyweds advice about marriage and family life. Every so often the colorfully robed women would ululate their approval and joy and spontaneously launch into the most amazing *a cappella* harmonies.

Toward the end of the proceedings, Edwin, my sixty-nine-year-old "date," leaned in and whispered, "I think they want some words from you." Minutes later, a man named Sadiki passed back a microphone and introduced me as "the special guest, the white Jew from America."

"Um, thank you so much," I stammered into the mike. I stood up and took a deep breath. "First of all, I want to thank the bride and groom and their families for so graciously allowing me to join you on this special day. I wish you the best of luck and much joy in your future." I looked out at the congregation of men and women, who were looking back at me expectantly. "It's really appropriate that we're all meeting for the first time today, at a wedding, because weddings are about joining families, and family is what we are. You are my brothers and sisters." I stopped here. This sentiment, though technically true, felt a little too We-Are-the-World-y, but the congregation was smiling openly now, so I pushed on. "So, finally, as we say at Jewish weddings in America, 'Mazel Tov!'" I bellowed, stomping my feet. No one had a clue that "Mazel Tov" meant "good luck" or that I was stamping on an imaginary glass per Jewish tradition, but they cheered just the same.

After the ceremony, men and women rushed up to shake my hand, and the groom's uncle ushered Edwin and me to a tidy, pastel-hued house across the street, which, like so many homes in the gentrifying township, beamed with a middle-class pride. Inside, Uncle hustled us to the front of the food line, where jolly ladies heaped rice, vegetables, grilled chicken, and corn porridge onto our plates. "There's no pork in this food," the auntie serving me reassured. Edwin nodded and repeated, "No pork, that's for sure."

When Edwin and I went back outside to eat, I spotted the two teen girls lingering nearby, staring shyly. I waved them over and introduced myself, and they launched into their interrogation about white Jews and life in America. "We are Jewish, too," one of the girls declared, but that seemed to be about as much as she knew of the matter. Like so many Lemba, who have long believed their tribe to be descended from ancient Israelites, these girls had only recently begun to understand what such a heritage—and what being Jewish—might actually mean.

To chart the start of the Jewish Diaspora, you have to go back in time, before the pogroms of Eastern Europe, before the expulsion of the Jews from Spain, before the birth of Christ. It began some twenty-seven hundred years ago, when Assyrians invaded ancient Judea and banished ten of the twelve tribes of Israel. To this day, what really happened to those tribes remains a mystery. But considering that nearly three millennia later, people in places as disparate as Latvia, China, India, and Yemen practice some form of Jewish ritual, it's pretty clear that those ancient

Jewish tribes spread to every corner of the world, even into Africa. In Ethiopia, the Falashas have long been recognized as one offshoot of the Diaspora, but few historians or theologians fathomed that wandering Jewish tribes penetrated sub-Saharan Africa.

Enter the Lemba. According to their own oral traditions, they are descended from those lost tribes, having fled Judea and settled in the ancient, and until recently unknown, Arabian city of Sena. The Lemba flourished there for centuries, but eventually a small band left for Africa. Here, the story goes, they established a second great civilization, called Sena II, where they remained until God cast them out for eating mice, which were considered impure and thus forbidden. The Lemba then scattered throughout Southern Africa, with the majority remaining in a band stretching from Zimbabwe to South Africa.

With no written record or other forms of proof, there was no corroborating the Lemba's story, and to be honest, few people from the outside world, Jewish or otherwise, have been all that keen to bother trying. The Lemba lived in remote rural areas, off the beaten path of other Jews. While over the decades local anthropologists and politicians showed a mild interest in the Lemba—South African president Paul Kruger reputedly referred to them as "Africa's Jews"—the Lemba remained an interesting, obscure tribe—a curiosity, a legend. In 1948, when the white South African National Party established its racist system of apartheid, the only categorization that mattered was skin color, and the Lemba lost any special status they may have enjoyed. Moreover, under apartheid South Africa became even more isolated from the

Western world, minimizing potential contact between the Lemba and other Jews.

But then, South Africa's world—and the Lemba's—began to transform. In the late 1980s, when apartheid was on its last legs, English anthropologist Tudor Parfitt traveled to Johannesburg, where he met a group of African men claiming to be Jewish. Skeptical at first, Parfitt traveled to Soweto to meet more Lemba and was surprised to discover that these Africans practiced many Jewish rituals. The Lemba don't eat swine and certain animals with cloven hooves. They ritually slaughter livestock, and many towns have a specialized Lemba butcher. They bury their dead wrapped in the skin of an animal. They wear skullcaps similar to Jewish yarmulkes. They circumcise their boys, although not at the typical Jewish age of eight days but at eight years and onward. They have Semitic-sounding clan names, like Hamisi and Sadiki, and many bear a distinctly Semitic look. And the Lemba's tribal sign is the six-pointed Star of David—albeit with an elephant in the middle.

Parfitt undertook a yearlong journey throughout Southern Africa and Yemen to see if he couldn't retrace—and confirm—the Lemba's fabled migration. In the end, he did just that, even locating the probable lost city of Sena in southeastern Yemen, an area that once had a sizeable Jewish population. Parfitt published a vivid account of his expedition and a compelling argument supporting the Lemba's claims in the 1992 book *Journey to the Vanished City*. But though his research anecdotally supported the Lemba's oral tradition, it didn't close the case. That the Lemba were of Semitic origins didn't necessarily mean they were Jewish; they could just as easily be descended from Arab traders who plied the coasts of Africa.

Meanwhile, in the 1990s historians were discovering a new way to peek into the past using DNA. Researchers in Israel had validated the existence of the ancient Hebrew priestly tribe known as the Cohanim by analyzing the Y chromosomes of Israeli men who claimed to be Cohen descendants. Membership in the Cohen tribe is passed down from father to son. As it happens, the Y chromosome is also passed from father to son without any interference from a woman's genetic material, so it remains virtually unchanged over time, providing an amazing genetic window into the past. The Israeli study found a high frequency of certain markers on the Cohanim men's Y chromosome. This so-called Cohen Modal Haplotype showed up in about 10 percent of the general Jewish population but in about 50 percent of the men claiming to be Cohanim—strong proof that these men had descended from a single line.

Using that study as a model, in 1997 Parfitt, along with a group of scientists from the Center for Genetic Anthropology in London, set about sampling the DNA of Lemba men to check for the Cohen Haplotype. The results were shocking—to everyone but the Lemba. One in ten Lemba had the Cohen Modal Haplotype. In one of the most prominent Lemba clans, the Buba, almost 50 percent of the men shared the same genetic markers as the Cohanim from Israel. These rates were the same as those found among the general Jewish population in Israel.

The missing link, connecting the Lemba to their Jewish brethren, was at last found.

Though Soweto is home to about five thousand Lemba, the heart of the community lies in the Limpopo (or Northern) Province, strewn around the Afrikaner city of Louis Trichardt, named after a famous Dutch *voortrekker*, or pioneer. Some twenty-six thousand Lemba, including many of the most active elders, call this region home.

"You must go to Vendaland," Edwin insisted, referring to the area in the apartheid-era bantustan terminology (the Venda is the dominant tribe in the province). "There you can meet the Lemba elders."

"Will people welcome me if I just show up?"

"No, no. I must come with you. I will provide introductions."

"You'll come with me all the way to Vendaland? I'd want to go for a week. It won't be too much?" Edwin was a sprightly fellow, eager to please, with a facial expression stuck somewhere between grin and grimace. But he was almost seventy years old, and it showed. He had gotten lost in Soweto for more than an hour trying to find the wedding, he had to catch his breath after the shortest of walks, and he often made a funny wheezing sound while breathing. I worried the trip might be too hard on him.

"I go there all the time. I have family there. I can stay at my son's house. I'm retired and it's no problem."

Edwin didn't have to ask twice. Back home, one of my best

friends was an eighty-eight-year-old Hungarian named Oly. Once a week I would visit her at her retirement home, eat the stale cookies she pushed on me, and listen to her recycled stories. Friends admired my do-gooderness; I left them to their illusions. The truth was, my motivation was selfish. I found Oly's company interesting and relaxing. But Oly had never invited me on a road trip. I told Edwin that I would love to go.

We had only gotten minorly lost finding the motorway on-ramp in Johannesburg, and once safely on the highway and traveling in the right direction, we whizzed through the incongruent cityscapes of South Africa. We drove past downtown Jo'burg's high-rises, now mostly deserted on account of crime, past the ugly mountains of brown earth of the city's gold mines, past the upscale shopping malls and gated housing communities of Sandton, past the crammed shacks of the Alexandra Township, past the isolated, glass-towered corporate parks where many of the businesses that once occupied downtown's skyscrapers have relocated, past the leafy environs of Pretoria, until at last the density of urban sprawl gave way to the open space of the veldt.

I turned up the radio and smiled. The sun was shining high, it was a straight shot to Louis Trichardt, and I was getting used to this driving-on-the-left-side business. I'd forgotten how much I loved cruising on the open highway, the wind-in-your-hair freedom of charting your own chariot, having control over your own radio. I looked at Edwin to share the glee, but he was napping and making an alarming rasping noise that made me worry he was having some kind of pulmonary breakdown. Mentally, I gave myself a CPR refresher course, and I was relieved when five minutes later Edwin made a mewling noise and shook awake.

"Are we at Pietersburg yet?"

"Nowhere near. We just cleared Pretoria."

"OK, man, I keep my eyes open so we can dodge the tolls."

As Edwin and I zoomed north, he asked me questions about America. "Do you have wide open spaces there?" he asked.

"Oh, plenty," I told him. "The middle of the country is full of open space."

"Do you have farms?"

"Lots of them."

"Can you drive from one end to the other in one day?"

"No. It's several thousand kilometers."

"You have black people there?"

"Yes, of course. Especially where I live, in New York. We have people from all over the world. You wouldn't believe it."

"Man," Edwin said, shaking his head and smiling. "It sounds like a good place."

Edwin periodically guided me off the highway to escape the toll booths, and we wound our way through towns with tongue-twisty names like Nylstroom and Naboomspruit. This was the Afrikaner heartland, home turf of the Dutch-descended farmers who colonized South Africa and then fought the Africans and British to rule it, which they did until 1994, when free elections put the African National Congress into power. If Capetown, South Africa's glamorous and urbane city in the south, represented the new South Africa, where whites, blacks, Indians, and everyone in between intermingled, the towns up north were still holding fast to the old South Africa. They were strictly segregated. Whites lived in tidy middle-class neighborhoods. Blacks lived in ever-improving but still shantytown-ships. Whites drove cars. Blacks mostly walked or took buses. I rarely saw them driving together, and when I did it was usually a bunch of black men in the back of a pickup truck and a white man and his dog up front. Perhaps this is why as Edwin and I drove on we started to get some cartoonish double takes.

By around three o'clock both our stomachs were gurgling, so we decided to stop for lunch. We turned into a shopping center, but I accidentally pulled into the exit lane (I guess I wasn't *completely* down with driving on the left). We were almost to the mouth of the parking lot when a car came the right way down the one-way road. The driver, a grizzled farmer, got out of his car and started screaming curses at us— or at Edwin, I should say. When I popped my head out to apologize for the mistake and suggest that it might be easier if he backed up to let us out, he was momentarily silenced; then the look on his face went from anger to shock to fury. The curses and screaming resumed, crescendoing in him calling me a "stupid bitch."

When we finally pulled into a parking place, my hands were shaking and my appetite was gone. Edwin apologized. "You have nothing to be sorry about," I said. "I can't believe people act that way. Let's take our lunches and go eat in the car."

Back on the road, as we munched on take-out mincemeat pies, Edwin started querying me about Judaism. He was curious if I'd always known I was Jewish. He also asked about which holidays I celebrated. He nearly whispered, "Do you celebrate Christmas?"

"Well, I don't, personally. But a lot of Jewish people do. It's become a kind of nonreligious holiday for some."

"But Christmas celebrates the birth of Christ."

"Right."

"And Jews have their own holiday?"

"That's true. In December I celebrate Hanukkah."

"With the candles?"

"That's the one."

He considered that for a while, then piped up: "We don't eat pork. When we slaughter an animal it must be done by a Lemba with a special Lemba knife. When I was growing up, my mother told me not to eat food at any neighbor's house because it was unclean. Did you do that?"

"Keeping kosher, you mean? I don't anymore, but when I was growing up my family didn't eat pork. Or shellfish. And I went to a Jewish school where I wasn't allowed to even bring meat in my lunch."

"But you knew you were Jewish?" Edwin asked again.

"I did."

"I know I am Lemba. I am president of the Lemba Burial Association. My father-in-law was the president of the Lemba Cultural Association. He was the one who went to Dr. Verwoerd"—former South African President Hendrik Verwoerd, one of the architects of apartheid—"and demanded that in the racial classification the Lemba be separated from the Venda. I was one of the Lemba who gave DNA to prove that I was Jewish. But I did not know that I was Jewish, or what Jewish meant, until ten years ago. And there is still so much I don't understand. But I'm trying to learn."

I knew he was. Back in Soweto I'd visited Edwin at his home before going to the wedding. Sitting together on a couch, while a clock depicting the Last Supper ticked overhead, Edwin had pulled a number of books from his shelf, and pieces of paperwork belonging to the Lemba Burial Society, the funereal group under whose guise the Lemba Cultural Association met in secret during apartheid. He'd shown me several basic books on Judaism. He'd displayed his "Jewish suit"—a fringed *tallit* prayer shawl and a yarmulke, a gift from visiting rabbis from America—which he kept in a velvet bag with a Star of David on it. Edwin's youngest son, Talani, eighteen, also showed me his Jewish suit, although he didn't know what it was for and asked if I did. I explained that Jewish men wore the *tallit* and *kippah* during prayer.

One of the books Edwin showed me was a guide advising Jews on how to handle Christian missionaries. For the Lemba, that horse is already out of the barn. During apartheid, missionary schools were among the few places where black Africans in rural areas could get educated. Along with reading, writing, and arithmetic, these schools provided lessons in the Father, Son, and the Holy Ghost. Consequently, many Lemba are Christian, as is about 60 percent of South Africa's black population. For the Lemba, however, this Christian business presents something of a prickly conundrum. If you are Lemba—and by extension, historically Jewish—what does it mean if you are also Christian?

Edwin and I set off to commune with the elders. Our first stop was at a lodge consisting of a series of *rondvales*, or round cabins, still under construction, on a beautiful parcel of land surrounded by rolling green hills in the shadow of the sloping Luonde Mountain. On the other side of the rondvales was a large, new house. We knocked on the double doors and a maid ushered us into an inner sanctum. There, amid gleaming marble and expensive electronics equipment, sat a diminutive sixty-year-old man in a gray safari suit. In his high-backed chair he looked like Mr. Magoo playing the last tycoon.

"I am a real Jew. I was tested both times for DNA," Ephraim announced to me before I'd even sat down. I nodded, but just to be sure I understood, he ordered me to write down his family's genealogy, noting which clan he came from (there are twelve Lemba clans; Ephraim was a Buba, Edwin a Hadzhi). After we'd established his background, he again proclaimed himself to be a real Jew and then launched into an oration to prove his case.

"I believe in what my ancestors did. I believe in hard work. I believe in obeying my father and grandfather. I believe, like my father told me, that 'the legs of the fish are in my children.'"

As further proof of his Jewishness, Ephraim spoke of his climb from humble origins. When he was a boy, he worked on a farm collecting animal bones as he plowed. He sold the bones and used the earnings to buy an amplifier and became a musician. With the cash he earned from playing shows, he bought a car, which he drove as a taxi, and when he had enough money he bought a taxi stand and more cars. When he had a chunk of change squirreled away, he went to a bank in Johannesburg and demanded a loan. "That was when our kind did not get financing," he said. He told the bank officer he was a Lemba, and he told me that this was why he was approved for a several-thousand-dollar loan. "I am the first black man to get such a loan." With that money Ephraim built a house, a guesthouse, and a liquor store. He also bought a farm, which he later sold to a white businessman for a tidy profit. He got another loan. He bought another farm, and now this one, which he hoped to turn into a game lodge for tourists. He was anxious to show off the first-class grounds. "Unfortunately, I have to drive because I recently had a minor stroke," he said.

Edwin and I got up with Ephraim, who clearly had suffered more than a minor stroke. Half of his body was paralyzed, and it took ten minutes to walk the fifty feet out the front door and to his truck. He drove and we walked down to the rondvales, where he showed off the top-notch construction quality while boasting of the success of his son,

Nicholas, who lived in Johannesburg and owned a computer shop, an imported-shoe store, and a beer and Coke distributorship. He also had another son, whom he described as a "shareholder," and a daughter who was a chemical engineer. "You see how well my children do. I am a Jewish man."

"What else makes you a Jewish man?" I asked.

"I am a clean man, a straight-talk man who doesn't believe in killing or stealing. A man who believes in hard work."

"Yeah, yeah," Edwin said, nodding in agreement.

"But I'm surprised because not all Jewish men I meet are like that," he said, going on to tell me a long, involved story about an Israeli who had come to South Africa to teach the Lemba about Judaism but had instead slacked in Ephraim's guesthouse for six months. "He didn't do anything but swim in the pool. He didn't want to leave the property," Ephraim said, disgusted.

"Have you always thought of yourself as Jewish? I mean, a lot of Lemba were brought up Christian, right?"

"I practiced Christianity when I was schooling. But now I build myself a synagogue. Come and see." He limped toward the main building, through the industrial-sized kitchen to a recreation-type room that overlooked the nearby dam and river. "This is my synagogue," he said. I nodded my head and then took a sniff. I swear I smelled bacon coming from the kitchen. Maybe it was something else, or maybe it was for the workers. Or perhaps the Lemba, like so many Jews I know, exclude bacon (and Chinese food) from their dietary restrictions.

The following day, Edwin and I went to the town of Thohoyandou—which means Elephant Head—to visit the distinguished local doctor Gedzu Mathiva. Gedzu was the son of Professor Mathiva, the great spiritual leader of the Lemba and the major force behind keeping their Jewish identity alive. Sadly, Professor Mathiva had died a few months before my arrival, and the whole community was in deep mourning and in a state of confusion, wondering what would happen to the Lemba without the Professor's guidance. Gedzu, more than anyone, seemed poised to step into his father's shoes. After I shook his hand, I told him how sorry I was to hear about his dad, how I regretted not meeting him. Gedzu, who had a bright, handsome face with sparkling, intelligent eyes, straightened his lab coat and sat behind his desk, motioning Edwin and me toward a pair of consulting chairs.

"The Lemba left Judea twenty-five hundred years ago, after the destruction of the second temple," Gedzu began. "We are descended from Yemenite Jews. We are Jewish. It is in the blood. It is because of circumstances. The Jewish Diaspora spread mostly to Europe, and the Jews there have a completely different *Halakha*"—or Jewish law—"but this law is not in the Torah. Not in the Talmud. The Lemba and other Jews don't differ in the rabbinic area." I nodded along, though Gedzu could've been telling me that the Lemba were descended from the Corinthians or the slayer of Goliath for all I knew of the matter. Gedzu continued, offering further proof and touching on the genetic testing. "We were willing to be guinea pigs," he said. "We didn't know of any advantage of being Jewish."

I got the distinct feeling that Gedzu, like Ephraim, was trying to prove something to me. Since their claims were validated by the DNA tests, many Lemba have found themselves having to make their case all over again, and this time to a much wider audience. Following the release of Parfitt's book and the subsequent genetic testing, the Lemba became international media darlings. In 2000, PBS's *Nova*, CBS's *60 Minutes*, and the BBC all ran stories on the amazing lost tribe. Journalists and scholars trekked to South Africa to find out more, publishing their accounts in newspapers, magazines, and on Web sites all over the world.

All of this attention, in turn, prompted a slew of Jews—rabbis, tourists, and curiosity seekers—to make pilgrimages to South Africa to connect with this long-lost tribe and bring it back into the Jewish fold. This should have been the happy ending (or beginning) for the Lemba, but it wasn't. Some visitors had come to meet the Lemba, expecting to find Western-style Jews in a slightly darker package. Instead they had been shocked to find Africans, many with only the barest understanding of mainstream Judaism. Other well-meaning-but-bumbling visitors had been openly horrified to find that so many Lemba were also practicing Christians.

Before I'd met Edwin, I'd spent a few days in Johannesburg, a city so dangerous that most guidebooks give tips for surviving it, not enjoying it. Crime may be rife there, but I happen to like Jo'burg, as it's locally called. The first time I visited, in 2000, I was immediately adopted by a group of crazy artists and spent an incident-free week cabbing around all parts of the city. This time I'd planted myself in the trendy and integrated area of Melville, eaten lots of delicious meals, re-connected with some local journalist friends, and tried to find someone who would introduce me into the Lemba community. That last part had been tricky. There was a lot of reluctance to expose the Lemba to any more outsiders, explained Miriam, a white Orthodox Jewish woman in Johannesburg. Miriam had set up a few camps to bring local Lemba children together with the white Jewish youth, but she'd had to do so through a Reform temple, so loath was the Orthodox community to in-clude the Lemba. "If I did this in my Orthodox synagogue, I'd be kicked out of the congregation," she'd said. For the same reason, she'd also asked me not to use her real name. It wasn't all bad news, however. Plenty of American and Israeli Jews had happily embraced the Lemba. One American organization named *Kulanu*—Hebrew for "All of Us"—had sent volunteers to teach classes, seminars, and had offered other outreach programs. But for every Kulanu there had also been Jewish forces within South Africa, the United States, and Israel that had chal-lenged the Lemba's Jewishness.

One major bone of contention is what makes a Jew Jewish. By Jewish law, descent is traced through the mother (Jewish mom gives birth to Jewish child), but by Lemba custom, ancestry is passed through the father. Intermarriage is permitted only for Lemba men marrying non-Lemba women, thus ensuring the couple's offspring remains Lemba. Some religious figures have suggested that the Lemba are no longer really Jewish because the line has been sullied by so much intermarriage. One Lubavitcher rabbi went on South African national radio, ostensibly inviting Lemba into the faith but then calling for them to undergo formal conversion to do so. For the Lemba, such demands are insulting. They have already lived through the prejudice and the exclusion of apartheid; the last thing they want is to invite that experience all over again from Jews, who, in so many words, were telling them that they weren't welcome in the family.

I wanted to interrupt Gedzu, to say that *I* believed him, that I wasn't here for proof or explanations. Besides, I'm the last person anyone should have to prove anything to. I'm not particularly observant or knowledgeable about Jewish tradition, having forgotten everything I was taught at Jewish day school. I don't attend synagogue regularly, and during my rebellious years I wouldn't even call myself a Jew. Yet for some reason, in my midtwenties, a Jewish identity became deeply important to me. Though I'm not entirely comfortable with many aspects of my own faith, or indeed of organized religion in general, Judaism has certain inherent values that I treasure: the importance of family, the emphasis on education and open debate, the work ethic, the call to be your most moral self. Even though I hadn't been looking for proof or parallels, I'd already noticed that many Lemba shared these values. While some of Ephraim's yarn was certainly fictitious, his rags-to-riches story reminded me of so many Jewish immigrant tales. Under apartheid, blacks' education was severely restricted, access to higher education particularly so, but somehow, so many Lemba I had been meeting had managed to get either for themselves or their children not only high school diplomas but college and professional degrees as well. Professor Mathiva had taught and served as chancellor at the University of the North, one of the few universities open to blacks in the apartheid era, and his son Gedzu and his daughter Rudo had gone to medical school. Rudo was currently the head of the ICU at Soweto's Chris Hani-Baragwanath Hospital, the largest medical center in Africa.

As we talked, Gedzu's cell phone rang often. He answered it with a Hebrew greeting of "Shalom." After one call I asked if any Lemba had thought to make *aliyah*—to emigrate to Israel, which is the birthright of all Jews. He made a face. "We have had discussions and seminars about that. The question is, how does one make aliyah when one doesn't know the reception one might get?" Gedzu said he had no interest in having to convert to Judaism or in proving anything to anyone. Besides, he noted that other African Jews, like the Ethiopian Falashas—thousands of whom were airlifted to Israel in the 1980s in Operation Moses—have had a notoriously difficult time assimilating into Israeli society.

"It will take the South African Jewish community years to accept us, for obvious reasons," Gedzu said. "But Israel is supposed to embrace everyone. We do not want to coerce anyone. We know that this Jewish heritage is ours as much as anybody's. And please don't give me any more Orthodox Jews. They give me ulcers!" He stopped and rolled his eyes. "We would be willing to have a rabbi come visit us, to tell us things. We are grateful for someone to come and say how to do things correctly. But this superiority complex: 'Don't do it this way! Do it this way!' No, we don't want that."

Gedzu was actually touching on what I consider a strange contradiction of my faith. We are a small people, historically a persecuted people whose numbers have been thinned by the most brutal of genocides. With such a legacy one would hope that Jews would embrace other Jews, be they converts or products of mixed-faith families. This is not always the case. There are great battles between Reform, Conservative, and Orthodox scholars over who is Jewish: the children of a converted Jewish mother? How about kids adopted into a Jewish home? There's also a lot of *sturm und drang* around intermarriage. Today, between 40 and 50 percent of American Jews marry outside the faith, and many Chicken Littles decry this as the death knell of Judaism. When I married Nick, a nonpracticing Catholic agnostic, we had a hell of a time finding a Reform rabbi who would do the deed. It was bad enough to be refused over and over, but worse was the animosity with which we were rejected, and the silent accusation that I was helping to speed Judaism's demise. *Please.* Had anyone bothered to ask about Nick's and my life, they would know that we already had a Jewish home (no pork, no Christmas, and a yearly raucous Passover Seder) and planned to raise our future children Jewish. Nick doesn't want me to be Catholic, and he participates in plenty of Jewish ritual, but he has no urge to join my tribe. As I huffed to one nay-saying rabbi, "My not being married in a Jewish ceremony is not going to prevent me from marrying the man I love. But it may alienate me from my faith."

I appreciate that mine is not a proselytizing religion, desperate for converts. Aside from the Jews for Jesus, you won't ever find yourself besieged at home by polite, suit-wearing missionaries wanting to sign you up to the god of Abraham and Moses. But denying me a traditional ceremony or forcing the Lemba to "convert" or casting aspersions on the Jewish legitimacy of a child born of a converted Jewish mother seems ultimately counterproductive. Why exclude someone who has a rightful claim to Jewishness and who wants to practice the faith, based on some anachronistic technicality? So much of Judaism is open and accepting and elastic, and I wished that Gedzu could see that side of it, could meet more rabbis like the wonderful woman who eventually did marry Nick and me.

"Not all Judaism is so exclusive," I told Gedzu. "In New York, where I live, there are all kinds of congregations. There's even a synagogue for gay and lesbian Jews."

"A gay and lesbian synagogue. Ha!" Gedzu whooped and clapped his hands. "I'd like to see that."

"Come visit, and I'll take you there. And to Katz's deli. Everyone should eat at a real Jewish deli at least once." Gedzu smiled and escorted us out to his now-crowded waiting room. He was too polite to say so, but he'd surely been to a Jewish deli before. On the way to the car I glanced at his office nameplate with his degrees listed: an M.D.

from South Africa's University of Natal and a master of public health
from Harvard.

On the way back to Louis Trichardt, Edwin, who'd been mute in the
meeting, chattered about Gedzu and his wisdom and then promptly
fell into a wheezy sleep. While I kept an eye on his breathing, I pondered the idea of acceptance and rejection and all the artificial walls
people erect to separate themselves from "the others." I thought about
South Africa's Jews, and why they had been so cool to their new
brethren. In the United States, only about 10 percent of the Jewish
population is Orthodox; in South Africa, 95 percent of the white Jews
are Orthodox, and on the who's-Jewish questions, Orthodox tend to
be the most exclusive. The majority of South Africa's Jews were also
white, having grown up, lived under, or been influenced by the
apartheid system. Though apartheid was abolished in 1991, the racial
divisions in the country are still blaringly present. Liberal white South
Africans I met, those who had opposed apartheid, still did not seem
all that comfortable with their new multiracial society. Many chan-
neled what felt like latent prejudice into a hysterical fear of crime. Yes,
Johannesburg was dangerous, but people barricaded themselves in
their homes as though they lived in a war zone. How much of that
fear was of guns and how much of it was of living side by side with
blacks? I couldn't tell.

A few times during my stay it felt as though apartheid had not
ended. When we'd arrived in Louis Trichardt two days earlier, before

dropping off Edwin at his son's home nearby, I drove to my bed and breakfast to let them know I had arrived. When I pulled into the driveway, the proprietor cased Edwin and asked me, "Where'd you get *him*?" I explained that we had been traveling together and I was just about to bring him home. The owner insisted upon doing it for me, warning that I shouldn't drive to that part of town. I declined his offer, took Edwin home, met his family, and returned to the guesthouse in time for dinner, which was included in the tariff. I sat down with the owner, his wife, and another guest, a white South African haberdasher named Richard. As we ate rack of lamb and mashed potatoes, talk turned to what I was doing here. I explained about the Lemba. The guesthouse owners were familiar with them and at least feigned interest, but Richard took it upon himself to educate me.

"These are blacks, right?" he asked.

"Yes."

He snorted. "You haven't lived in this country so you don't know this, but blacks will swing any old way if it'll get them a handout. Even swing to the Jewish side."

"They don't seem to want handouts. A lot are quite wealthy, actually. As for faking Jewish, there have been scientific tests to prove their claim."

Richard went on ranting about the wily ways of blacks, telling a story about some friends in Zimbabwe. At one point he referred to a black African man as *kaffir*, a racial slur that was once ubiquitously used here. He turned to me, paused, and apologized. I felt vaguely gratified that at least he seemed to have gotten the idea that I didn't share his views, but then he went on to clarify: "*Kaffir*; it means 'nigger,'" he explained.

Edwin and I spent the next few days visiting various Lemba, and one evening, as I drove him home, he asked if I minded making a stop. He guided me to a cemetery on the south side of town where his son, who had died a year earlier, was buried. I strolled around the cemetery, leaving Edwin alone at the grave. When he seemed finished I walked over and placed some rocks on the gravestone.

"This is a Jewish custom," I explained to Edwin. "I'm not sure why we do this. I've heard it's to show that the buried person has been visited, has not been forgotten."

Edwin walked away and returned, breathing hard. He stooped down beside me and placed his own stones next to mine. "Thank you," he said.

On our last day in the North we set out to the east of Louis Trichardt. A few miles out of town, the paved highway gave way to a rutted, red-clay road that led to a township called Sinthumule. Rain clouds had a clear preference for the west because where the country around Thohoyandou was green and lush, here, not forty miles away, the earth was flat, brown, scrubby, and very hot.

We made our way to the church where the Lemba Cultural Association occasionally met. We had arranged to meet two elder Lemba. (Aside for the sweet teen girls I'd met in Soweto, all of the active Lemba I'd met were either middle-aged or old, and there was some concern that without the leadership of Professor Mathiva, the upcoming generation would lose their link to Judaism.) Edwin introduced me to one William Masala and one Mr. Buba—no first name given. They cut a dapper trio. Mr. Buba wore a sweater vest and hat even in the broiling heat, and the gray-mustached William had on a lavender button-up shirt under a blazer. Edwin, too, had on his usual sport coat; I'd noticed he only removed it in the car. I greeted the elders with a clap of my hands and a call of *Mushavi*, the traditional Lemba salutation, for men at any rate; women must await a *Mushavi* and then reply with a *Msoni*. But my breech of protocol was humored with reserved smiles.

"Did you know you were Jewish all the time?" Mr. Buba asked me, in what had become a common query.

"I did. Did you?"

"I knew from my parents that the Jewish are also our people," William interjected. "But so many did not. That is why Parfitt's book was so important. It showed us how the Jews have scattered, how many of us there are. And it has ensured the Lemba survival."

"I grew up knowing I was Lemba and knowing I was from Israel. Even as a little boy, I did this," Mr. Buba said, clapping the *Mushavi* greeting. "And the girls replied with *Msoni*. But I did not know how the Lemba came here or know what Jewish was until I went to Johannesburg to work for a Jewish family. They gave me food. I wouldn't eat it because I thought it was pork. I threw it in the dustbin, and the man saw it there and said, 'Why do you throw this away?' I tell them the truth. 'I don't eat pork.' They say, 'We don't eat pork. What religion are you?' I say, 'I am Lemba.' This is where I found out I was Jewish. They gave me the book of the Jews, the Torah, and in that I found the verse of the Lemba coming to Sena, in Nehemiah 7:38 and Ezra 2:35. You see, I can recite the psalms."

Again I had the sense that like Gedzu, Mr. Buba and William were trying to prove something. They cited various biblical scriptures and re-iterated the Lemba's migration away from the tribes of Israel, to Sena and to Africa. I'd heard the story a dozen times, but I sat mesmerized by their low, rumbling voices. After a while, they abandoned their history lesson and took up more current matters. "Some white people phoning since yesterday morning, asking us to please come in to see them in my Jewish suit," William told Edwin. Apparently the request had come from a reporter who had asked the Lemba to dress up in their ritual outfits and meet him on a certain street corner. The request was as ludicrous to these men as an appeal that they wander the village in their underwear.

"These clothes are for our people, but when others see us they don't know what we're doing in our honorable clothes," William said. "You don't want them to use the pictures for the wrong purpose."

"You don't want to be like animals in a zoo," Edwin added. Mr. Buba and William nodded. All three were seasoned media pros by now. Both Edwin and William were among the first Lemba that Tudor Parfitt had met; both had offered up their DNA for the study, and both had participated in the BBC documentary (in fact, it was a Jewish BBC producer who had given William his Jewish suit). The attention, which had been flattering at first, had apparently grown tiresome to the Lemba, who, Edwin reminded me, have always been a private people.

"We are a secret society," he said. "During apartheid we had to be secret because we were afraid of the government and also of the Venda chiefs. We did not want them throwing us off our land. And now we are still a secret society."

"This is true. It is only out of respect to Edwin that we receive you," Mr. Buba said.

"And because she is Jewish, and a relative," Edwin added.

"Yes, you are OK because you are Jewish," Mr. Buba told me.

"How do you know I'm really Jewish?" I asked. "I could lie just so you talk to me. Journalists can be sneaky that way." The men just laughed at this.

"We cannot go somewhere and tell our story to people on the street," William said. "They must come to us and tell us what they need from us and then we decide if we will talk. We still must be secret, to look after our nation, to be careful of people who come after us like wolves."

"Who are the wolves?" I asked. The media? The Orthodox? No. William was referring to the same wolves Jews the world over fear, the twin preoccupations of killer Nazis and murderous Islamists.

"When I think about Hitler, I almost have a heart attack. When I see the people in the photos from that time I think of the people who hate the Jewish," William said, his eyes tearing and voice cracking.

Seeing this measured, wise old man grow emotional made me start to get misty. The men looked at me with equal parts concern and confusion, as they might appraise a weeping granddaughter. I wiped my face and got it together.

William, too, composed himself. "When we hear something today done by Arafat to the place of our grand-grand-fathers, we get hurt."

"It's terrible," Mr. Buba added. "A man goes inside a bus wearing a bomb. That man dies, but many Israelis die. Why isn't he afraid to die?"

We talked a bit about the idea of martyrdom, and then I pushed the envelope. "Some people say the Palestinians are driven to desperate tactics because they are so mistreated and oppressed. In fact, the Palestinians have been compared to Africans under apartheid." The men weren't buying any of this. After all, South Africa's liberation struggle had never endorsed killing. "Who is this God who rewards such things?" William exclaimed. "There is only one God, the God of Abraham, and those killers counter the law of God: 'Thou shall not kill!'"

"We are always worried about Israelis," Edwin said. "We black Jews would go fight there. We'd go fight Arafat like we fought apartheid."

As I watched these men rail on and offer themselves up to arms, I wished that those who had doubts of the Lemba's Jewishness could witness this exchange: fretting about Israel, fearing another Holocaust, decrying Arafat, lamenting the never-ending violence in the Middle East.

If there is anything that binds Jews, be they from Bukhara or Brooklyn, it is these particular obsessions.

Edwin and I made a few more stops around the village so I could meet more of my long-lost brothers and sisters, and they me. A couple of families even invited me to stay in their homes. I would have loved to, but it was time to go back to Johannesburg. My parents were due to fly in for a visit, and Nick was already there, languishing in a hotel room with a nasty case of food poisoning. I felt bad for him but was relieved that food poisoning was the worst of it. At the beginning of Edwin's and my road trip I had been in a slow-building panic, having not heard from Nick for more than two weeks. After our romantic interlude in Livingstone, Nick had planned to spend a few days at a camping resort on a remote island in the middle of the Zambezi, about four hundred miles from where I was now, before making his way from Zambia to Namibia and then to South Africa. I'd calculated when he'd be back in civilization's range—where he could find an Internet café to e-mail me or to get my e-mail with my South African cell number. When I hadn't heard from him two days after that date I'd started to worry. As two days turned to three, then four, then five, I started to panic. During the entire trip we had never gone this long without being in touch, and I began to imagine him dead in a car accident, beaten by bandits, delirious with malaria. Although I'm not a religious woman, I prayed to the travel gods to keep Nick safe.

Edwin was praying, too. After I almost crashed the car reaching for my cell phone—what if it was Nick?—I confessed my fears about Nick's silence to Edwin. He reassured me that Nick was fine and had taken to talking about him. He even began answering my phone while I was driving, in case it was Nick. And when it finally *was* him on the other end—instead of Namibia, he'd gone on a horrible safari in the middle of Botswana—Edwin prattled to him as though he were a long-lost son.

The drive back south was mostly uneventful, save for some drama when Edwin guided me onto a motorway on-ramp that turned out to be an off-ramp. Earlier in the trip I had mentioned to Edwin maybe visiting Leo Abrami, a Johannesburg Reform rabbi who had reached out to the Lemba, but now I was anxious to get back to Nick so I figured I'd catch the rabbi later by phone. On the drive home, however, Edwin started talking about the rabbi, about how much he would like to meet this nice man because he had questions to ask. I took the hint, and at a lunch break I called Leo, who said he would be happy to see us. He gave me directions to his house in the posh Johannesburg suburb of Sandton. "You can't miss it," he said of his house. "It's the only one on the block without a security fence."

Going gateless in Jo'burg can be construed as a revolutionary act, and it was easy to see that Leo and his wife Ruth were radicals among the white Jews here. For starters, they were from England and had only come to the synagogue after apartheid ended. "We wouldn't have lived here under that," Ruth said, waving her cigarette. We were sitting in their living room, a bright, cheery space full of bowls of candy and photos of family. Leo explained he had been visiting the Lemba in the

North, giving classes and seminars in beginner's Hebrew or on the various rituals of Shabbat. He had also opened up his congregation here to the Lemba community in Soweto, and at least one young man had become a regular at services. But Leo was very clear that such offerings were given in the spirit of inclusion. "We don't want to impose on them." Leo and Ruth were both disgusted with the heavy-handed way other members of the Jewish community had treated the Lemba. "What a disrespectful way to treat people," he said.

Edwin, who had been sitting quietly, starting moving around and making some throaty noises. He looked as shy as a ten-year-old in a college classroom. "Do you have questions for the rabbi?" I whispered. "He knows a lot more than I do."

Edwin began in a faltering voice. He wanted to know about Shabbat: Was it OK to work? To read? To cook? But mostly, Edwin wanted to know about funerals. What kind of coffin was acceptable? Which way should it face? North toward Jerusalem? What was the appropriate garb for the deceased? How soon must a funeral take place? I wondered if Edwin's interest was because of his role in the burial society, or because, as an old man, such concerns were heavy on his mind. The rabbi spent a good twenty minutes exhausting Edwin's death questions, and when they petered out we got up to leave.

Leo and Ruth walked us to my rental car, now red with the dust of the north. "You know you are welcome for Shabbat services anytime," the rabbi told Edwin.

Edwin beamed at this. "I would love to go to that, man."

"I know Sandton is far from Soweto, so it's difficult, but please let people know they are always welcome."

Edwin puffed up with pleasure and settled into the front seat. The rabbi reached through the open window to shake his hand. "Shalom," he said. "Goodbye."

"Shalom," Edwin replied, tentatively. And then, as we drove away, once again, but louder, he repeated, "Shalom!"

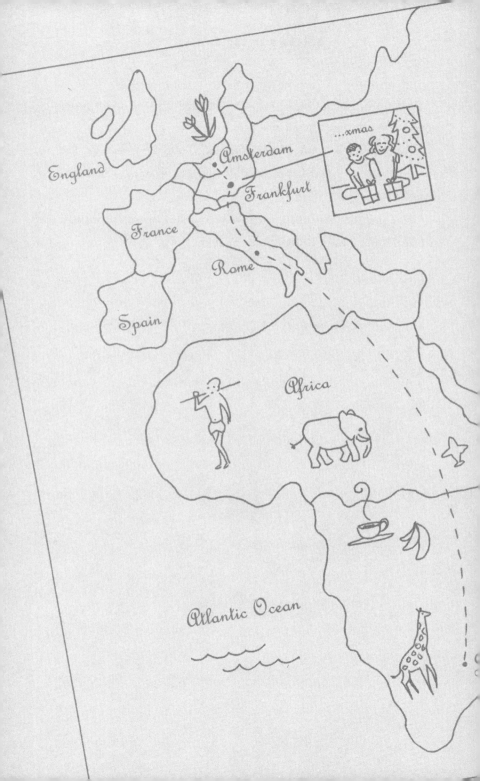

South Africa to the
Netherlands—December

We caught a ten-hour flight from Johannesburg to Rome, and
after two weeks of overindulgent eating and shopping and tourist-
peeking, we caught another flight to Frankfurt, where we spent a
quiet Christmas with Astrid and Martin, the German couple we'd
met in Tonga. Then we took a train to Amsterdam.

There were no delays, no breakdowns, no insane taxi drivers,
no fights. Travel in the First World may be boring, but it certainly
is easy.

Laid Off

For tourists of a certain generation, or predilection, a visit to Amsterdam often kicks off with one of two activities: a trip to a coffee shop to smoke out on one thousand varieties of hash or grass; or a trip to the red-light district to stare at one thousand varieties of G-stringed, nipple-pierced women. I didn't give Nick the choice. After we dropped off our bags at a friend's apartment in the Jordaan neighborhood, near the Anne Frank House, I dragged him through the central Dam Square and into the red-light district, known locally as *de wallen*. We ambled up and down the narrow lanes, weaving around the Christmas crowds taking part in this great Amsterdam version of window-shopping.

"What do you think of her?" I asked, pointing to a skinny Asian woman in black leather.

"She's pretty."

"Not your type, though."

"No, you know me. I like blondes."

We kept moving, past a group of curvaceous mulatto ladies—the Surinam and Colombian contingent—who flashed a tit or two, around the *Oude Kerk*, or Old Church, to the African women with skin so black their red negligees looked neon. We checked out a tired-looking party of heavy-lidded babes with gray eyes. Some of the ladies danced, some talked on their cell phones, some read, but many put on a little show, presenting their merchandise as much to me as to Nick. Which I found thoughtful.

"So, what do you think?"

Nick, who had never been to Amsterdam, wasn't thinking anything. He was gaping. We'd been all over the world, and he'd been hit up by all manner of prostitutes, but nothing compares to this international emporium of sex.

"Yeah," I said to Nick's nonresponse. "I know what you mean."

I had spent my own first night in the city almost fifteen years ago. I was eighteen, and Amsterdam was to be my first class in the University of Life. I had studied abroad in England for my junior year of high school, and during that period I'd become a vegetarian, a socialist, an animal-rightist, and a travel addict. "I'm not going to college," I'd told my parents during senior year, as all of my friends were filling out applications and taking SATs. "There's nothing some institution can teach me that I can't learn by experiencing the world." (I'd also become a self-righteous brat that year.) Lucky for me, my parents have always been the greatest travel-pushers in my life, and they seemed as proud to put me on a one-way plane to Europe as they would have been dropping me off at Yale.

I ended up railing around the continent, first with my English friend Rebecca and then by myself. I'd thought I would end up in Spain, but after a few days in Amsterdam I fell in love: with the winding canals and sloping rowhouses, with a Dutch bartender, and with the essential weirdness of the city. Amsterdam seemed to be an incubator for misfits.

The bartender turned out to be a fling, but my affair with the city endured. It was not, however, love at first sight. Rebecca and I had arrived at Amsterdam's Centraal Station at night, and instead of exiting via the front doors onto the bustling Damrak Avenue, we'd accidentally slipped out the back and onto the shadowy Ijsselmeer, where the junkie hookers worked. Then we'd proceeded to get lost en route to our red-light district hotel, arriving so late that we had to share a room with a Swiss guy shooting up heroin on his bunk bed. We'd dropped our backpacks and scurried outside to look around, getting jostled by crowds in the alleys of neon women and narcotized tourists. University of Life? More like primary school; I felt like a girl in pigtails.

"It's another world, isn't it?" I asked Nick. He just nodded. "Let's go find your blonde girls. Now where are all the Dutch ladies?"

We circled back onto the Oudezijds Voorburgwal canal near the Bulldog Café, which, as I told Nick in running commentary, was where Rebecca and I had gone for our first joints, although we hadn't known how to roll them. Finally, just down the road from Casa Rosso, the famous live sex-show theater, we found a cluster of windows showcasing several beautiful blondes.

"OK, check out that one," I said, pointing to a thin-faced woman with a ponytail and black-rimmed hipster glasses.

"She looks a little too schoolteachery."

"And she doesn't look Dutch, either. Look at her eyes. I bet she's Russian or Polish. Go talk to her."

"What should I say?" Nick asked. He wasn't accustomed to accompanying me on reporting trips, but he was making an exception this time.

"Ask how much."

Nick went to the window and the blonde opened the door. They talked, he returned. "She said sixty-five euros for a 'suck and fuck.'"

"That's pretty reasonable. Did you find out where she's from?"

"I didn't ask."

"What kind of accent did she have?"

Nick shrugged. "Fine," I said. "Let's try another."

We did. Same price, but Nick still had no clue whether the woman was Dutch or not. When we strolled up to a blonde with heavily painted black lids and a white merry widow, I told Nick I'd come with him. "She'll either think we're really kinky or the world's most codependent couple. Either way, there's nothing these women haven't seen." We approached the window.

"*Goeie avond,*" I said when she cracked the glass door.

"*Goeie avond,*" she replied.

"How much for my husband here?" I asked.

"Fifty for a fuck. Sixty-five for a suck and fuck."

"Is it extra if I watch?"

"No. Same price."

"That's a good bargain. Where are you from?" I asked.

"From Holland," she said, a bit nervous now.

Here was the point to make a deal and go inside, but we were only browsing. We thanked her and moved on. She seemed relieved. Maybe she thought I was Immigration, because she obviously wasn't Dutch. I can discern Dutch-accented English from a mile away. I'd lived here, my sister had married a Dutch boy, and for a year after returning home from Amsterdam in 1990 I'd used a Dutch fake ID, adopting a pretty decent phony accent every time I'd go into a bar. Point is, I knew she was faking it, too. Nick and I walked a bit more and got a few more price quotes from a few more blondes. None of them sounded Dutch to me.

We walked in circles until we found ourselves on the Warmoestraat, not only the oldest street in the city but the most famous block in de wallen, the center of the red light since the nineteenth century. The sex trade itself is much older. Amsterdam has been a major merchant-and-sailor center for more than five hundred years, and where there are traveling salesmen, there are girls to entertain them.

I knew the Warmoestraat well, having worked on it. No, not as that but as a maid at the sleazy backpacker hotel where Rebecca and I had first stayed. It had been a decade since I'd been back in the city, and I'd been hearing friends lament that my beloved Amsterdam was changing: becoming homogenized, "Europeanized," and losing its quirky, small-town feel. The Warmoestraat had certainly transformed. What had once been a dingy road crowded with cars, bikes, junkies, and touts handing out flyers for sex shows had morphed into a pretty pink-stoned pedestrian-only street. I guided Nick down my memory lane as we strolled.

"That condomerie just opened when I lived here," I said, pointing to Het Gulden Vlies, now a landmark on the street. "And the police station and the sex shops were here, of course, but all the modern hotels and restaurants are new. And the lack of junkies on the streets, that's new, too."

"Even the red light gentrifies," Nick said.

We walked to the end of the block and there it was. I had no idea if the hotel had the same owners—a former prostitute and a prison convict back in my day—but whoever was in charge had made an effort to keep up with the ever-tonier neighborhood. The painted window sign had been replaced by a proper hanging number, and the peeling facade of the four-story rowhouse had been recoated. But the renovations had only given the place a desperate feel, like an aging party girl gussying herself up.

"This is it," I told Nick. "This is where I worked. Maid. Cook. Waitress. Illegal alien."

"I can't imagine you as a waitress. You're too clumsy. And I definitely can't picture you as maid; you're such a messy girl."

"This is why. This is where I learned to hate cleaning!"

"Do you want to go in?"

I peered through the window. The saloon looked the same: a long wooden bar festooned with currency from all over the world, and around the bar the same sad mix of drunken tourists and locals. The bartender was yet another woman of indeterminate age, with bleached hair and optimistic cleavage.

"I don't think so. It looks depressing."

"What do you want to do now, eat?"

"Actually," I said in my best coy voice, "I had something else in mind."

"Oh, did you now?"

"Uh-huh. No one's at the apartment. And I won't charge you a cent."

"Aren't you nasty," he said, leaning in to give me a wet, sloppy, teenage kiss. Then he grabbed my hand and we hustled back to the flat.

Amsterdam was not my introduction to the world of prostitution. Growing up in Los Angeles, my family spent many Friday nights having Shabbat dinner at my grandparents' apartment in Hollywood. On the drives home my dad would often detour down Sunset Boulevard, which in those days was crawling with painted ladies in spandex and Corkies. I thought they were the most beautiful creatures ever.

It wasn't until I moved to Amsterdam that I met actual prostitutes. In addition to the ex-hookers on staff at the hotel, the bar's clientele included a number of ladies of the street who sometimes dropped in before or after shifts for a coffee or a beer. At first I kept my distance, not because I disapproved of their lifestyle but because I was too shy. I still felt vaguely pigtailed. But over the months, as I learned Dutch, I picked up snippets about the women's lives. I started talking to some of them after I got off work, when it was my turn to drink a coffee or smoke some hash that a departing hotel patron had left as a tip. There was Siska, who was divorced with two kids. Marike, who seemed to be a bit of a drunk. Yolanda, who was from Surinam but was now a Dutch citizen. She was married and had kids.

What struck me about these women was not what they did, but that they seemed to regard it as another working-class job. It's an overstatement to say that the twenty-five thousand prostitutes in the Netherlands—at least two thousand of whom work in Amsterdam—are regarded as career girls, no different than secretaries or nurses. But the sex business is far more normalized here than anywhere else in the world. These women were open about their jobs. They had husbands, boyfriends, girlfriends, and parents who knew what they did. They had health insurance. A union. They also seemed to have a community. They were friends. They looked out for one another. It was nothing like the image of prostitution in the States: a last stop on the road to depravity, peopled by drug-addicted whores and violent pimps.

The lives of Dutch prostitutes are unique, in part because the Dutch are uniquely tolerant. In 2000 the government finally got around to legalizing prostitution outright, a bureaucratic process that had been going on for seventeen years. But legalization was really just a rubber stamp. Like soft-drug use, also officially against the law, prostitution had long been decriminalized. You don't go to jail for smoking hash in Amsterdam, nor do you get handcuffed for selling your body or renting someone else's. Under the new laws, brothels are now legal, quotas on other sex businesses have been eased, and it's no longer against the law to "organize prostitution for someone else"—that is, be a pimp. Moreover, the government now regards sex work as an industry, subject to the same degree of regulation as, say, fishing.

The Dutch soft-on-vice approach—not to mention the progressive stances on euthanasia (legal) and gay marriage (also legal)—has given them a reputation as the most liberal folks in Europe. But really, they're just unfailingly pragmatic: Prostitution will happen, so you might as well control it. Soft drugs will always be abundant and don't do much harm, so you might as well regulate (and tax) them. Street prostitution creeping into other areas of the city? Why not set up special *tippelzones*, or tolerance zones, where street hookers can service their clients under discreet police supervision without fear of assault or harassment from clients or pimps? If cops provide protection, the middleman is made irrelevant.

Amsterdam went so far as to build an ersatz prostitution street for its tippelzone, complete with bus shelters and streetlamps. Men drive in, look at the girls, make a deal, and then get a hand job or blow job or more in their cars. There's even a bike shelter for two-wheeling Johns. Adjacent to the street is a so-called *huiskamer*, or living room, where the women hang out between clients, chatting amongst themselves or with on-site social workers, drinking coffee and stocking up on condoms and minipacks of Kleenex, which the huiskamer sells by the stack.

The Dutch tolerance of prostitution and pot may strike those outside of Holland as not just liberal but libertine, licentious, and profane.

In America we do things differently. Kids having sex? Teach them abstinence. People taking drugs? Declare a war and throw users in jail. I find the Dutch system healthier, and the data backs me up. By some statistics, up to 90 percent of prostitutes in the States are drug-addicted. In Holland, that number is closer to 10 percent. Certainly some Amsterdam girls I met at the hotel were down and out: runaways, drug addicts, victims of abuse. But many of them seemed to be "normal" women who found sex work convenient, easy, lucrative, and even interesting. As Siska once told me, "The sex part only takes two minutes. It's the rest that keeps me coming back." By "the rest" she meant the camaraderie, the companionship of the community, and the thrill of never knowing who would come through the door. A millionaire banker from Bangkok or a virgin college student from Dubuque?

The next morning Nick went off to explore the Van Gogh Museum while I went to the Prostitution Information Centre (PIC), a small storefront shop started by a former prostitute who wanted to provide support for working girls in the area. I hoped someone there could explain the mystery of the disappearing Dutch whores. Twenty years ago, the ladies in de wallen's windows were almost exclusively Dutch. By the time I had lived here in the late 1980s, the first contingent of foreign women had started to arrive, mostly South Americans and Dominicans, and a few Western Europeans, too. Now, with a new klatch of African and Eastern European girls working the area, the Dutch women seemed to have vanished. Where did they go?

"*Goede morgen. Kan Ik U helpen?*" asked the strapping blonde woman behind the desk.

"*Hallo. Ja. Ik wil graag een beetje informatie,*" I said in rusty Dutch.

"What kind of information would you like?" the woman asked, switching to English.

I explained that I used to live here and was curious about the dearth of Dutch hookers. Jacqueline smiled when I explained this. She told me that most tourists only want to know how much to pay or why a woman would do this job. She motioned for me to sit down and set about explaining things.

"We had the legalization, of course, so now there are all new taxes and regulations. Also, there are so many illegal girls these days. They don't pay taxes and they charge much less. It's been a very hard time for the local girls."

"That's too bad. I used to know a lot of women who worked here. I wonder what happened to them."

"They get other jobs. Or they do it part time."

"What about you?"

"Yes, I was a prostitute."

"I mean, did you have to quit?"

"Yeah. I'm out of the business."

"For economic reasons?"

"And a lot of other reasons. But I did love it."

Jacqueline offered me a coffee. I accepted and dashed out to a bakery on the Warmoestraat to get us some sweet rolls. Then we just sat down and started talking like old friends. We gossiped about boys (she was antimarriage), kids (ditto), and pets (she had six Sphinx cats and a German shepherd named Dixie who was napping in the corner). After about three hours, Nick came to find me, and I introduced them. Soon after, a young Austrian student shuffled in. She was in her early twenties and had dark hair and bad skin. She was broke and considering getting a job in the neighborhood. She wanted to know how to go about it. Jacqueline patiently explained that as a citizen of a European Union (EU) country, she could legally work in the Netherlands, including in the red light. All she had to do was find an open window, show her papers to the landlord, and pay rent (up to 100 euros, or around 120 dollars) for an eight-hour shift. After twenty minutes of conversation, Jacqueline sensed that all this might be too much for the girl and suggested that she might be more comfortable working in a brothel, where she would not feel quite so exposed and would have the company of other girls. After the Austrian girl left, it was time for Nick and me to take off. Jacqueline invited me to return the next day, promising to introduce me to a few remaining Dutch prostitutes in the neighborhood.

The following day I arrived to find Jacqueline sitting behind the counter with Dixie. She was on the phone—for me, it turned out.

"Hallo," she called. "I have been making appointments for you. Moniek, one of the Dutch neighborhood girls, will meet you here, and later you will meet Niko."

"Is he a male prostitute?"

"No, he is a client, but he is wonderful."

We waited for an hour or so until a woman with long blonde tresses, made much longer and blonder by a bushy hair fall, walked in. Moniek had worked in the red light on and off for fifteen years. She claimed to be in her thirties, which was about a decade short, but she was holding fast to her youth. She wore low-slung camouflage cargo pants, a black lacy thong peeking out the top, and a hoodie sweater, unzipped to reveal a black lace bra and just the right amount of cleavage.

Moniek talked in a bubbly, bordering-on-manic manner, jumping from topic to topic. She spoke in the local working-class brogue, which made her sound as though she was chewing her words. She told me that after all these years she still liked her job. She met interesting people, chose her own hours. It was difficult now and again, "like when you fall in love with a client, that's hard. Or when you have a boyfriend. That's tough to juggle," she said.

But even more difficult to manage were all the new rules. Since prostitution had become legal, Moniek had had increasing troubles with the government, specifically the bean counters at the tax revenue department. She'd been in a protracted battle over what counted as work time—waiting in the window?—and what was tax deductible—condoms? A lot of hookers were having similar dilemmas, and many local accountants were doing a tidy side business explaining the tax intricacies of buying and selling sex. To make matters worse, since 2002, when the euro replaced the Dutch guilder as the national currency, prices for day-to-day goods, such as food and clothing, had skyrocketed. This inflation had been a problem all over Europe, as businesses used the euro switchover as an opportunity to drastically raise prices. (Before 2002, a coffee in an Amsterdam café used to run about three guilders—or a buck fifty; now it's three euros, more than three dollars.) Worse still, wages haven't kept pace with this inflation, and thanks to ever-increasing competition in the Red Light District, prices there have remained stagnant or have even dropped.

"It gets harder to make enough money, so now I don't work full time. Just weekends and a few nights a week," Moniek said, before adding with a dose of pride, "During the day I am a newspaper girl."

"A newspaper girl? Like a reporter?"

"No, I sell the papers on the street."

When it was time for her shift to begin, Moniek invited me to come along and see her window. She bounced out the door and I trailed behind. As we made our way down the alleys, she flirted with and said hi to a dozen men. The bouncers from the bars and brothels waved to her. But she made no contact with the other girls. "Do you know any of these girls?" I asked.

"Of course I know some. The ones who work near me. They watch out for me. Last week I accidentally hit my panic button," she said, referring to the security device that by law every window must have. "My neighbors were there right away. But it's usually more competition with the girls."

"Do you still work with the same women you worked with ten years ago?"

"No," Moniek said. "Those girls have mostly gone."

We arrived at her office, which, like most red-light windows, was a simple street-front room with a single bed, a towel, a sink, a chair, and the professional necessities: an economy-size box of condoms and a big jar of lube. Moniek gave me the Dutch triple-cheek kiss and said she'd see me around, and I set off to the coffee shop to meet Niko. I entered the café to the whiff of coffee and hash, and spotted a goateed man with dancing blue eyes who bore a striking resemblance to Micky Dolenz of the Monkees. When Jacqueline had described him to me, she'd said that Niko had some kind of special energy about him. It had sounded hokey but it turned out to be true.

Niko was an eccentric. A saxophone repairman, he had moved to the red light in the early 1980s, when apartments could be had for next to nothing. Several years ago, in lieu of pursuing more traditional romantic relationships, he'd started visiting the girls in the windows, usually staying faithful to one woman for a matter of months before the relationship inexorably morphed into friendship. Niko was a local favorite, known for bringing home-cooked meals to the girls he visited, and for his amazing reiki-type massages. He was such a beloved neighborhood fixture that he'd been immortalized in a graphic novel about the red light called *De Fijnproever*, or *The Connoisseur*. But now the neighborhood that had nurtured him was changing. Yuppies were moving in, he told me, forcing old-timers out. And with more and more foreign girls working the area, he lamented, "It is becoming difficult to have the same friendship and intimacy with someone who cannot speak your language. Sex is now like everything else. It is becoming commercialized and globalized."

Three strong Dutch coffees later, I said goodbye to Niko and went back to the PIC, where Jacqueline had lined up another prostitute for me to meet—this time an adorable guy with floppy black hair who looked like a dark-skinned Leonardo DiCaprio. Jeroen immediately pulled a small silver case out of his expensive suede jacket and handed me a business card with Mondrian-like graphics, reading, JEROEN: MALE ESCORT, GIGOLO, MODEL, ACTOR, AND MORE along with his Web site, e-mail addresses, and cell phone number.

"Thanks. Take one of mine," I said, fishing out a crusty card from my bag.

Jeroen waved it away, and in clipped Queen's English said, "Don't waste it."

"Jeroen is another one of our local prostitutes," Jacqueline said. "He's very ambitious."

Jeroen made a face, grabbed a soda from the refrigerator, plopped a euro coin on the counter, and asked if I wanted to talk as we strolled around de wallen. When we got outside, he waved his hand in front of him like a royal. "Ask me anything."

"Where are you from?" He sounded British but spoke flawless Dutch.

"I'm Dutch. My family is Indonesian, but I was adopted by a Dutch family."

"How did you get the British accent?"

"I studied to be an English teacher."

"But you became a prostitute instead?"

"I'd been doing it since I was seventeen." He was now twenty-two.

"Isn't it illegal at that age?"

"Only for the clients."

"So how come you're not an English teacher?"

"This is more interesting, more lucrative," he said, waving his arms again. "Ask me another question."

I asked him about his clients, his rates, his offerings. He gave me the blow-by-blow. His clients were mostly gay men, though he offered anything and everything: straight sex, gay sex, light bondage, heavy S&M, onesomes, twosomes, threesomes or more, in a hotel, in his apartment, in the park. "There's no extra charge for outdoor sex." Prices ran about 200 euros an hour—he charged a little less for local men, a little more for Americans because he said they have more money—and he offered bulk-rate bargains. "If you're interested, I could give you a discount rate. Maybe a free S&M session?"

"That's very generous. I'll think about it."

Before Jeroen left to meet a client, I asked if I could use his real name when I wrote about him.

"Darling," he said, "use my name. Put my Web site in. And my photo. Publicity, publicity."

The next night, Jacqueline invited me to go out with her after work. She wanted to show me a gay bar where a bunch of straight Romanian boy prostitutes worked. "It is so good for the ego," she said. "All the guys ignore the clients and just pay attention to you. There is one gorgeous boy who I took home with me a few times. I shouldn't have. He's twenty-two"—Jacqueline was thirty-seven—"but oh, he is beautiful, with the most amazing body. We had the best sex together."

"Ohh, a new boyfriend?" I asked.

Jacqueline looked horrified. "No, not a boyfriend. Just sex. I don't want a boyfriend or a husband or children." It wasn't the first time she'd spoken of committed relationships as though they were some kind of hideous punishment.

"It doesn't have to be so bad," I said. "People have all kinds of relationships."

The Dutch are not known for their politeness, and Jacqueline gave me her typically blunt opinion. "Nick seems nice," she said, "but marriage is like prison."

The Romanian boy bar wouldn't get hopping until 1 A.M., so around eleven o'clock Jacqueline and I popped into Casa Rosso. We settled ourselves into seats in the balcony and peered down as a muscled, tattooed fellow and a skinny blonde woman went at it doggie-style on the revolving stage, looking as bored as children at a Latin mass. It seemed an appropriate time to ask when and why Jacqueline had become a prostitute.

"I was twenty-seven when I began. I was always so fascinated by it, and I remember asking my brother's friend to tell me what it was like to see a prostitute and he told me, 'If you're so curious, why don't you do it?'"

"So, that's why you did it, curiosity?"

"It was something more, like I was drawn to it. And after the first time with a client I just knew that this was what I was meant to be doing. This was like something I had done in another life, and I felt like I had found my home. I cried."

You hear a lot about girls crying the first time they sell their bodies, but not usually out of gratitude. I looked over at Jacqueline. She, like Jeroen and the women I'd met all those years ago, didn't fit the portrait of prostitute-as-victim. Jacqueline had walked into the business with her eyes wide open and claimed to have loved it. This was supposed to be a contradiction. I searched her face for signs of deception, but her giant blue eyes were awash with emotion, lost in a delicious memory. When she came back to earth, she continued her story.

"All my life, I felt ugly, weird. When I was younger at school, from about age eleven to nineteen, I was teased about my looks. I was too tall. I had bad skin, I was not slender enough. I was so unhappy. But this was like therapy. When I'm working I can be anyone. I feel beautiful. And it's the most interesting job. I've stayed at the nicest hotels, eaten at the best restaurants, met people from all over the world I would never have met otherwise. There is no other job where you have this kind of life."

Jacqueline was eventually forced to quit working as a prostitute full time. "When I had to stop, I felt like my life ended, like my identity had died. I went through a big depression," she said. She still had a few regular clients who she saw now and again, but she would prefer to have her old life back. She was vague and tight-lipped about why she had to quit, and several months later she divulged her reason, making me promise never to tell a soul. "But then I got the job at the PIC and at least now I can be back in that world."

"Have you ever done this?" I asked, gesturing toward the stage, where a woman with long black hair and perky tits was pleasuring herself with a lit candle, inserting only the unlit end, thankfully.

"I feel too insecure about my body to do this in front of a crowd. I did it once, though, with a friend. I gave a blow job onstage. But I've never done any porn or anything like that."

Later we walked to a narrow, smoky bar behind the Rembrandtplein. In the back, next to the bathrooms, a half-dozen young Romanian men were congregated. Most of them were straight boys and illegal immigrants—Romania's not yet a part of the EU—who had come to Amsterdam to find work only to discover that their options were limited to black-market work: selling drugs or selling sex, usually to other men. Christian, Jacqueline's nonboyfriend, doted on us. He stroked my wrist, which to him was inconceivably small. "Such a little hand," he marveled over and over. Most of his attention was for Jacqueline, whom he nuzzled as she grinned like the schoolgirl in love that she claimed not to be. The rest of the guys fawned all over us, while at the other end of the bar the neglected male clients sulked into their drinks.

More than anything, it is the illegal workers like Christian—or more specifically, his female counterparts—who are drastically changing the color of the Netherlands's red lights. In 2002 only about 15 percent of de wallen's 300 windows were occupied by locals. On a national scale it's estimated that between 50 and 70 percent of sex workers in the Netherlands come from outside the European Union. Part of the reason for this demographic shift is the sharp rise in importing sex workers from abroad. Oftentimes these women are forced into the business—a worldwide problem known as sex trafficking.

While the Netherlands's liberal prostitution policies are touted as the right example by some, antiprostitution advocates call it a worst-case scenario. They claim that legalization increases demand, which increases trafficking, which causes the glut of foreign and forced sex workers. They're partly right. Legalization has definitely opened the doors to outsiders. The Dutch government successfully petitioned the European Court to recognize prostitution as an economic activity, enabling women from non-EU and former Soviet-bloc countries to obtain work permits as prostitutes. Moreover, with all the new brothels and eased restrictions, Amsterdam has become the city of choice for traffickers, a lax place to set up business. According to one study from the governmental Budapest Group, as many as 80 percent of the non-EU prostitutes working in Dutch brothels have been trafficked.

But though sex trafficking has become the bogeyman of globalization, it's not a clear-cut issue. The rise in trafficked women in the Netherlands has as much to do with shifting geopolitics as it does legalization. In 1989 the Soviet Union began to loosen its grip on Eastern-bloc countries, and a year later disintegrated itself. Suddenly millions of women from Russia and Central and Eastern Europe, whose countries were in economic and political turmoil, were able to go West. Many did, hoping for a better life. But without papers or a common language, many wound up working in the world's oldest profession. The rising Russian mafia also did its share, expediting the transportation of women, even deceiving and forcing some of them into the sex trade. Meanwhile, as the European Union became more formalized, borders between many of the member states were opened, making travel—and trafficking—within Europe that much easier.

Jacqueline introduced me to Sophia, a pretty, hazel-eyed twenty-five-year-old student from Latvia. A few years ago Sophia applied for what she thought was an au pair job in the Netherlands. The interview took place at a nice office in Riga. It all seemed legit. But when Sophia got to Amsterdam, her passport was confiscated by her handlers and she was installed in a sex club, where she was forced to work from eight o'clock at night until five in the morning. By day she was transferred to a small brothel where she worked from ten in the morning until five in the evening. She never saw the money she made. The pimps, mobsters, and keepers would not let her go out alone, threatening to kill her son back in Latvia if she went to the police. So she spent three months drunk and on her back, until the sight of the other girls getting beaten jarred her into action. She went to the Dutch authorities, told her story, agreed to testify against her traffickers, was granted asylum, and was moved to a safe house.

Deception, coercion, rape—it's all atrocious, the ultimate cautionary tale. But there's more to Sophia's story than melodrama. While living in the safe house, Sophia met another girl who was a prostitute. "One day she asked me to bring her some of her things to work," said Sophia. The woman worked at a private house, which is like a brothel but smaller and serves no alcohol. "It was such a nice place, so different from where I had worked. There was no one to boss you around or watch you, no one controlling your money. And this girl made a lot of money." Sophia was living off a few dollars a day, smoking pack after pack of cigarettes to keep her hunger at bay. She could have returned to Latvia, but she was waiting for her Dutch working visa to go through. Eventually she decided to get a job at the private house where her friend worked. She spent a year as a prostitute, and, she says, it wasn't a bad one. She made friends, and made money. "I knew it wasn't a job forever, but it was fine for then," she said. Eventually, after coming into a windfall—she claims a client gave her a bag full of cash and then disappeared—she quit the business, enrolled in law school, sent for her son to come live with her, and got a job working with an immigration attorney.

Sophia's experience reveals a gray area of trafficking you don't often hear about: There can be an element of choice involved. Maybe it's a choice necessitated by economic desperation, but it's a choice nonetheless. Though Sophia did not know what she was getting herself into back in Riga, she went on to willingly become a prostitute after she escaped her traffickers. And, unlike Sophia, many girls *do* know what they're signing up for when they accept a trafficker's offer of a free ride to the Netherlands. They understand they will be working in the sex industry. What they may not anticipate is the level to which the traffickers and pimps will control their lives.

It was Sophia herself who told me this. Part of her job was to offer immigration law advice to the prostitutes in Alkmaar, a quaint city twenty-five miles north of Amsterdam, known for its giant cheese market and for its Red Light District. "When tourists come to visit, the wives go shopping for cheese and the men go shopping for sex," Sophia joked as she showed me around the warren of windows in Alkmaar's city center.

A client in Alkmaar these days will most likely be serviced by a foreign girl. The prostitutes come in waves, explained Sophia. After the collapse of the Soviet Union it was the Russians, Ukrainians, Poles, Czechs, and Hungarians. In 2002, most of the girls were coming from Romania and Bulgaria. "There are buses in Bulgarian towns leaving specifically for Alkmaar. It's known that this place is more relaxed," she said, referring to the town's more liberal window policies. Amsterdam authorities, in an attempt to stem the flow of illegally trafficked girls, had begun checking window occupants for papers and penalizing landlords who rented to illegals. In Alkmaar there were fewer questions asked.

As we walked down the lanes, the girls recognized Sophia and popped open their windows to ask about visa forms and deportations. Many were worried that the laws might change—they're in flux and vary all over the Netherlands—and that they might somehow be sent home. I was struck that none of them seemed to want to go home. I asked Sophia if they qualified as trafficked.

"Yes and no," she said. "They are physically transported here. And sometimes there is a pimp or a boyfriend who is in control, even though in the windows they don't need that kind of protection."

"Why do they want to stay here then? If they aren't forced?"

"Money. They can make so much here. Save it and go home and do a lot of things. If they could make that money at home, they would."

Part of Sophia's job was to inform these women of repatriation programs that would enable them to return home free of charge and without risk of jail or penalty. Some women took her up on this offer. Many more did not. They wanted to stay. Which got me thinking: You could call these women exploited, but if you removed morality from the equation and ceased to see prostitution as one rung up from hell, how exactly were these girls different from illegal and ill-paid chambermaids or any of the other migrants who work hard, crappy jobs in foreign countries? I don't mean to minimize the horror of being forced to sell your body, but there's a reason that prostitution is one of the oldest jobs in the world. Sex is always in demand and, face it, women control the supply. Prostitution is one job a woman can always do, with no tools other than her body. Is that exploitation? Or is it power?

Either way, prostitution is a field that plenty of women are clamoring to work in. In May 2004, ten new countries, including Poland, Latvia, Hungary, and the Czech Republic, joined the EU, making it legal for a new crop of citizens to work in Holland. In 2007, Bulgaria and Romania will also become EU member states. These additions will cause further demographic earthquakes, again shifting the way business—including the sex business—operates.

Jacqueline invited me to Rotterdam to meet her friend Marleen, another former hooker who was in her midthirties. Like Jacqueline, Marleen looked prototypically Dutch: tall, blonde, big-boned. Also like Jacqueline, Marleen had become a prostitute to scratch an itch. "Curiosity killed the cat," she said, laughing, after I asked her why she went into the biz. She landed her first job at Yab Yum, one of the most upscale brothels in the country, and over the next ten years she went on to work at a number of escort agencies and houses.

In recent years, with all the changes in the industry, it was becoming more difficult to get the same buck for the bang, so Marleen decided to go from worker to owner. She invested all of her money and, with her boyfriend, opened Marleen's Privè, a small private house. At first, everything went swimmingly. Marleen, whose boisterousness and warmth had already made her well-known in town, was the perfect Madam. The place had plenty of customers and a loyal staff of girls. It was going so well that Marleen decided to expand to another floor of the building they rented.

That's when the troubles started. With prostitution officially sanctioned, brothels, private houses, and clubs are now held to the same workplace standards as other businesses, even when those standards make no sense. By-the-book authorities began hassling Marleen about her ceilings and her bathrooms. "The government forced me to have male and female toilets. In a brothel? Men and women want one bathroom, to bathe together." When she fought back, cops began raiding the house, which scared away some of the clients. In the end, Marleen drove herself into deep debt expanding the house, only to get shut down because her ceilings were a few inches short of regulation. "The government, they drive me *bannaccas*," Marleen complained. "Here you think that I'm what they want, a female entrepreneur, a woman running a private house, and they make it impossible. With all the competition and difficulty they should be supporting us, but now that we're legal the government doesn't know how to treat us."

Marleen wasn't the only one going through such tribulations. With legalization comes legitimacy, and with legitimacy comes bureaucracy. All over the country, owners of brothels, private houses, and clubs were struggling to make sense of the cumbersome employment and tax policies. In Amsterdam, Jacqueline said that one-third of brothel owners had gone out of business since legalization. For independent girls, legalization has also brought its own economic headache—taxes. Prostitutes were always meant to pay taxes, but before legalization it was easy enough to sidestep them. No more. Taxes plus rising expenses and dropping prices are proving to be a lethal combination for today's working girl, especially if she's a legal resident. "The gap between the legal, taxpaying prostitutes and the illegals is so huge that the legal girls cannot charge as little as the illegal girls do," Jacqueline said. "They can't charge as much as they need to survive." In the end, many go bust.

I asked Marleen to describe her house for me, and she offered to take me to a similar one nearby. We rang a discreet doorbell, looked into a camera, and were buzzed upstairs into a den of red-velvet decadence. A gaggle of girls spilled into the hall. Most of them sounded and looked Eastern European but I couldn't be sure. You don't storm into a brothel in the Netherlands and start demanding passports, especially these days. When they saw that we were not clients, the girls disappeared back into the living room to watch TV. The housemother invited us into the kitchen for cappuccinos and then took me on a tour of various rooms equipped with showers, hot tubs, sex toys, velvet tassels, and, behind one mirrored door, an S&M dungeon. Prices were clearly listed. Exits were clearly marked. Every floor had a swinging fire door and a male and female bathroom. "It's all by the book," Marleen said, sighing. "So much money put into this."

After the brothel visit, Jacqueline and Marleen had an informational interview about a job as a sex surrogate working with (i.e., having sex with) mentally ill men at a psychiatric home. (It is so Dutch to include sex as part of psychiatric treatment.) Jacqueline had told me that her dream was to become a sex therapist, and Marleen, it turned out, was now studying for her nursing degree in hopes of going on to do sex therapy. This gig seemed like a good intermediate, and Jacqueline agreed to participate once the program was up and running.

Interview completed, we caught a water taxi to the Hotel New York for high tea. While we demolished a three-tiered plate laden with finger sandwiches, scones, and petit fours, Jacqueline and Marleen bitched about the government regulations, complained about the influx of cheap labor, and then Jacqueline started railing against the pervasiveness of what she called "hobby sex."

"It's really the fault of people like you," she said, turning on me.

"What do you mean?"

"Sex should be professionalized. It shouldn't be in marriage or relationships. It's never good in those anyhow. But if people get it for free, why will they pay?"

"You mean we should visit a prostitute like we see a dentist?"

"Yes."

I looked at Marleen to see what she thought. She lived with her boyfriend and was helping to bring up his son, and she had admitted to loving the little family they'd created. She was busily stirring her tea.

"That's silly, Jacqueline," I said. "And besides, what about you? You're having, what did you call it, 'hobby sex' with your Romanian boy."

"That's different, she said. "We're both professionals."

Speaking of professionals, there were a couple of Dutch pros who were thriving in the new economy. The day after I got back from Rotterdam, Jeroen text-messaged me with an invitation to join him for lunch at De Bijenkorf, one of Amsterdam's nicest department stores, which was conveniently located at Dam Square on the edge of the red light.

When we entered the store, Jeroen guided me to the escalators. "First, a little shopping," he said. "I had a good night last night."

We rode up to the top floor, then browsed our way down through the menswear (which Jeroen rejected as too conservative), housewares, electronics, and music, where he bought a couple of classical CDs. When we reached the ground floor, we walked over to the café, which was populated with pairs of perfectly coiffed Dutch women, their scarves tied just so, having afternoon coffee and cake.

"We're like the ladies who lunch," I said, as we slid into a window-side table.

"Speak for yourself, darling," he said, and, as if to prove me wrong, added, "Have you given any thought to my offer?"

"Which one was that?"

He raised his eyebrows.

"Oh, you mean giving me the courtesy discount."

"A freebie, darling. A free S&M session."

"What would that entail, exactly?"

"First, we would have a conversation. I would ask you what you like, what your fantasies are, what your limits are."

"Then what?"

He paused to appraise me. "I'd get you undressed and tie you up. Maybe a blindfold. I'd leave you there a while."

"I'm getting cold now."

"Patience. Let's see. Do you have big tits?"

I scooped up each of my breasts. "A decent handful's size."

"I'd get the nipple clamps on. Then some spanking, with my hand or a small whip. Maybe some candle wax dripped on your tits. From there it depends on you. If you like water sports, I'd piss on you."

It was a generous offer. I knew he charged 200 euros an hour for this kind of bondage. Still, I passed.

Jeroen shrugged. "You know where I am if you change your mind."

"How come you're offering me a freebie in the first place?" I asked, spearing a leftover piece of quiche from his plate.

"Business has been slow. I don't want to get out of practice."

"Why's business bad?"

"Oh, the usual: 9-11, the war in Iraq. The economy is bad here. Luxury items are the first thing people give up when times are rough, and I am a luxury item."

I told Jeroen that I'd been hearing a similar complaint from other Dutch prostitutes. But if I thought he was at all like them, he quickly disabused me of that notion.

"Look, prostitution has been around for thousands of years. Do you expect it to stay the same? You have to be adaptable. Yes, business is slow, but that's temporary. The world is changing, and change is good." Jeroen went on to detail his plans. Now that prostitution had been legalized, he could deduct business expenses, like marketing, so he had set up a new Web site with photos, descriptions of his services, and other offerings (a pair of cum-stained boxers for 30 euros; a series of photos of him urinating for 50). "My plan is to do this until I'm twenty-seven and then open a club of my own."

"That's great for you. I'm just saying that some of your colleagues aren't adapting so well."

Jeroen looked quizzical and, staring me right in the face, asked, "What do I care about them?"

If the golden rule of globalized business is adapt or perish, Jeroen was clearly the prostitute most likely to succeed. I had more sympathy for the others than he did, although I wasn't sure the economic shift was so bad for Dutch women. As normalized as it is, for most women prostitution is still a so-so-paying, potentially dangerous job—though condom use is so prevalent that STD rates in the red-light district are supposedly near the national average (though there's no mandatory testing). Even though Marleen's business had failed, hadn't legalization catapulted her from laborer to entrepreneur? And now she was studying to be a nurse. Jacqueline had also become a respected professional. As part of her job with the PIC she traveled to conferences all over Europe, giving lectures on prostitution. In a sense, what was happening in de wallen struck me as a replay of what happens when low-wage manual labor and industrial jobs leave the United States or become the domain of illegal workers. The displaced local workers cry foul at first, blaming the foreigners for usurping their livelihood. But eventually those original workers are propelled a rung or two up the socioeconomic ladder; in the end, so, too, is that first generation of foreign migrants. In Amsterdam there are plenty of former prostitutes now happily working as social workers and teachers or studying for their PhDs. As opportunities increase, sex work is becoming a low-wage job, one that is increasingly outsourced, although in this case the outsourced jobs aren't going abroad, but workers from abroad are coming in to Holland.

I wasn't so sure it was prostitution that some of the women were truly mourning anyway. Though Jacqueline had seemed more put out by the changes in the industry than anyone, I couldn't help but wonder why. Prostitution had not made her rich, after all, though she said it had made her happy and fulfilled. Sex, even paid sex, can provide a connection, and for someone who'd been as lonely and outcast as Jacqueline had been, the nightly couplings probably provided an elixir against the hurts of her past. But as Siska had told me all those years ago, sex was just a small part of the deal. Jacqueline, I believe, loved being a prostitute for the sense of family it had given her. The red-light district, whether you're talking about the physical boundaries of de wallen or the virtual kinship of the broader community, was a haven: for hookers, junkies, artists, con men, and life's other castoffs and strange birds. It was a place where eccentric johns baked cakes for their paid escorts. It was a place where "neighborhood watch" had a whole new meaning. It was a place where weird girls fit in.

The day before I was due to leave Amsterdam, the PIC hosted a sex fair in the square outside the Oude Kerk. The afternoon was bright and sunny, and a lot of people milled about the booths that the PIC and other advocacy groups had set up. There was a festive feel in the air. A stage had been erected for entertainment. Food and candy had been laid out. There were even party games, including my favorite, a timed contest for putting on a condom without looking by rolling a rubber onto a dildo in a box. Jeroen was there, stationed behind an STD-info counter stacked with *Rood Lantaarn* (Red Light) magazines, a publication by and for sex workers. Ever the salesman, he had opened several copies to a page featuring an article about him—complete with full-spread photo—and had fanned the magazines on the table, along with a stack of his business cards. Jacqueline was there, too, Dixie behind her. She lit up when Christian, her Romanian not-boyfriend, arrived.

While Christian went to test his condom-placement skills, Jacqueline started talking to a handsome older man with dark blond hair and a short beard. This was the infamous Joep, who had been the beat cop in de wallen for thirty years. He had recently been transferred to another division, much to the chagrin of the locals. Joep was a legend in the red light, a uniquely Dutch, open-minded, blunt, tolerant, and caring cop who had no interest in policing the whores, only in helping them. When many spotted him they hugged him or called out "Joepie!" causing the taciturn man to smile. Joep was also internationally famous, having served as the inspiration for Harry Hoekstra, the red-light cop in John Irving's novel *A Widow for One Year*.

Joep knew as much about the changing neighborhood as anyone, so I dragged him inside the PIC and began peppering him with questions. Joep told me that thirty years ago the red-light was full of factories. "That one there made billiards," he said, pointing across the way. "Along with factories were the prostitutes. All were Dutch women; many of them had children out of wedlock and were pushed to the margins. Prostitution has always been on the margins. The streets in this small area were the only places these girls were accepted. The feeling in the neighborhood was that they were our whores. They were welcome here. It was like a village." Joep stopped for a moment to look around the neighborhood. "Everything is changing. No more factories. No more working class. Now we have yuppies. And the whores don't live in the neighborhood anymore."

Joep went on to tell me about other demographic shifts in the red light, and how with the recent glut of foreign workers, every year the amount of money the girls earn has gone down. All this was changing the tenor of the sex trade. "Before, when you visited a girl you spent three-quarters of an hour. You would eat something, talk a while. Now, it's fifteen minutes, fuck, and get out." Joep shook his head in dismay. He told me a story about one older German whore who was seventy-six years old. She didn't offer intercourse anymore, but she still had plenty of clients who came to her window because her fridge was always full, her ear always open, and the men could spend an entire hour with her. "But she is the exception, and she is old. For the young prostitutes it all changes, and for the men, too. The community, the camaraderie, all of that is going."

I thought about what Joep said. He was not only echoing the complaints I'd heard from the Dutch prostitutes but from fringe groups all over: The shrinking world was undoing the social villages in the same way the Starbucks were swallowing up the bohemian cafés, or the Barnes & Nobles were strangling the corner bookstores. By now I'd seen this phenomenon all over the world—from Tonga to China, from Kazakhstan to South Africa—yet I didn't see these changes as a permanent loss. No culture is static. People have proven themselves to be incredibly dynamic. They don't lie down and die when things change. Sure, the little villages fall apart, but they also re-form. Maybe the fakaleiti will cease to be fakaleiti but maybe they'll become part of a larger global queer community. Maybe the Kazak kids had lost their Soviet identity, but look at the bonds they were creating from the ashes. And maybe the Dutch whores were moving on, but wasn't a new community forming in their wake?

I backed away from the fair and sat down on a bench. Onstage, two cabaret performers were doing a burlesque show. Christian jumped up to dance like Elvis, and everyone cheered. Moniek had stopped by and was chatting with Jeroen and eating chocolate. Niko was there, too, shooting pictures with his vintage camera. Joep and Jacqueline stood to the side, thick as thieves and deep in conversation. One of the fresh-off-the-bus Romanian prostitutes, who'd come into the PIC to ask questions about a visa, was shyly talking to a health worker. A bearded, bedraggled, barefoot guy was picking up scraps of garbage and muttering to himself. A group of tourists, led by a man dressed as a medieval page, arrived, cameras at the ready. And all around us, the ladies in the windows danced.

The sun was shining, glinting off the spires of the Oude Kerk. The church bells started to ring. As I watched this menagerie of worlds intermingle, I was struck by how *gezellig* it all felt, gezellig being a distinctly Dutch term that is often translated as "cozy," although cozy doesn't quite cut it. Gezellig is a warm fire on a cold, rainy day. It's singing songs with friends at the tavern. It's the little village in the big city where everybody belongs.

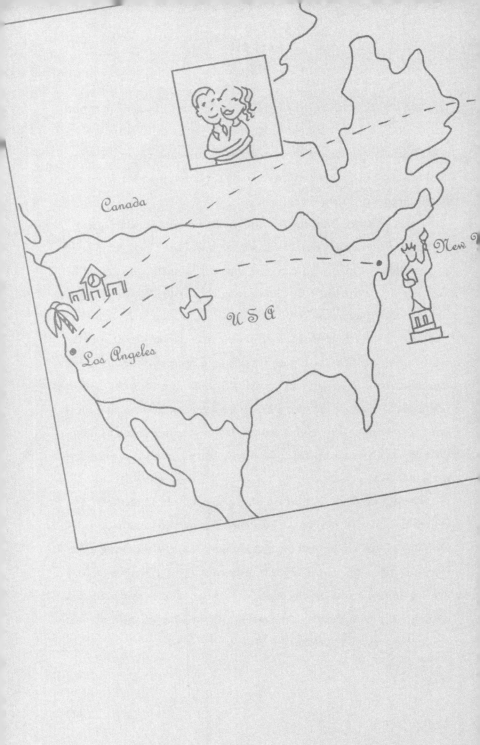

The Netherlands to Home—
January

An hour after the plane took off from London, I started to cry. This was surprising considering that for the past several weeks I had been thinking of nothing but home. Even though Europe had been relatively stress-free—a sort of vacation from the trip, during which the few disagreements Nick and I had were laughable, like whether to take a cab or a bus—I had been counting the weeks *until this trip was finally over. The cumulative effect of over-crowded African minibuses, $4 cups of Parisian coffee, and the frightening precipice to which Nick and I had taken our relationship had me weary and longing for the comforts of home. Home, where Nick and I could sleep in our own bed and wake to the sounds of our cats racing up and down the hall. Home, where I could meet friends and not have the conversation start with some variation of, "So, have you ever been to Lake Titicaca?" Home, where I could get a cup of coffee without having to get dressed first. Home, where I could talk on the phone with my sister for as long as I wanted.*

And yet, here I was crying on the plane because I was going home. Nick looked at me, at the tears streaming down my face. Ostensibly I had started weeping because the awful woman in front of me had tilted her seat all the way back immediately after takeoff—and, annoyingly, kept it like that for the whole twelve-hour flight, even during meals—leaving me claustrophobic and requiring me to move to another seat, away from Nick. It wasn't the lack of legroom I was crying over, I told a bemused Nick. It was the symbolism of the seat-switch: separation. The end of our intense year together.

A funny contradiction, I know. All that intensity and togetherness had been anything but pleasurable at times. But if I had learned anything this year it was that contradictions are complementary, that a truth and its opposite exist in harmony. It's how the shrinking world was destroying cultures just as it was creating new ones. And it's why the qualities that make me love Nick—his quiet, his calm, his being the opposite of me—and those that make him love me—my assertiveness, my gregariousness, my being the opposite of him—almost drove us apart.

But now this otherworldly existence Nick and I had inhabited alone together was coming to an end. In fact, it was already disappearing into the fog before the trip ended. For the last six weeks we had traveled like normal people, among friends and family, and to familiar places. In South Africa we'd been with my parents. In Germany we'd celebrated a quiet Christmas with friends, and in Amsterdam we'd stayed in an actual apartment with people we'd known for years. In Paris we'd spent ten days sightseeing like typical tourists with two of our best pals from home. By the time we reached London, where I battled throngs of commuters on London's tube, plotting a path through the crowds the same as I do in New York, I had the sense that I was already home.

Instead of going straight back to New York, we flew from London to Los Angeles to see family. Our relatives were greedy for us, and after clearing customs, Nick was whisked off to Palm Springs by his mother and grandmother, and I was driven to my suburban home by my father, sister, and nephew.

Standing in the terminal after Nick had gone, I had the sense not just that the adventure was over, but that it had never even happened. Was I the person who had taught crazy Doctor Bi Chinglish? Who learned to joust? Who had prayed with the

Lemba? Was I even married? Was there really another person to whom I could say, "Remember that meal in Samarkand?"

Nick and I were to be separated for only two days. We had endured far lengthier times apart under more painful circumstances, but I started crying again at the airport anyway. When I got to my childhood home in the San Fernando Valley, I grew even more melancholy. That evening I went with my father to the new strip mall, fashioned to look like a quaint European town, complete with fake cobblestones and a clock tower—"largest Rolex in the world," the residents boast—to pick up some Mexican food, which I had been craving for months. I was jet-lagged and disoriented, and I suddenly felt like I did when I was seventeen. Back then I had just flown home from England after spending twelve months abroad as an exchange student. If drama camp had been my coming out in life, the year in England was my coming into myself. At my wild anarchist school I joined a band and edited the literary journal. I marched against apartheid. I discovered how to put my social conscience into action. And I became enmeshed in the biggest, coolest group of weirdos I'd ever met. Consequently, I fell in love—with travel, with the thrill of plunging myself into the unknown, and with the joy of coming up connected. When I'd returned to the LA suburbs all those years ago, I'd also cried my way across the Atlantic, and when I'd landed I'd had the sense that the amazing year I'd just experienced hadn't happened at all, that the clarity and community it had wrought would be as temporary as my affected English accent. I worried that life would never feel so big again.

A week later, Nick and I boarded one last airplane for home. We held hands on takeoff, and as we circled New York City, I no longer felt sadness, just excitement and anticipation. I now understood that this momentous thing that Nick and I had gone through together would not vanish. After all, that seventeen-year-old girl hadn't gone anywhere. She was the reason I'd taken this trip; indeed, she had been with me all along.

Life, it turns out, is as big as you're willing to make it.

Acknowledgments

For an entire year, strangers from every corner of the world opened up their lives to me, put up with my endless questions, and let me tag along to their beauty contests, rap shows, and bug-catching sprees. Their stories fill these pages, and without them, there wouldn't have been a book—or indeed, much of a trip.

I am indebted to my entire family, especially my parents, Ruth and Lee Forman, for getting me addicted to travel and never raising an eyebrow when I announce I'm leaving town again, and to my sister, Tamar Schamhart, for keeping me stocked in *New Yorkers*, Kiehl's, and hope while on the road. Tamara Glenny kept the home fires burning and the cats happy. Many thanks to Prateek Chawla, Dawn Keall, Lucy N. Painter, Debbie Vaccaro, and the writers of the *Lonely Planet* guides for helping with the planning and logistics, and to the following people, who provided ports of comfort to a pair of weary travelers: Daniel Baltzer, Alyssa Banta, Rama Bhatia, Aigul Berdygulova, Matthew Bloch, Martin Buder, Ruchira Gupta, Wolfgang Kellers, Isaac Kenyajui, Anne

Acknowledgments

McFerran, Frederic Nowak, Astrid Pfenning, Giacomo Pirozzi, Lucy Pritchard, Adam Roberts, and Michele Spinello.

While writing this book, I had the pleasure of working with an extraordinary group of smart people: The inimitable Nina Collins is the kind of agent I didn't think existed—someone who is guided by her love of writing and her belief in writers. Also thank you to Matthew Elblonk and Leslie Falk for their hard work. At Rodale, Stephanie Tade acquired and championed this book, and the talented and thoughtful Chris Potash raised the bar while editing it; there ought to be more editors like him. Thank you also to the two Jessicas, Roth and Titel, for their tireless efforts. Aaron Cometbus, Greg Forman, Milo Schotz, Lisa Schwartz, Rachel Louise Snyder, and Joel Weber offered valuable research assistance. Diane Rios supplied the personalized maps. Eliza Griswold has been this project's biggest cheerleader since we outlined the idea for it on a cocktail napkin, and her support has been steadfast and astonishing. Marjorie Ingall cried when she read the draft and went on to cut through my clichés with her savage humor. Kim Sevcik's perceptive guidance became so necessary that during the muddled times, I would ask myself WWKD (What Would Kim Do?) and usually find my way to clarity. Sean Smith pushed me to go deeper and then pushed aside his own deadlines to groom the final draft like a monkey looking for fleas.

Finally, my deepest thanks go to Nick Tucker, for taking me on this trip, and for being the home to which I always want to return.